Contesting Globalization

What is the nature of the world economy as a terrain of political struggle? Is global civil society a political, or ideological, construct and what autonomy can it have from governing institutions? What is the best way to effect radical progressive change?

Contesting Globalization is an original addition to the literature on globalization which examines the challenges faced by those wishing to develop a critical understanding of the nature of power and counter-power in the contemporary world economy. The author traces the history and development of the institutions of global governance (such as The World Bank, IMF, WTO) as well as the emergence of the anti-globalization movement. He argues that we are at a critical juncture in the history of global capitalism, where the world economy itself has become a defining terrain of struggle, as global cities were in the nineteenth century.

Drawing lessons from the London dockworkers' strike of 1889 and the politics of Tammany Hall in New York, Drainville further argues that we need to understand the fundamental contradiction between, on the one hand, hegemonical attempts to organize the world economy as a levelled space to be administered on purely business principles, and, on the other, struggles to make it a place of politics. The former tries to empty the world of politics, while the latter are preparing the ground for a successful, self-supportive and self-governing global neighbourhood. This important volume will interest students and researchers of politics, sociology, geography and urban studies.

André C. Drainville is Professor of International Political Economy at Laval University, Québec, Canada.

RIPE Series in Global Political Economy

Series Editors: Louise Amoore (*University of Newcastle, UK*), Randall Germain (*Carleton University, Canada*) and Rorden Wilkinson (*University of Manchester, UK*).

Formerly edited by Otto Holman, Marianne Marchand (*Research Centre for International Political Economy, University of Amsterdam*), Henk Overbeek (*Free University, Amsterdam*) and Marianne Franklin (*University of Amsterdam*).

This series, published in association with the *Review of International Political Economy*, provides a forum for current debates in international political economy. The series aims to cover all the central topics in IPE and to present innovative analyses of emerging topics. The titles in the series seek to transcend a state-centred discourse and focus on three broad themes:

- the nature of the forces driving globalization forward
- resistance to globalization
- the transformation of the world order.

The series comprises two strands:

The *RIPE Series in Global Political Economy* aims to address the needs of students and teachers, and the titles will be published in hardback and paperback. Titles include the following:

Transnational Classes and International Relations
Kees van der Pijl

Gender and Global Restructuring
Sightings, sites and resistances
Edited by Marianne H Marchand and Anne Sisson Runyan

Global Political Economy
Contemporary theories
Edited by Ronen Palan

Ideologies of Globalization
Contending visions of a new world order
Mark Rupert

The Clash within Civilisations
Coming to terms with cultural conflicts
Dieter Senghaas

Global Unions?
Theory and strategies of organized labour in the global political economy
Edited by Jeffrey Harrod and Robert O'Brien

Political Economy of a Plural World
Critical reflections on power, morals and civilizations
Robert Cox with Michael Schechter

A Critical Rewriting of Global Political Economy
Integrating reproductive, productive and virtual economies
V. Spike Peterson

Contesting Globalization
Space and place in the world economy
André C. Drainville

Global Institutions and Development
Framing the World?
Edited by Morten Bøås and Desmond McNeill

Routledge/RIPE Studies in Global Political Economy is a forum for innovative new research intended for a high-level specialist readership, and the titles will be available in hardback only. Titles include:

1 Globalization and Governance*
Edited by Aseem Prakash and Jeffrey A. Hart

2 Nation-States and Money
The past, present and future of national currencies
Edited by Emily Gilbert and Eric Helleiner

3 The Global Political Economy of Intellectual Property Rights
The new enclosures?
Christopher May

4 Integrating Central Europe
EU expansion and Poland, Hungary and the Czech Republic
Otto Holman

5 Capitalist Restructuring, Globalisation and the Third Way
Lessons from the Swedish model
J. Magnus Ryner

6 Transnational Capitalism and the Struggle over European Integration
Bastiaan van Apeldoorn

7 World Financial Orders
An historical international political economy
Paul Langley

8 The Changing Politics of Finance in Korea and Thailand
From deregulation to debacle
Xiaoke Zhang

9 Anti-Immigrantism in Western Democracies
Statecraft, desire and the politics of exclusion
Roxanne Lynn Doty

*Also available in paperback

Contesting Globalization

Space and place in the world economy

André C. Drainville
With a foreword by Saskia Sassen

LONDON AND NEW YORK

First published 2004
by Routledge
11 New Fetter Lane, London EC4P 4EE

Simultaneously published in the USA and Canada
by Routledge
29 West 35th Street, New York, NY 10001

Routledge is an imprint of the Taylor & Francis Group

© 2004 André C. Drainville

Typeset in Baskerville by RefineCatch Limited, Bungay, Suffolk
Printed and bound in Great Britain by The Cromwell Press,
Trowbridge, Wiltshire

British Library Cataloguing in Publication Data
A catalogue record for this book is available from the British Library

Library of Congress Cataloging in Publication Data
Drainville, André C., 1963–
Contesting globalization: space and place in the world economy/
André C. Drainville.
p.   cm.
Includes bibliographical references and index.
1. Globalization – Social aspects. I. Title.
HF1359.D73 2003
337–dc21   2003004602

ISBN 0–415–31929–3 (hbk)
ISBN 0–415–31930–7 (pbk)

Chicane Ben

Contents

Illustrations

Foreword

Saskia Sassen

Globalization and the international human rights regime have contributed to the emergence of conditions that weaken the exclusive authority of national states and thereby facilitate the ascendance of sub- and transnational spaces and actors in politico-civic processes once confined to the national scale. Drainville's radical and provocative thesis is that the global economy has become a place where social forces are operating but that the categories in use to capture this are spectral. Many of the 'global projects' from cosmopolitanism to global civil society, or constructs such as 'international public opinion', or 'the poor of the world', prevent us from recognizing the emergence of real global actors. These older categories actually veil the existence of such actors and they hide the possibility of their project.

In earlier phases of the world market, inventing these spectral forms was a way of 'breathing life into a world economy where social forces did not meet'. Today, Drainville argues, there is no need for simulating presence. This is the specificity of today's phase of the world economy compared with past phases, when world market notwithstanding, it was at the national scale where the struggles that gave concrete, historical shape to capitalist accumulation took place.

Are global subjects that can stand between society and the world market indeed emerging? Drainville recognizes that global social relations and social forces have barely begun to take form, and are still pre-political. But, he argues, this should not keep us from a serious analysis of the possibilities and limits of global social relations. We need to understand the particularities of the world economy as a terrain for social relations. He rejects some of the current globalizing representations of putative common good. He finds that such representations 'may actually stunt rather than stimulate political thinking about what might be born in the world economy'. The people (or women, or poor) of the world may amount to less than real historical subjects – 'daydreams about how to humanize social and political relations in the world economy' – when in fact more radical possibilities can be investigated.

Drainville posits that it is in the concrete spaces of locality that we can observe and detect this assembling global subject. He wants to imagine the world economy as a city, to help think critically about the making of world order. He invokes the concreteness of the urban for questions of social order and social movements: cities are both critical and permeable sites for social relations. Urban politics in the latter part of the nineteenth century saw the working class rise up in protest; cities as the centre of the world economy became key terrains of struggle. We see the emergence of a new type of political subject or actor: this subject emerges at the intersection of place-based politics (such as the dockworkers' strike in London) and the world economy (the various interests of the financiers and traders in the City of London). This differs from other strategies evident at the time, such as the use of spectacle. He sees this epitomized in Tammany Hall's large outings for immigrant constituencies in New York City, which kept workers on the outside of the political realm.

The detailed dissecting of events and conditions in this book makes for a sharp contrast with current notions of the new cosmopolitanism and of global civil society. Drainville is rather merciless in his assessment of such categories. He finds them to be operating on behalf of an imaginary subject, 'humanity', which never asked to be represented. For him, global politics is placed politics, being invented and articulated in actually existing localities. (And 'global governance' is found in localizations of neoliberalism.)

This line of thought does not sit comfortably with what are today's master narratives around global civil society, yet I strongly concur with what Drainville is getting at. I have long sought to locate the importance of place for two strong emerging social forces – global corporate power and the multitudes of disadvantaged actors. Along these lines Drainville posits that walking and being in the would-be global city of the world economy allows him to explore contextualized local orders without losing a sense of the overall global coherence of governance (which he sees as the political handmaiden of global corporate neoliberalism). His use of the concept of 'the global city' as a would-be city works well in this intellectual project of identifying placed politics as part of the global economy.

Recognizing that the place-based actions and activisms we see today around the world can be the elements for bringing politics into the world economy signals that there is something happening in the domain of non-formal politics. In my own work I have been grappling with the emergence of new types of subjects and spaces (Sassen 1998, ch. 1, 2002). The global city is a site where global corporate capital and multitudes of disadvantaged can engage with each other, where place-based politics (e.g. anti-gentrification struggles) becomes a form of global politics. The global city makes possible the emergence of new types of political, as yet not formalized subjects.

The space of the city is a far more concrete space for politics than that of the nation. It becomes a place where non-formal political actors can be part of the political scene in a way that is much more difficult at the national level. Nationally, politics needs to run through existing formal systems: whether the electoral political system or the judiciary (taking state agencies to court). Non-formal political actors are rendered invisible in the space of national politics. The space of the city accommodates a broad range of political activities – squatting, demonstrations against police brutality, fighting for the rights of immigrants and the homeless, the politics of culture and identity, gay and lesbian and queer politics. Much of this becomes visible on the street. Much of urban politics is concrete, enacted by people rather than dependent on massive media technologies. Street-level politics makes possible the formation of new types of political subjects that do not have to go through the formal political system. It is in this sense that those who lack power, those who are disadvantaged, outsiders, discriminated minorities, can gain *presence* in global cities, presence *vis-à-vis* power and presence *vis-à-vis* each other. This signals, for me, the possibility of a new type of politics centred in new types of political actors. It is not simply a matter of having or not having power. These are new hybrid bases from which to act.

Drainville speaks of the would-be global city of the world economy; yet he is getting at these concrete dimensions. It allows him to make the argument that categories such as global governance, global civil society and cosmopolitanism are abstract, rationalist efforts which have the effect of voiding the world economy of politics. This is a truly provocative book, but one that constructs its provocation through detailed and nuanced observation.

Series editor's preface

Contesting Globalization is, in the author's own words, an 'experimental work of theory', the 'artisanal work' of a single and fallible author whose intellectual ambition far exceeds his (or indeed any mortal academic's) ability to provide robust and rigorous evidence for the claims he makes. It is an intellectual expedition into unmapped territory, bound to unsettle many of the unspoken assumptions stowed away in the excess storage space of the reader's brain.

André Drainville's book is for adventurous readers willing to take a risk. The journey it takes readers on will be neither easy nor comfortable but for those who persevere the rewards are great. Drainville writes in a very personal language and style that integrates fields such as urban geography and the avant-gardism of the *internationale situationiste* into an unorthodox critique of the contemporary global economy and that bridges Anglophone and Francophone cultural and intellectual spheres.

Contesting Globalisation offers a provoking critique of the burgeoning literature on global governance. Drainville mercilessly exposes the normative and ideological underpinnings of the problem-solving approaches at the heart of 'transnational public policy'. He identifies this as one of three theoretical strands in the literature on 'governance in the age of globalisation'.

He is equally merciless in his critique of the two other strands, the sociological and the neo-Marxian. Sociological approaches, Drainville argues, posit an imaginary (and essentially apolitical) transnational subject of 'cosmopolitan democracy', namely that of an 'inferred, habitudinal and globally-reflexive humanity'. On the other hand, 'transnational historical materialism', whilst ostensibly understanding globalization as a dialectic dynamic, is also limited. Drainville argues that this approach actually proves unable to provide much meaningful insight into how social forces 'make themselves' in real, concrete and historical ways, both in national contexts and increasingly in the context of the world economy.

Drainville finds lacking in both an understanding of the ways in which social forces are rooted in concrete *places* rather than existing only in imaginary *spaces*, as so many fashionable contemporary approaches tend to argue.

The task Drainville then sets himself, and the challenge he poses to readers, is to explore the relationship between space and place in the world economy in order to provide a better understanding of the global political economy as 'a field of concrete and situated practices'. We invite the reader to take up this challenge. We are confident that it will be well worth the effort.

Marianne Franklin, Otto Holman
Marianne H. Marchand and Henk Overbeek

Acknowledgements

I depend more than I readily admit on others to stimulate and challenge me, and often neglect to thank peers, comrades and friends who have been generous enough to listen to my ideas and share their thoughts. Among those to whom I feel most indebted are Leo Panitch and Robert Cox, who will both be surprised to figure so prominently in my acknowledgements. In the past decade and a half, each has, in his own distinctive way, provided honest, insightful, sometimes ruthless, critiques that have influenced my intellectual work more than puerile pride has let me say. Both have provided models of integrity; to them, I wish to express all my respect and heartfelt – if belated – thanks.

I am thankful as well to scholars from other places and disciplines who have invited me to their gatherings during the time I was working on this book. It is quite fashionable these days to present one's work as being 'of the margins'. There is, as Bhabha, Rushdie, Said and many others have emphasized, freedom and creativity in the margins: 'Out there', on uncharted lands and in interstitial spaces, can dwell creative intellectuals weary of disciplinary gregariousness, willing to risk displacement to create. But, as I learned from my experience at the edge of the academic continent, margins are sometimes petty, stultifying worlds of their own, ruled by powers that are no less constraining for being so small. To keep from drowning in the muck they make, one needs shelter and a sense of other places. Among those who offered me both, I am most grateful to: Gregory Baum, Duncan Cameron, Barry Carr, Alejandro Colás, Luis Eduardo Guarnizo, Kimberley Hutchings, Edward J. McCaughan, Margie Mandell, Bruce William Morrison, Henk Overbeek, Saskia Sassen, David A. Smith, Michael Peter Smith, Kees van der Pijl and Peter Waterman.

Sincerest thanks as well to friends, librarians, archivists and research assistants who worked, with integrity, imagination and intelligence to gather the fragments without which it would not have been possible for me to engage in such broad theorization: Pierre Beaudet, Sébastien Bouchard, Éric Boulé, Alexandre Brassard-Desjardins, Christina Buccica, Étienne Cantin, Jean-Pierre Carrier, Jim Catterson, Marc Dean, Radu Dobrescu, Nicolas Drouin, François Fortier, Jacques Grenier, Robert Jasmin, Susan M. Jenkins,

Suzuki Keiko, Evelyne Pedneault, Dilys Rennie, Véronica Rioux, Jean-François Savard, Jeffrey J. Segall and Simon Thibault.

In Québec city, acknowledgements are due to students and militants at Laval University and in the *faubourg Saint-Jean Baptiste*, who, now and then, create wonders in the margins. Without the invaluable sense of worth and belonging they provided, I would undoubtedly have retreated into wholly academic abstractions, or folded into myself.

Research for this book was made possible in part by a grant from the *Fonds FCAR (Formation des Chercheurs et l'Avancement de la Recherche)*, and by the generous hospitality of the International Social Science Institute of the University of Edinburgh. As endnotes acknowledge, I have drawn extensively from published texts. Specifically, parts of the Introduction, as well as sections of Chapter 4 dealing with matters of governance, draw from my 'On the Relevance of the Avant-Garde', published in *Telos* (120, summer 2001). The presentation of the 'counter-revolutionary humanity' wished into theoretical existence by recent works of international political economy builds on my 'International Political Economy in the Age of Open Marxism', published in the inaugural issue of the *Review of International Political Economy* (spring 1994). The first section of Chapter 3 draws on ideas originally elaborated in 'Left Internationalism and the Politics of Resistance in the New World Order' published in *A New World Order: Global Transformations in the Late Twentieth Century*, edited by D. Smith and J. Böröcz (Westport: Praeger 1995). Brief parts of the Introduction, the discussion of Québec city's Summit of the America found in Chapter 2 and the analysis of the structuring of social relations in the Americas in Chapter 4 owe everything to my 'Québec City 2001 and the Making of Transnational Subjects' published in the *Socialist Register 2002*, edited by L. Panitch and C. Leys (London and New York: Merlin Press). Concluding comments on more recent happenings draw from a conference organized by the Socialist Studies Association of Canada on 'Quebec City one year later: debating strategic lessons'. I wish to thank conference organizers as well as the other participants in the round table: Judy Rebick, Jaggi Signh, Hassan Yussuf and Leo Panitch. On a night when I taught less than I wanted to, I learned more than I expected. I hope that much is evident in the Conclusion of this book. Although it does not directly quote it, the discussion of global governance presented in Chapter 4 builds on 'The Fetishism of Global Civil Society: Global Governance, Transnational Urbanism and Sustainable Capitalism in the World Economy', published in *Comparative Urban and Community Research* (6). I am grateful to Telospress and Taylor & Francis (www.tandf.co.uk) who gave their permission to reproduce portions of published texts.

I have made every reasonable effort to acknowledge and clear copyrights of the illustrations used in this book but may have made some mistakes. I would be grateful to copyright owners to signal any such mistake, and will be happy to correct them in subsequent editions of this book.

Finally, I wish to thank anonymous reviewers for their sympathetic and intelligent reading of my manuscript, as well as editors of the RIPE series and Heidi Bagtazo, who accepted and supported a book that has less to do with international political economy than they might have wished. I took great comfort in their support and am honoured as well as excited to have my first academic book published with RIPE/Routledge.

André C. Drainville

Introduction

We have now reached a junction, a kind of crossroads, and we could do worse than to examine the lie of the land before we proceed any further.

(Lefebvre 1978, 17)

Holy ghosts of all sorts are haunting global politics: 'global civil society', 'international public opinion', 'the peoples of the earth', 'the global NGO community', 'the peoples' (or 'the women' or 'the workers' or 'the poor') of the world. On their behalf, seemingly incessant celebrations of planetary oneness are being held (see Table 0.1), 'functional utopias' (Falk 1993, 49) imagined, and numerous political and academic parleys organized. In politics, transnational protests are being waged and global programmes and blueprints drawn that range from plans for a people's UN assembly, to ideas for good governance and global social contracts or 'alternative humanist projects of globalization', to more radical schemes for the reinvention of the sum and substance of the world economy.[1]

When global capitalism was a 'minority phenomenon' – of consequence to many but steered by a few (Braudel 1985, 93–94) – inventing cosmopolitan surrogates was a necessary means to breathe social presence into the world economy and to think about politics in a place where it was not actually being made. From the long sixteenth century to the end of the Bretton Woods order, global capitalism expanded but the nation-state remained as the privileged place for social forces to meet and, consequently, the defining context for capitalism accumulation, where took place the struggles that gave concrete, historic shape to accumulation. By contrast, the world economy was not a place of significant encounters. There, financiers and capitalists (from the Fuggers to the transatlantic bourgeoisie) met like-minded competitors, as well as soldiers and diplomats, but as a class they did not meet another. In this context, more could be imagined on behalf of cosmopolitan spectres than what could actually be made on the terrain of the world economy (think of the projects for perpetual peace that the Abbé Saint-Pierre and Jean-Jacques Rousseau conceived for the *citoyens du monde*, of the cosmopolitan rights that Immanuel Kant or Flota Tristan argued for on behalf of wandering

Table 0.1 Calendar of cosmopolitan observances*

Date (first)	Name
1 Jan. (2001) to 31 Dec. (2001)	International Year of Volunteers
1 Jan. (2000) to 31 Dec. (2000)	International Year for a Culture of Peace
1 Jan. (1999) to 31 Dec. (1999)	International Year of the Elderly
1 Jan. (1998)	International Year of the Ocean
1 Jan. (1996) to 31 Dec. (1996)	International Year for the Eradication of Poverty
1 Jan. (1995) to 31 Dec. (1995)	United Nations' Year for Tolerance
1 Jan. (1995) to 31 Dec. (1995)	World Year of People's Commemoration of the Victims of the Second World War
1 Jan. (1995) to 31 Dec. (2005)	United Nations' Decade for Human Rights Education
1–7 Jan. (1995)	Universal Letter-Writing Week
1 Jan. (1993) to 31 Dec. (2002)	Second Industrial Development Decade for Africa
1 Jan. (1993)	Asian and Pacific Decade of Disabled Persons
1 Jan. (1992)	International Day for the Eradication of Poverty
1 Jan. (1991) to 31 Dec. (1992)	United Nations' International Year of the World's Indigenous People
1 Jan. (1991) to 31 Dec. (2000)	United Nations' Decade Against Drug Abuse
1 Jan. (1991) to 31 Dec. (2000)	Second Transport and Communication Decade in Africa
1 Jan. (1991)	Fourth United Nations' Development Decade
1 Jan. (1990)	Third Disarmament Decade
1 Jan. (1990) to 31 Dec. (1999)	International Decade for Natural Disaster Reduction
1 Jan. (1990) to 31 Dec. (1999)	International Decade for the Eradication of Colonialism
1 Jan. (1990) to 31 Dec. (1999)	United Nations' Decade of International Law
1 Jan. (1988) to 31 Dec. (1997)	World Decade for Cultural Development
1 Jan. (1985) to 31 Dec. (1994)	Transport and Communication Decade for Asia and the Pacific
1 Jan. (1983) to 31 Dec. (1992)	International Decade of Disabled Persons

1 Jan. (1983) to 31 Dec. (1992)	Second Decade to Combat Racism and Racial Discrimination
1 Jan. (1981) to 31 Dec. (1990)	Industrial Development Decade for Africa
1 Jan. (1980) to 31 Dec. (1989)	Third United Nations' Development Decade
1 Jan. (1978) to 31 Dec. (1989)	Transport and Communication Decade in Africa
1 Jan. (1975)	International Women's Year
1 Jan. (1973) to 31 Dec. (1982)	UN Decade to Combat Racism and Racial Discrimination
1 Jan. (1970) to 31 Dec. (1979)	Second United Nations' Development Decade
1 Jan. (1960) to 31 Dec. (1969)	United Nations' Development Decade
3 Jan. (1954)	Nuclear Free and Independent Pacific Day
11 Jan.	International Thank-You Day
15 Jan.	Humanitarian Day
15 Jan. (1950)	World Religion Day
24 Jan. (1995)	Abolition 2000 Day
27 Jan. (2002)	International Internet Free Day
1–28 Feb. (1995)	International Embroidery Month
28 Feb. (1950)	International Pancake Day
1–7 March (1995)	Universal Human Beings Week
8 March (1910)	International Women's Day
14 March (1997)	International Day of Action Against Dams: For Rivers, Water and Life
15 March (1997)	International Day Against Police Violence
Week beginning 21 March (1979)	Week of Solidarity with the People Struggling against Racism and Racial Discrimination
20 March (1991)	Journée Internationale de la Francophonie
21 March (1999)	World Poetry Day
21 March (1966)	International Day for the Elimination of Racial Discrimination
22 March (1995)	World Day for Water
23 March	World Meteorological Day
24 March (1997)	World Tuberculosis Day
27 March (1962)	World Theatre Day
6 April (1995)	International Day for Nonviolence
7 April (1950)	World Health Day
8–14 April (2001)	Pan-American Week
14 April	Pan-American Day

Date (first)	Name
22 April (1970)	Earth Day
23 April (1995)	World Book and Copyright Day
26 April (1996)	International Day of Prayer for Land-mines Victims
28 April (1995)	Workers Memorial Day
28 April (1984)	International Day of Mourning
29 April (1982)	International Dance Day
1 May (1890)	May Day/Labour Day
3 May (1994)	World Press Freedom Day
3 May (1972)	Sun Day
6 May (1992)	International No Diet Day
8 May (1999)	International Migratory Bird Day
15 May (1994)	International Day of Families
17 May (1969)	World Telecommunication Day
18 May (1977)	International Museum Day
Third week in May (1948)	World Trade Week
21 May	World Day for Cultural Development
24 May (1996)	Women's International Day for Peace
24 May (1991)	International Jazz Day
25 May (1963)	Africa Day
31 May (1988)	World No-Tobacco Day
5 June (1972)	World Environnment Day
17 June (1994)	World Day to Combat Desertification and Drought
19 June	World Sauntering Day
26 June (1988)	International Day against Drug Abuse and Illicit Trafficking
First Saturday in July (1992)	International Day of Cooperatives
11 July (1989)	World Population Day
6 August (1945)	Hiroshima Day
9 August (1995)	International Day of the World's Indigenous People
13 August (1976)	International Lefthander's Day
8 Sept. (1966)	International Literacy Day
14 Sept.	International Cross-Cultural Day
16 Sept. (1995)	International Day for the Preservation of the Ozone Layer
29 Sept.	International Day of the Deaf
Last week in September (1978)	World Maritime Day
Third Tuesday of Sept. (1982)	International Day of Peace

Last Sunday in Sept. (1996)	International Day of Prayer for the Persecuted Church
1 Oct. (1995)	World Vegetarian Day
1 Oct. (1991)	International Day for the Elderly (alternatively International Day of Older Persons)
First Monday in October (1986)	World Habitat Day
4 Oct. (2000)	International Walk to School Day
5 Oct. (1990)	International Teachers' Day
6 Oct. (1995)	Black Solidarity Day/International Day of Education
9 Oct. (1984)	World Post Day
Second Wednesday in October (1990)	International Day for Natural Disaster Reduction
16 Oct. (1979)	World Food Day
19 Oct. (1996)	International Day of Dialogue
24 Oct. (1948)	United Nations Day
24 Oct. (1972)	World Development Information Day
24–30 Oct. (1979)	Disarmament Week
1 Nov. (1995)	World Communication Week
11 Nov. (1919)	Armistice Day
Week of Nov. 11 (1989)	International Week of Science and Peace
13 Nov. (1988)	International Day Dedicated to the Mime
16 Nov. (1995)	International Day for Tolerance
17 Nov. (1995)	International Day of Action Against Violence Against Women
20 Nov. (1989)	Africa Industrialization Day
20 Nov. (1953)	Universal Children's Day
21 Nov. (1996)	World Television Day
27 Nov. (1992)	Buy Nothing Day
29 Nov. (1977)	International Day of Solidarity with the Palestinian People
1 Dec. (1995)	International Day Without Art
1 Dec. (1987)	World Aids Day
Whole of December	International Calender Awareness Month
Whole of December	Universal Human Rights Month
2 Dec.	Pan-American Health Day
3 Dec. (1993)	International Day for Disabled Persons
3 Dec. (1992)	International Day of Disabled Persons
5 Dec. (1986)	International Volunteer Day for Economic and Social Development

Date (first)	Name
7 Dec. (1992)	International Civil Aviation Day
10 Dec. (1950)	Human Rights Day (followed by Human Rights Week)
12 Dec. (1994) (to 2003)	International Decade of the World's Indigenous People
12 Dec. (1993)	Third Decade to Combat Racism and Racial Discrimination
12 Dec. (1983)	Second Decade for Action to Combat Racism and Racial Discimination
12 Dec. (1973)	Decade for Action to Combat Racism and Racial Discimination
15–21 Dec. (1887)	International Language Week
Third Sunday in December (1995)	International Shareware Day
29 Dec. (1994)	International Day for Biological Diversity

Note
* Excluded from this calendar were one-time celebrations and events linked to specific campaigns (e.g. The Rainforest Action Network's International Day of Protest against Mitsubishi Corporation, 16 October 1996; The International Longshore and Warehouse Union International Day of Action in support of Mersey dockworkers (Liverpool), 8 September 1997; the International Anti-Dam Movement's International Day of Action Against Dams and for Rivers, Water and Life, 14 March 1997). Global Exchange has set Wednesday, 11 August as a national day of flooding Gap's customer service department with phone calls and faxes. Gap's toll-free phone line is 1–800–333–7899.

foreigners, of the revolution Marx theorized for the worldwide proletariat or, most recently, of the struggle against colonial alienation waged by Franz Fanon's wretched of the earth).

But now, the world economy itself has become a significant place for social forces to meet. Whether they have been brought there by global regulatory agencies working to consolidate the social foundations of planetary neoliberalism or they have taken to it in the course of variformed struggles against the ways and consequences of globalization, crucially conflicting social forces have set foot on the terrain of the world economy. Arguably for the first time in the history of capitalism organized on a world scale, the world is no longer a 'no man's land', beyond place and context (Lipovetsky 1983), and social presence need no longer be simulated by cosmopolitan artifices in order to be studied at the global level. In this context, cosmopolitan reveries may actually stunt rather than stimulate political thinking about what might be born in the world economy. Abstracted, blown up and ensconced in reverent absolutes, 'global civil society' or 'the peoples' (or 'the women' or 'the workers' or 'the poor') of the world may amount to less than real historical subjects; ghostly, they may make us daydream about ways to humanize social and political relations in the world economy when, in fact, more radical possibilities can be investigated.

To develop what Robert Cox would have recognized as 'critical awareness of potentiality for change' (as distinct from 'utopian planning'), we need to enquire into the making of global subjects rather than take them for granted. To do that, we need to stay with global practices long enough to see what they might carry that is significant and, perhaps, transformative. Only thus can we look – realistically and radically – beyond ways to humanize global capitalism, about revolutionizing it. This is what this book is about.

That inhabitants of this planet share a common humanity is, of course, unquestionable, as is basic 'human solidarity' (Falk 1995b), 'human community' (Boutros-Ghali 1996) and 'the inevitability of being . . . together' (Petrella 1996). 'We', indeed, are all human beings. On this we can agree with Karl Marx, Victor Hugo, World Bank officials, Bob Geldof (of 'Live Aid' fame), U2's Bono, Subcommandant Marcos and all the Bennetton ads in the world. Above and beyond knowledge of this elementary humanity, however, political questions remain whole: Is there any substance to imagined, inferred and assumed cosmopolitan ghosts? Is a global, or transnational subject indeed assembling itself that can stand between society and the market? Should we rather think about a plurality of global subjects making themselves, or being made? How and by whom? What are the possibilities and limits of global practices? Of ideas for global reform and global revolution? Notwithstanding the cosmopolitan ambiance of our time, answers to these questions remain very much matters of empirical enquiry and theoretical consideration.

To answer them, we need to problematize what cosmopolitan reveries take for granted. To do this, we will turn against itself the civic discourse of the World Bank *et al.* and make of it what Walter Benjamin would have called a *thought-image*: a heuristic device giving concreteness and intelligibility to often implicit, diffused and abstract social structures.[2] Taking global civic pronouncements more literally than discourses usually want to be taken, we will conceptualize the world economy as a meeting place of social forces, a 'place of encounters', to borrow Henri Lefebvre's definition of cities.[3] In the age of Dutch hegemony, Amsterdam presented René Descartes with an evocative and readable 'inventory of possibilities' opened up by the fast-expanding capitalist world economy.[4] In the period of *Pax Britannica*, London offered Henry James 'the most complete compendium of the world'.[5] In the age of *Pax Americana*, 'a whole world of commerce and money exchanges collapse[d] into a confrontation on New York's Fifth Avenue' (Harvey 1985). In the age of *Pax Planeta* (Ramphal 1997), we will imagine the world economy as a city, to help us think critically about the making of world order.

Civic and urban idioms are perhaps the richest store of modern images of social order and movement. Tapping into this trove will, hopefully, give our investigation into global practices a coherence comparable to that which

Michel Foucault gained by carrying with him the language of concrete places of enclosures (prisons, schools, asylums, factories, galleys) into abstracts diagrams and *épistémès*, or – closer to our field of enquiry – that which Robert Cox gained by combining Fernand Braudel's vivid historical imagery (where *nébuleuses* gather and analytical ships are floated) with Antonio Gramsci's geographical and tactical vernacular (where protagonists occupy positions across terrains, organize and sustain sieges, dig or dig not trenches of hegemony, and fight wars of position and movement).[6]

Thinking urban thoughts will also enable us to make sense of attempts by global regulatory agencies to animate, but also to contain and structure, the global movement of social forces. As we will see, 'global governance' (the political companion of global neoliberalism) is an attempt to organize the passage of social forces to the world economy and to regulate their movement in it. To understand this absolutely crucial, and critically undetermined attempt, we must keep in mind that global politics is placed politics. Although it appears to float above places and contexts, it is, as Manuel Castells, Mike Davis, John Friedmann, David Harvey, Anthony King, Michael P. Smith and many others have emphasized, being invented and articulated in actually existing localities, that, together, make up what Saskia Sassen called a 'worldwide grid of strategic places' (Sassen 1998). In this context, thinking with reference to cities, 'the place where social conflicts [are] most exacerbated' (Tschumi 1998) will prove invaluable.

Global from the point of view of the social forces it represents, 'global governance' is also locally fragmented from the point of view of the policy initiatives it animates. Accordingly, some of the most telling artefacts of 'global governance' will be found in local programmes that both signal a tightening of global regulatory parameters and increased efforts to fine-tune global regulation to local and regional contexts. 'Walking and being' in the would-be global city of the world economy will allow us to explore increasingly contextualized local orders without losing a sense of the overall global coherence of governance. Structured with references to a broad process akin to what Walter Benjamin (and Engels before him) would have called the 'Haussmanization' of the world economy, our local enquiries will gain perspective and intelligence.[7]

Most importantly, fashioning a heuristic device from civic appeals will help us think through the politics of change in the contemporary world economy. Where most contemporary studies think of the world economy as a site so well ordered that it can be reordered only by cosmopolitan *proxies – deus ex machinas* for the global age – we will look into it as a relatively open and indeterminate place where actually existing social forces really do meet. This will encourage us – to paraphrase Frank Lloyd Wright on creativity – to 'see into' global practices rather than 'look at' them.[8]

Emerging modes of social relations to the world economy

In significant ways, the world economy is a new, relatively indeterminate and permeable field of political practice. Social and political relations that are made on this terrain remain episodic, intimately linked to happenings elsewhere, and, to paraphrase Patrick Geddes about lives in cities, they are still folded in the 'manifold warp of circumstances, [the] changeful weft of life' (Geddes 1908, 2). To date, global social relations have not produced ideologies or programmes of their own, or even a broad sense of political perspective to help us think critically about the world economy. Thus, to rise above the present bewilderment (of which the popular expression 'global anti-globalization movement' gives a sense), we will not be able to stand on others' shoulders.

Unprompted by endogenous political referents, many authors simply fail to problematize global social relations at all, but rather comfort themselves with cosmopolitan certainties, assuming that, indeed, some kind of global civil society is somehow rising that will, at some point, stand between the World Bank and markets. Students of Gramsci will recognize this course of thought as a late, global variation on the 'empty and inconclusive economic moralism' characteristic of nineteenth-century liberalism. From such impolitic work, we can expect no help in thinking critically about order and change in the world economy.

Others do try to think politically about global social relations, but reason from intuitive rather than analytical categories. Running through the literature, for instance, are distinctions – both explicit and implicit – between what is radical and reformist, or between what seems to come 'from below' (and is thus deemed somehow 'authentic', 'embedded' or 'popular') and what seems to come 'from above' (and gets branded 'authoritative', 'fabricated' or 'inauthentic'). Robert Cox, for one, often works from a division between

> the forces at work . . . that operate from the top down, which tend to maintain the trajectory of existing power relations, and those that operate from the bottom up, which may challenge existing power relations.
>
> (Cox 2001)

Reasonable on the face of it, these distinctions have in fact more to do with ideological presuppositions than with a serious analysis of the limits and possibilities of global social relations. For that, they need to be questionned, or suspended for a while, until we have a broader sense of the specific context of the world economy. Rather than intuitive certainties, we need to question what is being taken for granted. What if what comes 'from below' is also being structured, or over-determined (to raise the spectre of Althusserian structuralism), or manufactured (*à la* Chomsky), 'from above'? What if what is taken to be most authentic was most fabricated? What if what does come from the bottom does not make a civil society that has any autonomy from politics? What if 'grass-roots' means nothing at all? What if, more to the point, 'global civil society', 'international public opinion', 'the peoples of the earth', 'the global NGO community', 'the peoples' (or 'the women' or 'the workers' or 'the poor') of the world are not trans-national subjects in any political sense, but discursive, or ideological, mir-ages? What if they are *political* creations, 'real copies' of global civil society (to borrow from Umberto Eco on 'hyper-reality): perfectly fabricated, per-fectly still and acceptable substitutes to contain more contentious reality (Eco 1986)?

Still others in the literature reason by analogy, often drawing from nineteenth-century political vocabulary to write of socialism, or anarchism. This is a course of thought that can be more fruitful, but only if it is followed with more conceptual rigour than is often the case. Marginalized in the mod-ern *épistémè* (Foucault 1966, 36), analogies are often a stopgap measure in the social sciences, a way to tie over reasoning until a new field of enquiry arises that can produce a scientific reason, and a vocabulary of its own (by what Barthes called 'the semantization of usage').[9] Without a doubt, this marginalization gives analogies an impunity that, in turn, can lead to unrig-orous, or immodest, work. In a moment when what is known vernacularly as 'globalization' challenges all existing conceptualizations (this in spite of the reassurances of world-system theorists and other students of the capitalist *économie-monde*, who tell us that globalization is not in fact new at all, but related to 500- or 5000-year-old processes), the analysis of global social rela-tions is too often bent out of shape by political and historical analogies applied mechanically, without enough thought to the particularities of the world economy as a terrain of social relations, as if lessons learned and con-cepts born in one moment in one place could simply be transposed to another place at another moment. Often, categories and lessons of the past are used as benchmarks, most often to fault global social movements for not yet having made something of themselves that can compare to what was made by the old social movements. From such thinking we can learn little beyond what we already know: that global social relations have barely begun to take form, and that they have not yet moved much beyond what Alberto Melucci called 'the pre-political dimension of everyday life' (Melucci 1989, 222).

To learn whatever lessons analogies can teach us, we need to use them not as substitutes for critical analysis, but as their beginning point. From images frozen in time, analogies have to be made heuristic devices. This is what *thought-images* are. Famously, Walter Benjamin used them to think about the erosion of urban experience, and to penetrate the crucial moment when 'the continuum of traditional experience and remembrance embedded in spatial forms, once thought to be the ordering structure of the city and the generat-ing device for memory, was impoverished beyond recognition' (Boyer 1996, 23–24). Looking to the future, I want to use urban thought-images to explore both the manner in which global social relations are being severed from their political context and the manner in which they are being connected, not to know, as Benjamin did, what once was, but to unearth possible futures that risk becoming buried in cosmopolitan ideology.

More explicitly (by borrowing still another structuralist term in need of rescuing): I will use urban *thought-images* to make *real-abstract concepts*, that is to say concepts drawn from practice (what Althusser called *le concret de l'action*) and linked to it, but relatively autonomous from conjunctural happening. Although like them abstracted from practice, *real-abstract* concepts (*le concret de pensée*) have nothing to do with the vulgar analogies that are so prevalent now in the analysis of global social relations. Rather than provide an external viewpoint from which to judge global social relations, they are internal to practice. Closer to conjunctural happenings than ideal-types, they are theoretical expressions of a latent, politically unarticulated coherence; a unity that is still – and that may always remain – unrevealed, or unactualized, by concrete struggles.

Specifically, I will think with reference to *modes of social relation to the world economy*.

From the onset, something needs to be said about 'modes', a concept that has found more currency – at least in the post-war period – in French than in English (for reasons that have everything to do with the differing popularity of structuralist rereading of Marx). In the vernacular, 'modes' are relatively coherent and enduring sets of manners and habits, fixed for a while by societies, groups or individuals. How long the while varies: 'modish' ways of speech and dress last but a season, until people tire of 'moding it' or of following particular fads. More enduring modes (of thought or understanding, for instance, or in grammar or music) belong to the *longue durée* of mentalities, and can last for several lifetimes. For Boswell's Johnson 'modes of conceit' sometimes lasted as long as did relationships with individuals worthy of them.

In social scientific usage, 'modes' most often refer to relatively invisible but enduring, and structuring, products of specific historical circumstances. Dialectically, they are both artefacts of historical struggles and part of the conditions under which histories are made. Born of the meeting of social forces, they structure, inform, shape or over-determine historical conjunctures. Most famously, Marx used the concept of 'mode of production' to highlight how societies resolved the contradictory development of the means and the social relations of production. Regarded by contemporaries as ethereal bonds out of history, 'modes of production' were, for Marx, contradictory and contingent historical arrangements lasting for a while, and helping set the stage for further historical developments. Thus was slavery born of the specific contradictions of primitive communism, feudalism of slavery, capitalism of feudalism, and thus would socialism be born of the specific contradictions of capitalism. More recently, authors from the Parisian *école de la régulation* wrote of 'modes of regulation' as historically specific ways to manage contradictions between the extraction of surplus value and its realization, and to stabilize the social act of production (Boyer 1986; de Bernis 1990;

Jessop 1995). Also wanting to 'express concrete historical forms of the ways in which production has been organized', Robert Cox wrote of 'modes of social relations of production' (Cox 1987). In the same vein, David Harvey recently wrote of 'modes of competition' to describe 'Institutions, rules, and regulations [that] ensure that only one sort of competition ... prevail' (Harvey 2000, 211). More concerned with everyday life, Marshall Berman described modernity as a 'mode of vital experience' of space and time, self and others, and life's 'possibilities and perils'.[10] In the same spirit, Michel Freitag wrote of modernity as a *mode d'existence du réel lui-même* (Freitag 1995, 10). Against modern alienation, Raoul Vaneigem made it his project to restore *le mode d'être de la vie humaine* (Vaneigem 1999, 30).

Thinking from modes, then, will encourage us to reflect on what is being born of present circumstances that may later set limits to political possibilities.

About 'social relations' little can be said for now, except that needed distinctions (between material and ideological practices, or between social relations of production and reproduction) will be drawn as we progress.

About 'to', a small but significant preposition, something does need to be said. If the world economy was a social formation unto itself – self-contained and relatively autonomous from other social formations – we could think of modes of social relations made *in* the world economy as the *école de la régulation* thought of modes of regulation *in* national social formations. But the world economy is not a social formation like nation-states, at least not like nation-states at the centre of the world economy – the social formations of reference from Marx to the *régulationnistes*. Although it is becoming a significant place for social forces to meet and a defining context of capitalist accumulation, it is not (yet?) a container of social relations, a place where they are 'fixed' (to echo David Harvey's term, to which we will return below).[11] Little if anything has been made by global social relations that has had a structuring impact, either on global social relations themselves or on social relations elsewhere. On the contrary, what has been made in the world economy that has had the most impact is what was made most autonomously from social relations, by globalizing *élites* gathered in discreet, almost clandestine, places ('neoliberal concepts of control' for instance, that will be discussed below). Certainly, there are no global 'modes' of any sort, made solely from the global meeting of social forces. To write of modes of social relations *in* the world economy, then, would be to presume much too much from the world economy and, perhaps, force us to bring back through the back window cosmopolitan assumptions we chased out of the front door.

What are being constructed in the present juncture are ways to enter the world economy and to organize the occupation to the new terrain: modes of social relations, then, not *in*, but *to*, the world economy. Born in circumstances that are ours – and that we have the responsibility to try to understand – these ways will structure, inform, shape or over-determine what kind of subject will be present in the world economy, and what kind of politics will be made.

To recapitulate: between the vernacular and science, concerned with social relations of production, reproduction as well as with the organization of daily life, we will think of 'modes of social relations to the world economy' as relatively coherent, and perhaps enduring, ways to organize both the passage of social forces to the terrain of the world economy and their relationship on it.

Again, thinking with references to cities – that are both critical and permeable sites of social relations – will help us clarify our intent. Inspired by urban politics in the latter part of the nineteenth century, when 'the working class rose up in protest' and cities as the centre of the world economy became central terrains of struggles (Boyer 1996), we will contrast two 'modes of social relations to the world economy': a 'unitary' mode and a 'civic' mode.

In cities, people move about who were not brought there by invitation, who would not be thought of as proper citizens by civic-minded urbanites, whose wanderings contrast radically with the would-be geometric order of urbanists and civic-minded notables. Even aseptic city cores reinvented for the tourist trade, namely shopping centres, gated villages or synthetic 'edge cities', harbour people and modes of social interaction inexplicable from the point of view of planners. *Flâneurs*, of course, were of that type, as are – less romantically perhaps – people who come to cities in search of (material, cultural or political) sustenance, be they farmers selling produce in city markets, cultural tourists who left the periphery for urban heartlands of civilization, or, more to the point, social forces who move about in the city and explore it, circumstantially and purposefully, one step at a time, looking for like groups to exchange with and draw from and protective societal relationships to build. For them, cities are fields of tactical and strategic experiences, crowded sites of bound knowledge, contextualized 'places' rather than abstract, Cartesian 'spaces' (Ivain 1958; Khatib 1958).[12] Theirs is an experiential relationship to cities, born in discrete, bounded places and, to borrow Kafka's image of urban civility, in the 'traffic' in between (Boyer 1997, 29).

This, as we will see in Chapter 3, is the model from which we will try to make sense of the contemporary flight of social forces to the world economy. It is at the heart of the 'unitary' mode of social relations to the world economy.

The 'civic' mode is ideal-typically cosmopolitan. From sophists and cynics (who stood between *polis*, above citizens) to enlightenment philosophers (citizens of the *cité de l'esprit* who scorned real cities) and contemporary cosmopolites (who dwell in global conferences, universal exhibits, digital cities and other interstitial *non-lieux*), cosmopolitans have stood outside, or above, the miseries of context. From their miradors, they have viewed cities with detachment, as abstracted, bundled and levelled spaces where could be installed 'geometric freedom' (Le Corbusier 1994 [1925]). In what may be thought of as the birthing moment of modern urbanism, Le Corbusier saw Paris thus from the Eiffel tower:

> Ascending the Eiffel tower he felt was a solemn moment, for little by little as the horizons rose, the mind was projected onto a wider screen. When

Figure 0.1 The city of placed experiences
Source: *Guide psychogéographique de Paris*, G.-E. Debord, Asger Jorn, 1956.

the eye took in the urban panorama, optimism reigned and there the imagination conceived of vast new arrangements of space. . . . From this vertical perspective Le Corbusier noted, the eye sees clearly, the mind makes wise decisions, and the city planner knows what to do.

(Boyer 1996, 43)

As we will see in Chapter 1, urbanism is the extension of civic reformism that fought against the working class for the city to be administered in business fashion, as a space functionally divided, 'where everything had a place, and every place its order of things'.[13] From it, space 'came to be represented, like time and value, as abstract, objective, homogeneous and universal in its qualities' (Harvey 1985). This, as we will see in Chapter 4, is the model from which we will try to make sense of the neoliberal governance in the world economy.

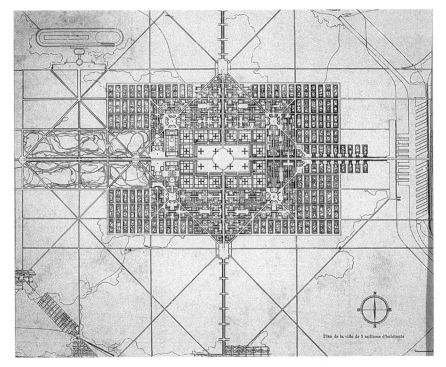

Figure 0.2 The city as a levelled space: *Plan Voisin*, '. . . the prototype for the grade-flat-and-build urban development that has defaced cities all over the world' (Sennett 1992, 171)
Source: Le Corbusier 1925. © FLC (Paris)/SODRAC (Montréal) 2002

What will be included in this book and what will be left out

In the thirty years or so that have passed since the beginning of the Bretton Woods crisis, all manner of social forces have rushed to the world economy, from globalizing *élites* gathering in exclusive places to define terms of global order, to social movements struggling against the ways and consequences of globalization. In doing so they have engaged in such diverse practices, and have created so many institutions, meeting places and events, that ten thousand E.P. Thompsons working with as many Walter Benjamins and a million philologues and area specialists helped by an infinite number of research assistants forever surfing the Web could not begin to document them well enough to rescue them from the oblivion of cosmopolitan generalities. The artisanal work of a single author, with minimal research assistance, this book cannot, of course, aim to present a credible *catalogue raisonné* of global practices at the beginning of the twentieth century. Admittedly, what is presented here, especially in Chapters 3 and 4, is neither as exhaustive nor as detailed as I would have liked, or as it would have been had my means to do research been a better match for the ambition of my theorizing.

Short of assembling exhaustive, or even convincing, documentation, what I can do is travel intelligently enough between the small, particular world of conjunctural practices and abstract, synthetical, *modes of social relations to the world economy*, to make leaps of faith seem reasonable and perhaps to help theoretical work catch up a little with the pace of events. Heuristic travelling, then, is my method; back and forth, between the subjectivity of practice and scientific detachment, thinking about the broadest possible worlds and the most abstract structures from the smallest, most concrete fragments.

Because of administrative and family responsibilities, and because of the exigencies of funding institutions in Canada – that give little to scholars who want to raise their own questions independently of the strategic priorities of the state – this book was a long time in the making. I began writing it in 1998, an epoch ago. Some events discussed here are more dated than I would have wished, others are more recent, but not as well digested as they could be. The resulting book, of course, risks not being as well received by the immense industry of rigorous and perfectly apolitical scholars who work in the field of international relations than if I had confined myself to a smaller domain within the boundaries of normal science. However, as I will argue in Chapter 1, to think politically about social and political relationships in the world economy, one has to question what normal social science takes for granted.

Whatever influence this book will have will depend entirely on its resonance among those who are curious enough to want to enquire, against cosmopolitan certainties and normal social science, into how humanity may be making itself, perhaps in ways and places we are only beginning to suspect.

For all the care I took to document case studies and to get stories right, I would like this book to be read as an experimental work of theory. I hope it offers needed tools to think beyond contemporary attempts to settle matters in the world economy. We have reached a crossroads and we need to examine the lie of the land before we proceed any further. This, above all, is what this book is about.

Chapter outlines

Contesting globalization is divided into five chapters. Chapter 1 begins conventionally, with a survey of the relevant literature. Rather than work from established categories in the academic field of international relations – where too many theoretical carcasses have been picked over for too long by scholars who are too close to governing agencies to feel any sense of urgency about politicizing struggles – the survey will divide studies of social and political relationships in the world economy by the cosmopolitan ghosts they create. First will be works of 'transnational public policy' that make up a *problem-solving humanity*. In the second cluster will be works (mostly of sociology) that infer from the study of global processes and practices that a *sociological humanity* has appeared, without looking into how it made itself or was made.

Third will be works of 'transnational historical materialism' that look into how globalizing *élites* have created a world in their image, who wish into existence a *counter-revolutionary humanity* to remake it.

In the second part of the chapter I will introduce concepts invented, or worked on, by the *Internationale Situationniste* (IS), a self-described 'international association of workers in the advanced domain of culture' that met, in different places and in differing numbers, between July 1957 and the early 1970s (the dissolution of such a small and quarrelsome bunch was a non-event not easily dated). Although their surrealist playfulness and avant-garde disdain for concrete matters of political organization appear far removed from the purposefulness of transnational campaigns, the IS will help us break through cosmopolitan romanticizing.

In Chapter 2 we will look at three moments in urban history when the movement of urban social forces highlighted very different modes of relation to cities at the core of the world economy: the dockworkers' strike in London (August to September 1889), the election of the first reform mayor in the history of New York City (November 1894) and protests surrounding the 'Summit of the Americas' in Québec city (April 2001). To emphasize most clearly differences that will be useful later – when we look into emerging modes of social relations to the contemporary world economy – these episodes will be visited twice: first, to enquire into the unitary politics of place; second, to look at the civic organization of space.

In Chapter 3 we will look into the hurried and disorderly flight of social forces to the world economy. In the first part of the chapter we review key moments in the history of 'left internationalism' from the 1840s to the Bretton Woods crisis. In the second part we take our first measure of contemporary happenings. Specifically, we characterize the contemporary movement of social forces as a collection of campaign-centred movements that are both (i) increasingly linked to one another by transnational institutions, and (ii) grounded by, and constitutive of, a sense of place.

In Chapter 4 we will look into global neoliberalism as a mode of social relations to the world economy. Our examination is divided into three parts. First, we look at the global level proper, beginning with 'global summits' organized by the United Nations at the beginning of the 1990s that are to global governance what universal exhibits were to free-trade internationalism: idealized representations of a projected order.[14] Where, as Charlotte Brontë put it, universal exhibits gathered a 'unique assemblage of all things' promised by free-trade capitalism (Malamud 1997, 15) in celebration of the universalist appeal of exchange value, global conferences gather and organize citizens of the world severed from context, rooted in generic problems. More specifically, we will proceed with a more systematic and sober analysis of less conspicuous sites where are tentatively defined the terms of global civility, from the periphery of power (e.g. the United Nations Department of Public Information's 'NGO Resource Center', ECOSOC's 'Committee on Non-Governmental Organizations', the UN's Environmental Liaison Center and so on) to the centre (e.g. The World Bank Inter-agency Group on Participation, the 'NGO-World Bank Committee,' IMF-sponsored 'town hall meetings').

In the second and third sections of the chapter, we look to specific policy initiatives at the global level, but also within regions, countries and, especially, cities of the world economy. There will be found some of the most eloquent initiatives born of global governance.

In Chapter 5 we will move towards a more synthetical and political understanding of the present juncture. Specifically, situationist concepts of *positions, dérive* and *détournement* help us draw the contours of a political articulation between hitherto particularized experiences.

1   More than ghosts

Subjects in places in the world economy

> [J]ust as postmodernism was *the* concept of the 1980s, globalization may be *the* concept of the 1990s.
>
> (Waters 1995, 1)

The academic literature that deals with social and political relationships in the world economy has grown enormously in the past decade. Whereas but a generation ago the only scholars who enquired into such matters were either engaged politically (in social movements old and new, in the Fourth International and so on) or else belonged to relatively circumscribed schools of analysis outside mainstream paradigms (world-system theory, for instance, or 'neo-Gramscian transnational historical materialism'), now several academic fields of enquiry have grown up around the concept of globalization that are giving significance and confidence to scholars of all lineages and tendencies, whether engaged or not.

Holding these expanding fields together is the certitude that we live in an historical moment when some kind of transnational subject has appeared to make unprecedented, globally democratic politics. This is the defining paradigm of normal social science in the age of globalization. As I made clear in the Introduction to this book, I want to question this paradigmic certitude, by re-establishing the continuum of experience – severed by cosmopolitan ideology – between contextualized politics and the making of transnational subjects.

Here, I begin by reviewing relevant works published in the past two decades, both to garner what I can that will be useful later, and to penetrate the critical moment in analyses when contextualized experiences get abstracted beyond politics. This, to put it crudely, is where the materialist analyses of politics ends and cosmopolitan ideology takes over. In later chapters I will start from there, to forge a different way forward.

Specifically, the first part of the chapter deals with three clusters of literature that all think global politics apart from contextualized experiences and each invent a cosmopolitan ghost that has little to do with actually existing politics. First will be works of 'transnational public policy', principally preoccupied with goings-on within what Anne-Marie Clark termed the 'international governmental arena' (Clark 1995). Working acritically from 'global problems' (that surfaced as political issues in the 1980s as they had in the 1840s, the dawn of another critical phase in the history of globalization[1]), these works make up a *problem-solving humanity*. As we will see below, this duty-bound global subject is a perfect fit for the global partner that neoliberal governing institutions are working to fabricate. In the second cluster will be works (mostly of sociology) that infer from the study of global processes and practices that a *sociological humanity* has appeared, without looking into how it made itself or was made. Third will be works of 'transnational historical materialism' that enquire into how globalizing *élites* have created a world in their image, and wish into existence a *counter-revolutionary humanity* to remake it.

Missing from all clusters is what *Contesting Globalization* hopes to add: a theoretical argument, informed by the study of concrete – contingent and situated – practices, for how transnational subjects are being made or may be making themselves on the terrain of the world economy. In the second part of the chapter I will move closer to making this argument, by surveying works that look at specific sites of politics in the world economy. This is a rich literature, whose lessons need to be critically synthesized rather than ideologized, as they often are these days. To operate this synthesis we will turn to concepts either invented or worked on by the *Internationale Situationnniste*, as part of their critique of modern urbanism.

Ghosts in three machines

So prevalent have cosmopolitan postulates become that we can, without excluding any major *problématique* or strand of literature, divide academic studies of social and political relationships in the world economy by the ghosts they create or allow to haunt what they have constructed.

Although there are arguably as many global ghosts as there are books about global politics these days, three principal figures do stand out: a *problem-solving humanity*, a *sociological humanity* and a *counter-revolutionary humanity*.

A problem-solving humanity (functional and apolitical)

Problem-solving theory 'takes the world as it finds it, with the prevailing social and power relationships and the institutions into which they are organized, as the given framework for action . . . to make these relationships and institutions work smoothly by dealing effectively with particular sources of trouble' (Cox 1986b, 88). When Robert Cox wrote this, the crisis of state-centred modes of regulation was only beginning (as we will see in Chapter 4), and social relations were still largely fixed to national social formations. Then, problem-solving theories, loosely gathered under the umbrella of 'realism', generally took as a given a difference of kind between intra-states politics (assumed to be the domain of 'authentic politics') and inter-state politics (seen as a place of 'mere relations').[2] When they did look into global political relationships and institutions, problem-solving works usually studied them as places of little intrinsic significance, where politics was almost wholly derived from state-bound processes. Or else they busied themselves, *à la* Allisson and Aron, with micro-sociological studies of soldiers and diplomats working within the confines of a set world. Only works informed by critical theory that did not 'take institutions and social power relations for granted but call[ed] them into question' looked to global relationships and institutions as relatively autonomous loci of power, where terms of global order could be defined and limits to political possibilities set (Cox 1986b, 88).

A generation later, numerous international institutions are addressing global problems and labouring to devise strategies 'to bring more orderly and reliable responses to social and political issues that go beyond the capacities of states to address individually' (Gordenker and Weiss 1996, 17). We will argue below that these strategies are part of a hegemonical design to tranform the world into a levelled space to be gridded functionally and managed economically. Although these strategies have not yet brought about anything like a new world order (if they had, this book would make no sense, except as a lament or a pamphlet), works of 'transnational public policy' already concede, acritically, that the framework for global actions has been set, and that humanity has fallen into problem-solving ranks.

Key here is the idea that 'global issues' (or challenges, or problems) are, by themselves, forcing 'collaboration or cooperation among governments and others who seek to encourage common practices and goals' (Gordenker and Weiss 1996, 17). Among the most studied are: environmental troubles (acid rain, ozone depletion, whaling, the trade in ivory from African elephants, global warming, overfishing, pollution, loss of biodiversity and genetic diversity, the degradation of human habitats); gender troubles (the private–public split, structural violence, militarization, prostitution, sexual division of labour, ecological responsibility, unequal distribution of resources); security troubles and issues (land-mines).

For works of this first cluster, global issues, challenges and problems are kernels around which naturally coalesce purposeful units, sometimes called 'transnational issue networks' (Burgerman 1998; Price 1998), or transnational 'networks of knowledge and action' (Lipschutz 1992), or 'epistemic communities' ('a network of professionals with recognized expertise and competence in a particular domain and an authoritative claim to policy-relevant knowledge within that domain or issue area').[3] There beaver away state representatives, labour representatives, international emissaries, experts, as well as various and sundry CBOs, GONGOs, NGOs, QUANGOs, GOINGOs, CONGOs and INGOs, that are the 'torch-bearers and stake-holders' of global civil society (Donini 1995, 83).[4] Some work 'upstream' to aggregate societal demands, others 'downstream' to retrofit the local to the global (Gordenker and Weiss 1996; Lipschutz and Mayer 1996). Among states, there are 'lead states' with a strong commitment to effective international action, 'supporting states' that 'speak in favour of the proposal', and 'swing states' whose commitment is crucial but fragile (Porter and Brown 1996, 40ss.). The experts' job is to foster innovative thinking, to deal effectively with sources of trouble (Porter and Brown 1996, 51).

Synthesized into global agendas (Porter and Brown 1996), moral programmes (Nussbaum 1996) and global ethics (Midgley 1999), the regimes, norms and policies that are made by global policy units, and the solutions that are found to global problems, are, without further thought, considered the building blocks of a more global, and more human politics (what Edgard Morin called une *politique de civilization*).[5]

Thus is a first cosmopolitan ghost created, by simultaneously pulverizing humanity into functional bits and reassembling it into an abstract bearer of rights, responsibilities and moralities. This double process, we will see, is an exact match for neoliberal governance, which aims to create a global civil society that is a strategic site of decontextualization, occupied by a politically neutered humanity, held to purpose and efficiency, never whole except when fulfilling appointed duties.

To think critically about this attempt and perhaps envision more than the apolitical reform of the world economy, we will obviously need to conceptualize global politics in a manner that does not just replicate, but actually question, the ways of neoliberal governance.

A sociological humanity (inferred, habitudinal and globally reflexive)

One of the founding myths of sociology – an academic discipline born in the golden age of internationalism – is that a truer, more intrinsically human, humanity exists in the ether above and between positions occupied by actually existing, conjuncturally bound, human beings. If earthly boundaries could be peeled away, the founding fable went (Auguste Comte wrote of a 'religion of humanity'), this truer subject would be revealed to us.[6]

In the twentieth century, as the academic field of sociology constituted itself on the acceptance of state-defined boundaries of social interaction, society and the nation-state came to be taken as coterminous (Giddens 1985b; Holton 1998) and this myth fell into desuetude. Only mavericks (Marshall McLuhan and Alvin Tofler, for instance), or engaged intellectuals (Franz Fanon, Johan Galtung), or those, like Immanuel Wallerstein, who were consciously working on 'a protest against the ways in which social scientific inquiry was structured . . . at its inception' evoked or studied human sociability beyond the nation-state.[7]

Now, the myth is surfacing again, in a moment when all social boundaries (and all bounded conceptualizations) are being challenged by dynamics of globalization. Most remarkable in this regard is the literature that focuses on new information and communication technologies, which has tended to embrace rather than problematize the 'renewal of the expectations for social change and the recomposition of human communities' that has been spurred by this latest technological revolution (as earlier expectations had been stimulated by previous technological revolutions).[8] Running through this literature is the assumption that new technologies, by freeing human beings from the misery of context, are allowing for the opening of what Howard Rheingold termed a 'computer-mediated social formation' (Rheingold 1993b) and Jean-François Lyotard 'a universal speech community'.[9] In these new realms, members of many global 'non-place' communities are deemed free to invent new, more human ways of politics, as far above the fret and worry of life in the real world as were William Gibson's avatars (who lived unfettered lives 'in a new informational network of computer matrix called cyberspace' that looked 'like Los Angeles seen from five thousand feet up in the air'), as freely as game players reinvent themselves in MUDs, MUAs, MUSEs, MUSHes, MOOs, *maskenbals* and Populopolis of all sorts.[10] Above and beyond all parochialisms (to borrow McLuhnan's celebratory phrase), new actors 'intervene, sometimes to resist, to organize, to legislate, to plan and to design' (Mitchell 1995).[11] This is what the 'ultimate flowering of community' is in the age of 'technosociality'.[12]

The new fable, then, goes thus: new (despatialized, desynchronized) agoras will make new citizens, unsullied by context, immaculately conceived.

> Within these places, social contracts will be made, economic transactions will be carried out, cultural life will unfold, surveillance will be enacted, and power will be exerted.
>
> (Mitchell 1995, 160)[13]

More seriously concerned with the profane world of material practice (and therefore closer to mainstream sociology), but still as swayed by cosmopolitan mythology (and often as guilty of reasoning by metonymy) are works that offer global variations on the theme of what futurologists in the 1970s used to call the 'information society' (Spybey 1996, 104), and sociologists of the 1980s and 1990s have come to study as 'post-industrial', or 'informational', society. By and large, this literature – too rich and varied to be treated here in anything but the most cursory manner – has tended to argue that improvements in managerial and production practices, as well as radical changes in transportation and communication technologies (e.g. wire, coaxial and fibre optic cables, wireless broadcasting, earth satellites) have opened up a planetary 'space of flows' (in Manuel Castells' celebrated idiom) that now exists above and beyond (or outside and between) the 'spaces of places', where political struggles about the collective organization of daily life were hitherto located.[14]

Crucially, the global 'space of flows' is not, as was the 'space of place', a contested terrain, where social relations relativize power and create contingent, historically specific and contradictory modes of production and regulation. It is not a place for the 'quotidian' making of social rules, where 'every day in every context, people acting individually or collectively produce or reproduce the rules of their society' (Castells 1983, xvi). Rather, it is conceptualized as an immaterial vacuum, where disembodied processes flow unimpeded and technology itself is a 'mode of social development', set behind actually existing actors, either busily networking and flextiming with the flow, or folded into themselves, in identity politics.

> [O]ur society is constructed around flows: flows of capital, flows of information, flows of technology, flows of organizational interaction, flows of images, sounds, and symbols. Flows are not just one element of the social organization: they are the expression of processes dominating our economic, political, and symbolic life.
>
> (Castells 1996, 412)

Thus, just as liberals imagined that 'markets maketh citizens' (MacPherson 1977), so does contemporary sociology assume that flows make humanity, thereby absolutely over-determining what futurologist Alvin Tofler used to call 'virtual social futures' (Tofler 1970). Social forces that are taken to preside over the flow, or profit from them, are taken to be part of what Manuel Castells called the 'technocratic-financial-managerial elite', a cartoonish character whose power is so absolute and transcendental, whose hegemony is so complete, that social forces opposed to it can be thought of only as rhetorical subjects, in whose name political plans and agendas need to be drawn. Neither winners nor losers, of course, get to be studied as subjects of their own history.

Somewhat removed from concerns about technology and communication, and more seriously concerned with the historical constitution of societies, are works situated within what Malcom Waters called 'a new sociology of globalization' (Waters 1995, 62). This is a relatively recent, and fast expanding, body of literature, that does look into what Marx would have recognized as real historical subjects, but most often not as *transnational* subjects per se. Rather than having made themselves – or having been made – on the terrain of the world economy, subjects studied here exist in, and belong to, other spatially and historically specific social formations. There, they are historical subjects in the full sense of the term. But in the world economy they are abstract subjects, bearers of all sorts of manners and strategies, but still as unmade politically.

A quick glance at the works of Immanuel Wallerstein (the principal figure of 'world-system theory', one of the most influential research programmes in the field for more than three decades), provides us with a kind of intellectual maquette of the argument most often presented here.

Building on Braudel (whose influence can be felt on all historical enquiries into the making of world order), Wallerstein conceives of the capitalist world system as a relatively contained, self-sufficient and organic *économie-monde*, structured by trade and production relations, bolstered and reproduced by inter-states arrangements. In this system, states (of three sorts: core states, semi-peripheral and peripheral states) 'stabilize capitalism by absorbing its costs and managing the social problems which it creates' (Waters 1995, 24). States, then, are significant milieux, where classes and fractions of classes make history: '[to] be "social" [is] to be "national" '.[15] For its part, the world economy is not a place in the material sense of the term, where struggles are played out and significant social relations of production happen, but an empty space. There, transnational subjects literally have no place of their own, except as idealized or objectified wholes ('the family of world anti-systemic movements').[16]

Likewise, Rolan Robertson presented a 'necessarily minimal model of globalization' (Robertson 1992) that divided the history of globalization into five phases:

1   The germinal phase ('lasting in Europe from the early fifteenth until the mid-eighteenth century')
2   The incipient phase ('lasting – mainly in Europe – from the mid-eighteenth century until the 1870s)
3   The take-off phase ('from the 1870s until the mid-1920s)
4   The struggle-for-hegemony phase ('from the mid-1920s until the late 1960s)
5   The uncertain phase ('beginning in the late 1960s and displaying crisis tendencies in the early 1990s).

In the first four phases, the world gradually came to be a place 'in itself', for reasons of trade relations and inter-state arrangements familiar to all authors working within the fold of world-system theory. In the fifth phase it has become a place not only 'in itself', but 'for itself'. How, of course, is the key issue here, that carries with it the determining question related to the making of transnational subjects and, ultimately, to the analyses of the limits and possibilities of the present time.

How then does the world come to be for itself? How has the consciousness 'to build transnational cooperation around shared goals' by which Jackie Smith defined transnational social movements (Smith *et al.* 1997, 59–60) come about? How did what Richard Falk called 'non territorial reality of global consciousness' (Falk 1995a; 1995b), Peter Beyer 'global awareness' (Beyer 1994), Jan Aart Scholte a 'world perspective' (Scholte 1993) and, most famously, Anthony Giddens (Giddens 1990) and Ulrich Beck, 'global reflexivity' (Beck 1999; 2000) emerge?

For Robertson and other principals of global sociology, uncertainty, risk and cost/opportunity structures are the ethereal bounds that unite humans and over-determine the 'consciousness of the world as a whole', by which humanity thinks and acts for itself (Robertson 1992). It is not global troubles, then, or global flows that beget humanity, but a global 'system of cognitive and motivating structures' that determines (managerial risk-avoiding) practices and makes (careful) transnational subjects.[17]

Formulated a decade ago, ideas of global reflexivity have become key tenets of the new sociology of globalization, a field that is often 'innocent of systematic attention to contentious politics' (Tarrow 2001). A measure of their influence is the number of recent works that have taken for granted that subjects active in the world economy are indeed conscious of global happenings, and proceed from there to fact-gathering activities, without enquiring into how consciousness and reflexivity are activated politically.

This is especially remarkable in works that enquire into global (or transnational) 'advocacy networks' active in a variety of fields: the environment (Lipschutz and Mayer 1996; Newell 2000), human rights (Dunne and Wheeler 1999; Keck and Sikkink 1998; Risse-Kappen *et al.* 1999; Sikkink 1993), religion (Beckford 2000; Beyer 1994), women's issues (Cockburn 2000b), labour activism (Munck 2000; Waterman 1988; 1995), and gay and lesbian politics (Adam 1987, 82–89). As works of the first cluster took prevailing social and power relationships for granted and fit humanity to existing institutions, so do these most often take for granted an order of consciousness and imagine a political subject to carry it. In Ronnie D. Lipschutz's excellent study of environmental activism, for instance, what are essentially bound and contextualized case studies are wrapped within a broad, ideological discussion of something called 'global civil society' about which we know very little except that it does not exist in reality and cannot speak for itself but must be taken as the ensemble of reference (Lipschutz and Mayer 1996). In like manner, Robin Cohen and Shirin M. Rai's accomplished anthology of the *Global Social Movements* literature (Cohen and Rai 2000a) begins and ends with an argument for a new form of global politics that is not actually carried in any chapter in the book, but rather is concerned with issue areas. What, or who, is the transnational subject that is to articulate and carry this new politics is not discussed.

Missing here is a sense of the political making (and, perhaps, the unmaking) of transnational subjects. I am talking here neither about discursive, nor ideological, subjects, nor about bearers of abstract rights and responsibilities (a much debated question here as well as in the introductions and conclusions of many works considered here), but of real, historical, transnational subjects present at their own making (if not necessarily in control of it). In other words – those of Ernesto Laclau and Chantal Mouffe, to whom we will come back in Chapter 5 – what is missing in the sociological literature is a concern for how an 'articulating subject' may be making itself, not above conjunctural happenings but through them. Works that do concern themselves with how political syntheses get made that rise above immediate, or corporatist, interests (see e.g. Rucht 1993) remain for the most part descriptive, or they content themselves with generalities about the linking of the global and the local (Cohen and Rai 2000b), the opening of a Habermasian 'global public sphere' (Devetak and Higgott 1999, 491–492) or the network form of it all (Klein

2000a; Vertovec and Cohen 1999; see also Graeber 2002). Again, then, what is most global about global politics remains most ghostly.

That global social movements may be inventing a repertoire of their own may be a crucial political development. For that, the comparative, issue-specific work most often undertaken by global sociology is fundamental. In what Alberto Melucci called 'the pre-political dimension of everyday life' (Melucci 1989, 222), similarities and coherences are sometimes observed that have not yet found conscious, or clear, political expression (the language of class can be more telling than the politics of it). Indeed, Braudel himself emphasized that much when he stressed the analytical importance for the study of *économies-monde* of what he called *la vie matérielle 'l'habitude . . . la routine . . . mille gestes qui fleurissent, s'achèvent d'eux mêmes . . . hors de notre pleine conscience . . . des incitations, des pulsions . . . des façons ou des obligations d'agir'.*[18] For this reason, we will certainly keep works of transnational sociology in mind when the time comes to theorize the making of transnational subjects in the contemporary period. We will, for the same reason, carry with us ideas of global reflexivity (and of 'transnational imaginary', 'transnational diaspora consciousness', or what Arend Apparduai termed 'global landscapes and ethnoscapes').[19] We will also keep in mind the importance of new communication technology (this was certainly crucial in the making of anti-summit protests in Seattle, Prague and elsewhere). However, we will not take it that central political questions related to the making of transnational subjects have been dealt with once we have assembled a store of global practices. Cosmopolitan ideology notwithstanding, global networks, 'world risk' assessment (Beck 1999), late modern reflexivity and a pouch full of global practices do not of themselves transnational subjects make. As A. Colás put it recently, what is missing here is a theory of agency (Colás 2002).

A counter-revolutionary humanity (anti-systemic and counter-hegemonical)

A third cluster of relevant works looks at the bourgeois making of global order and imagines a humanity that will remake the world in its image.

In polemics about global political relationships, figures of order are often answered by cosmopolitan *superoumos* that have more life in rhetorics than in politics. Thus, for instance, is Arthur Kroker's 'technological class' met, in the end, by a fantastic kind of cyberproletariat. Seemingly closer to actually existing politics and apparently more reasonable (but neither more material nor less fantastic) is Ricardo Petrella's work, in which *padronis de la Terra* (a theatrical stand-in for financial capital) is confronted by an assumed humanity, on whose behalf may be drafted global social contracts (Petrella 1995).[20] *Abyssus abyssum invocat*, absolute order begets an absolutely resolute, and absolutely definite, humanity.

Remarkably, the same mirror-images appear in the writings of what Stephen Gill has labelled 'transnational historical materialism' (Gill 1990, 46), arguably the most critical and politically conscious framework for the study of world order. Also drawing from Braudel, transnational historical materialism looks at the world economy as a minority phenomenon (Braudel 1985, 93–94). In Braudel's own study, such merchant capitalists as Jakob Fuggers and Laurent Medicis stood at the helm; they were the ones without whom the capitalist *économie-monde* was inconceivable (Braudel 1979). In the work of Karl Polanyi (whose imprint may be discerned in all works on 'transnational historical materialism'), world order was also conceived as the issue of a minority, as *haute finance* made a hundred years' peace for itself, from the end of the Napoleonic Wars to the First World War (Polanyi 1957). In works of transnational historical materialism, there are 'political gods at the center of the system' (Gill, 1991, 64), variously labelled the 'transnational managerial class' (Cox 1986b, 358; 2001), 'globalizing *élites*' (Gill 1994), the 'international cadre class' (van der Pijl 1984; 1997; 1998), the 'transnational capitalist class' (Sklair 2001) or the 'global ruling class':

> those who own and control [transnational corporations], their allies in the state (globalizing bureaucrats) and in political parties and professions (globalizing politicians and professionals) and consumerist élites.
>
> (Sklair 1999, 334)

Conceived *in vitro* – in meetings in Bilderberg, Basle, Rambouillet and elsewhere – relatively unconstrained by goings-on within national social formations (van der Pijl 1979), working with coherence of purpose and ideology (Cox 1987), linked into networks – here too a form that begets its own subjects – (Gill 1990; 1991), global rulers are the vanguard of the bourgeoisie (van der Pijl 1989, 30). In their miradors, they form a class both in itself and for itself, imbued with a 'highly developed consciousness' (Gill 1990). Informed by ' "internationalist" elements within the state bureaucracies of the major capitalist states' (Gill 1986, 212) as well as by such organic institutions as the Trilateral Commission and the Bank for International Settlements, (Gill l991), they are free to invent 'comprehensive concepts of control' (Burnham 1991, 87) that are

> coherent formulations of the 'general interest' which transcends narrowly defined fractional interests and which combine mutually compatible strategies in the field of labour relations, socioeconomic policy and foreign policy on the basis of a class compromise.
>
> (Overbeek 1990, 26, 178)

Carried 'across a wide range of countries' (Gill *et al.* 1992, 24) by an international state structure that has 'at its heart the central governmental agencies of the most important industrialized ... economies, together with key multilateral agencies' (Germain and Kenny 1998), translated and 'locked in' by neo-juridical (or 'neo-constitutional') reforms (Gill 1998), 'applied' nationally (van der Pijl 1989, 4, 7) by states acting as 'a kind of transmission belt for globalizing forces' (Cox 1986a; Gill 1992; Gill *et al.* 1992), transnational 'concepts of control' are devices by which the global ruling class makes world order.

For works of transnational historical materialism, then, the world economy is a place of absolute, unilateral power. The internationalization of the state and of political authority (Gill and Law 1988, 90–91) are, for all their authors' concerns with Gramscian analyses, quite literally political expressions of the globalization of production and finance (Gill *et al.* 1992, 8) and unproblematized 'sociological corollary to the internationalization of capital' (Gill 1990, 37). By contrast, all that is contingent, relational and relative about global power is assumed to be contained within national social formations (seen here, as in mainstream sociology, as the defining space of capitalist accumulation). It is there, and not on the terrain of the world economy, that significant social relations are deemed to take place, that class and class power become more than things, that civil society exists as a true source and theatre of history, that globalization may 'arouse oppositions that could strive to confound and reverse them' (Cox 1987), that concepts of control become matters of political contention and that in the end, the terms and limits of hegemony are negotiated. Significantly, it is also there, and not in the world economy, that Robert Cox (the principal figure of this literature) imagines transformative struggles taking place: 'the task of changing world order begins with the long, laborious effort to build new historic blocs within national boundaries' (Cox 1983, 174).

Having filled the world with transcending figures of order, transnational historical materialism has to step out of itself in order to think politically about processes of change in the world economy. To fight off neoliberal pretensions about the end of history and reconcile the optimism of its will with the pessimism of its intellect (a Gramscian *bon mot* that appears often in works of transnational historical materialism), it has to reach out for remarkably immaterial ideas and express unexplainable confidence in 'the human capacity to be able to create alternatives' (Gill 1997, 223). After having written a remarkable study on the making of transnational capital, for instance, Kees van der Pijl can only wish for counter-hegemonic concepts of control to fall out of the sky and 'lend coherence to political decisions in different countries' (van der Pijl 1989, 10). Similarly, Stephen Gill's study of 'Global Hegemony and the Structural Power of Capital' ends with an indeterminate wish for an 'ethically based counter-hegemony' that could control 'the power of capital and the unfettered market' (Gill and Law 1993, 380). In a later article, Gill means to clarify his politics by issuing a broad, undiscriminating invitation to

> organizations and movements that might form part of a counter-hegemonic bloc includ[ing] Amnesty International, green parties and ecological groups, socialist think-tanks like the Transnational Institute,

peace groups such as Oxfam, and religious organizations such as the
World Council of Churches.

(Gill and Law 1993)

Quite naturally, then, without political intervention to animate it, hegemony
is seen to beget counter-hegemony: 'Any attempt, therefore, to construct a
hegemonic system of rule will tend to generate, dialectically, a set of counter-
hegemonic forces' (Gill and Law 1993).

In the same manner, Martin Shaw theorizes an unfinished 'global-
democratic revolution' (of which globalization is only a moment) that he
wishes to see carried further by a ghostly movement only grounded 'in the
extent to which ... democracy and human rights have become universal
values to which individuals and groups can appeal, if need be over and
against national institutions' (Shaw 2000, 167). How, by whom and to what
purpose are these values constructed and installed, whether their universal-
ism challenges or completes that or neoliberalism, and what are the links to
actually existing struggles are matters not discussed by Shaw.

Leslie Sklair – whose work is rooted in world-system theory – also theorizes and documents the absolute domination of the transnational capital
class and ends with a brief conclusion – an afterthought really – that
expresses unexplained confidence and support for social movements of
resistance to globalization:

> The knowledge that worker, citizen, religious, and other concerned
> groups in communities all around the world are monitoring their activ-
> ities clearly encourages some TNCs to act more responsibly than they
> otherwise might be doing. New technologies of communication help
> transform local disruptions of TNC activities into global challenges to
> capitalist hegemony.
>
> (Sklair 2001)

That it invokes such immaterial spectres so late in its analysis says something crucial about the limits of 'transnational historical materialism' as a
framework for the study of global social and political relations. The resistance
of social movements to globalization might indeed present a challenge to
capitalist hegemony, and socialist think-tanks and green parties might, as Gill
wishes, make something of radical importance. But to think politically about
these possibilities and to build on them, we need, more than we do wishful
thinking, a theory of politics that does not exclude global social relations from
the beginning only to reintroduce history-saving ghosts by the back door.
Dialectically, we have to incorporate and relativize what 'transnational historical materialism' has to say about the making of world order, by looking into
the possibility that the world economy itself may be a significant context for
social forces to meet, where might be defined new modes of social relations.
Excluded here by theory, such global social relations have to be brought into

the analysis, and made subjects of critical investigation. To theorize global change as well as the making of global order, we cannot take the world economy to be a social formation where no social relations actually take place.

This, of course, is not to presume anything about the actual importance of global social relations, or indeed about their very existence. What, if anything, gets made in the global meeting of social forces, the relationship between this and what gets made elsewhere, in other social formations, as well as the limits of transnational power – if any – remain, of course, matters of empirical enquiry. To conduct this enquiry – to verify, as my positivist colleagues would put it, the hypothesis that transnational capital class may actually be making itself not outside of social relations, but within them – we need to think politically about global social relations. Concretely, this means broadening the scope of enquiry to include all social forces that might actually be engaging in global social relations.

In his latest article, Robert Cox conceived of three force lines of world order:

> The first is the mode of concentration of the dominant world-economic forces. . . . A second power area that merits further study is the private power that is effective in world financial markets. . . . A third set of forces have the cumulative consequence of sustaining existing power and can be loosely described as involved in political corruption and clandestine activities.
>
> (Cox 2001)

To these we have to add – at least as a hypothesis – social forces brought to the world economy by governing institutions to buttress the process of globalization and, crucially, social forces that have brought themselves to the world economy to contest neoliberal governance. If these are excluded from the start of our analysis of global power, we are easy prey for cosmopolitan wishful thinking.

To sum up: to problematize what cosmopolitan ideology takes for granted and look into the possibility that transnational subjects – not cosmopolitan ghosts but real, concrete, historical, subjects – may be making themselves in the world economy, we will need (1) to assume less than do works of 'transnational public policy' that existing institutions and social power relations have installed themselves as a given framework for action; (2) to question more than do works of 'global sociology' the political meaning of global reflexivity and to enquire into the political significance of what is being made, or can be made, in global flows and networks; and (3) to think more than do works of 'transnational historical materialism' about what is specific, contingent and relational about global power, and about the relative separatedness of the world economy as a terrain of politics. Most often treated as an absolute, this separatedness has to be problematized and relativized (as it was, indeed, in Braudel's own work).

To do this, and develop critical awareness of potentiality for change, we need to reason from concrete, contingent and situated practices.

Subjects in places in the world economy

At the periphery of the many academic fields of enquiry that have grown up around concepts of globalization, still below the radar of general theories of global order and change, are works that look critically into global power as a relational, contingent and situated arrangement. This is a rich and varied literature that has not yet been brought together into a theoretical ensemble. To my knowledge, there is no academic field that deals explicitly with situated instances of global power.

Were we to constitute this new field, that core work would come from what Anthony King called 'globally-oriented urban research'.[21] For the most part, this is a literature that has looked to 'world' (or 'global') cities as places that have been uncontestedly 'produced' by global capitalism (uncritical readings of Lefebvre's groundbreaking work on the production of space abound here). Thus seen, 'world cities' are conceptualized as 'technopoles' (Castells and Hall 1994), 'command and control centers able to coordinate, innovate, and manage the intertwined activities of networks or firms' (Castells 1996), tourist destinations, global 'shock cities', or places where transnational capital is recycled into the buying of cultural products and the development of property.[22] More interesting from our point of view are works that have looked into cities of the world as sites where global struggles get played out. For Saskia Sassen, for instance, world cities are crucibles where social forces meet that occupy markedly distinct positions in the globally structured movement of people, things, ideas and capital. Literally worlds apart, these social forces are brought together by urban propinquity. The social relations they engage in, as well as what Sassen calls their 'presence', are part of the dialectics of order and change in the world economy (Sassen 1998). Less inclined to theory-building, but closer to the kind of work that urban sociologists did in the 1970s, before cosmopolitan ideology encouraged global functionalist abstractions, Mike Davis (1992) and John Walton (1987) have both looked brilliantly at cities as specific sites of global power and counter-power.

Of interest to the new field would be works that look into still smaller instances of global power. Included here would be works on the particular forms of power and counter-power in export zone factories (Graham 1995; Harvey 2000; Ong 1987; 1996), on beaches and bases (Enloe 1989), in environmental sites (Mittleman 1998), during anti-summit protests in Seattle, Prague and elsewhere (Drainville 2001), or in many discrete 'spaces of resistance' (Pile and Keith 1997). Through these works, the world economy begins to look like an assemblage of contested sites, and world order like a relative, negotiated, contingent arrangement.

But, for all that they tell us about the contingency and situatedness of global power, these studies have not yet added much to our understanding of the making of transnational subjects. As do sociological works in the age of globalization, they have most often jumped from studies of specific instances to waxing cosmopolitanly about grand absentee subjects (indeed, David Harvey himself jumped from specific studies of export zones in Dhaka, Jakarta amd Bombay to talk of a 'transnational working class' (Harvey 2000, 42). Politically, this is still a literature that thinks by spectral procuration.

To think politically about the link between situated practices and the possible making of transnational subjects, we need intermediary concepts. In answer to these preoccupations, we will work with two concepts, both related to experimental works of the *Internationale Situationniste: dérives* and *situations.*

As many exegetes have pointed out, situationist scorn for programmatic unity makes it difficult to write of 'Situationism' as a coherent ideology, or even a relatively congruent collection of theoretical proposals (indeed the *International Situationniste* explicitly forbade such an adjectivation of its name). As a political phenomenon, the IS was neither a party (though Guy Debord's miserly disciplining does evoke a little party boss), nor a movement (though it was in a movement that the IS took its most concrete form), but a clique, both cemented and broken up by intensely reflexive, and pettily personal, politics.

Beyond their quarrelling, what IS principals did share – and what makes their work worth recalling when looking for ways to escape the immobilism of current thinking about social relationships in the world economy – is a radical critique of the benumbing *ennui* of everyday life under what might properly be termed 'settled modernism': Now that the modern spirit of exploration and discovery has been installed as a governing regime – and transformed into a quest for new commodities – creativity (or so went the IS critique) has been captured and cornered, reduced to a specialized activity of sanctified experts. Art, to take but one creative instance, has become the thing of officialized artists, mandated to produce picturesque images to be hung in designated places. There, art sits in a corner, detached from lived lives, making a spectacle of itself (Debord 1992, 3). Hypnotized, deadened by deference, alienated spectators become but shadows of themselves, absentee subjects inattentive to the creative possibilities of everyday life.

In politics, the IS denounced the spectacular division of labour curtailing the creative possibilities of everyday life. In the age of settled modernism, designated experts produce political spectacles consumed by alienated others living quotidian lives that appear increasingly banal by contrast (Ivain 1958).

Thus, the spectacle was not just an event for *Situationnistes*, but a social division of labour. Alienated, convinced of their own insignificance, non-experts lose a sense of their place in the world. They cease living creatively and become easy prey for rationalist ideologues, bureaucratic purveyors of functionalist efficiency, aesthetic or technical instrumentalists, ideologues and other fear-mongers; all specialists working to order. Thus is humanity

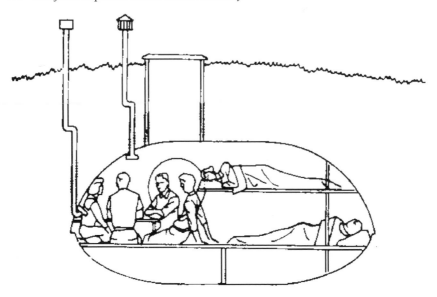

Figure 1.1 Humanity buried by ideology for its own good
Source: *Internationale Situationniste*, vol. 7, April 1962

contained and, sometimes, quite literally, buried for its own good (IS 1962, 245).

Against the alienating authority of the spectacle, the IS wished to reclaim all that was lived and significant in everyday life. Posing as a gathering of 'professional amateurs', IS members spoke and wrote of everyone becoming 'artists in their own lives', creating quotidian meaning (IS 1959b; IS 1960). Against experts at the vanguard of the revolution, who wish only to replace the ruling spectacle by another, they argued for the radical ordinariness of passionately lived moments:

> Those who talk of revolution and class struggle without explicit refer-
> ence to everyday life, and without understanding what is subversive
> about love and positive in the quotidian refusal of constraints, such
> people carry a corpse in their mouth.
>
> (Vaneigem 1967, 19)

In the first period (1957 to 1962) the IS concerned itself particularly with a critique of urbanism, which it saw as the most concrete expression of modern ways to create insignificant unity and disempower citizens (IS 1961; Kotanyi and Vaneigem 1961). Urbanists, or so went IS's critique, look down on the city as a location where problems happen that need to be solved expeditiously, with as little political interference as possible. In urbanists' eyes, cities are 'projection into space of a social hierarchy without conflict'.[23] For urbanists, people need to be housed, goods and capital moved and production organized

(IS 1961). These circumscribed imperatives correspond to myopic prescriptions: at times things and people need to be fixed in place, in houses that shelter workers and give them time and space to recharge exhausted batteries, in factories where commodities are produced, or in parks and other designated places, as desired by Haussmann (1979). At other times the purposeful movement of things and people needs to be directed efficiently, with minimum leakage and no vagrancy. Above all, there are to be no games, no wantonness, impetuosity, or playful meandering in the Cartesian city. LES JEUX SONT INTERDITS. Everything, movement and immobility, must be for a purpose (IS 1959a; Ivain 1958; Kotanyi and Vaneigem 1961). Modern thoroughfares born of urbanists' desires for efficient passage kill 'traffic' in Kafka's sense of the term.

Were it to succeed in its attempt to grid and rationalize, that modern urbanism would create efficient, settled and perfectly moribund cities where everyday life would no more be pregnant with radical possibilities. Cities would be, as Richard Sennet put it, spaces 'for economic competition, to be played upon like a chessboard . . . a space of neutrality', absolutely divorced from the social (Sennett 1992, 55). 'Struggle, with nature, with the body, with space, and with class [would] . . . come to an end' (Sadler 1998). The orderly spectacle of urban unity would prevail and alienated urbanites would become absentee subjects, incapable of creating significant lives in the city. In the end, the modern city would kill those who dwell within it: 'had Nazis known modern urbanism that concentration camps would have been made subsidized housing' (Vaneigem 1961).

Against urbanism and the hegemony of Cartesian gridding, the IS invented *l'urbanisme unitaire* (defined by Peter Wollen as 'integrated city-creation' (Wollen 1989b). Rather a critique of modern urbanism than an alternative to it, *l'urbanisme unitaire* was an attempt to rescue city dwellers from instrumental rationality and the deadening purposefulness of modern urbanism. Moved by the will to create, *l'urbanisme unitaire* wanted to transform the gridded city into a terrain of shifting decors, where quotidian jostling would beget tactical experiences and new meaning. Then, the city would know no set boundaries. It would form an unalienating 'unitary milieu' where divisions between work and leisure, and between private spaces and public places, would wither away (Situationists heaped equal scorn on parliaments and bedrooms). Thus would be unmade the separation between what is and what could be. Then, city dwellers would regain a sense of the significance of their lives and recapture the capacity to create radical meaning and relationships (IS 1959a; Ivain 1958).

Closer to political practice, two concepts were at the heart of *l'urbanisme unitaire* that seem particularly relevant to our purpose, to make sense of current practices of opposition to global neoliberalism (as we will see in Chapter 3), to see through neoliberal governance (Chapter 4), and to think about radical practice in the contemporary world economy (Chapter 5): *dérive* and *situation*.

Defined as 'a technical mode of behaviour tied to the specific conditions of urban life . . . to facilitate quick passage through most varied ambiances' (Debord 1958), *dérives* were both practised and theorized. In avant-garde fashion, actually organized *dérives* were seriously ludic affairs meticulously recorded.

> On Tuesday, 6 March 1956 at 10 a.m., G.-E. Debord and Gil J. Wolman meet in the rue des Jardins-Paul and head north in order to explore the possibilities of traversing Paris at that latitude. Despite their intentions they quickly find themselves drifting toward the east and traverse the upper section of the 11th arrondissement.
>
> . . .
>
> On the North side of rue des Couronnes a staircase gives them access to a network of alleys similar to the previous ones, but marred by an annoyingly picturesque character. Their itinerary is subsequently inflected in a northwesterly direction.
>
> . . .
>
> Upon studying the terrain the Lettrists feel able to discern the existence of an important psychogeographic hub [plaque tournante].
>
> . . .
>
> Debord and Wolman continue to walk north along the beautiful and tragic rue d'Aubervilliers. They eat lunch on the way. . . . Passing by the lock once again, they roam about for a while in Aubervilliers, an area that they have traversed dozens of times at night but which is unfamiliar to them in daytime. As darkness descends, they finally decide to put an end to a *dérive* that they deem to be of little interest as such.
>
> . . .
>
> Undertaking a critique of their operation, they establish that a *dérive* that starts out from the same point would do better to head in a north-by-northwesterly direction and . . . that the number of systematic *dérives* of this sort should be increased.
>
> (Debord 1989)

Importantly, *dérives* were not the detached and carefree deambulations of surrealists (Artaud 1979; Breton 1952) that owed everything to 'objective chances' and were more in keeping with bourgeois promenading and displaying. Nor were they like spontaneous 'happenings' fashionable in New York at the time, that the IS thought barren spectacles overloaded with aesthetics born of poverty ('material poverty, poverty of human contact, poverty inherited from the artistic spectacle, poverty of the specific philosophy driven to ideologize the reality of these moments' (Clark and Nicholson-Smith 1997; IS 1997; Kaufmann 1997). Rather, *dérives* were experimental struggles in the realm of culture, 'exercises in territorial reconnaissance . . . exploratory forays into singular surroundings', intended as means to reclaim the creative possibilities of city life against the deadening compartmentalization of urbanists' maquettes (Kaufmann 1997). Engaged and purposeful, partici- pants in *dérives* performed work of 'cognitive mapping' (to evoke Jameson, to whom we will return in Chapter 5).

In marked contrast to the individualizing meanderings of bourgeois *flâneurs*, Situationist *dérives* did not presume the existence of a collective subject, but were constitutive of it. In *dérives* through Amsterdam or Strasbourg for instance, participants carried walkie-talkies (Ross 1997) to link not only segregated neighbourhoods, but also each other:

> he walks, he deciphers the surrounding environment, but at the same time he communicates with other *dériveurs*, and together they transform the urban space into a clandestine communication network devised to elude power . . . The *dérive* is, simultaneously, the street reclaimed and com- munication reestablished. In the end, the only authentic communication takes place in and through the streets, which is the *bête noire* of the society of the spectaclé.
>
> (Kaufmann 1997)

Thus exposed, the situationist city became a fertile terrain for radical politics. To describe the radical possibilities of *dérives*, Guy Debord borrowed from Marx and spoke of 'the withering away of . . . alienated forms of communi- cation' and the birth of psycho-geography (Levin 1989).

With *situations* we arrive at the end of, and the reason for, Situationist agitation: total, unalienated experiences, synchronic moments of collective transcendence when spectators shatter their alienating identification with shadowy heroes and false images of their collective selves, and stand ready to become revolutionary agents (Debord 1985; Jappe 2001). This, I suggest, is a better beginning point – heuristically as well as politically – for thinking about what might be born of the present, global moment.

Conclusion

In his most recent book, David Harvey surveyed accounts that have been offered of 'how capitalism has structured its geography', citing

> Lenin's theory of imperialism, Luxemburg's positioning of imperialism as the savior of capitalist accumulation, Mao's depiction of primary and

secondary contradictions in class struggle, Samir Amin's account of accumulation on a world scale, Immanuel Wallerstein's analysis of the capitalist world system, Andre Gunder Frank's development of under-development, Arrighi Emmanuel's unequal exchange and Fernando Cardoso's dependency theory.

(Harvey 2000, 55)

To these seminal works we need to add accounts of the manner in which power and counter-power are formed in an infinity of discrete places within the world economy. Synthetized by concepts such as *dérive* and *situation*, this literature can help us contextualize the findings of transnational public policy, global sociology and transnational historical materialism, and help us think about global politics not as the thing of ghosts, but as a situated relationship between transnational subjects.

2 Three episodes from cities in the world economy

Events 'take place.' And again. And again.

(Tschumi 1998, 160)

In the 1880s and 1890s, the two most important cities at the core of the world economy were loci of political struggle. In London and New York, skilled and unskilled workers, trade unionists, ward heelers, precinct captains, district bosses and sundry roughs, the disreputable, the respectable and the residuum ('not a class, but the drift of all classes'), both men and women, stood in defence of their turf.[1] They picketed work sites and squatted tenements, parks and public places, organized vigils, formed gangs and neighbourhood clubs, sometimes bursting riotously out of place, or marching in processions and parades, 'dramatizing the power they still lack[ed]', trying to capture – at times symbolically, at others quite literally – hitherto inaccessible sites of power (Berger 1968; Marston 1989).[2] Through placed struggles and in movement across neighbourhoods and districts, what Peter Hall economically described as 'the evils of 19th century cities' (Hall 1996, 7) became matters of political contention; stakes of struggles were created and the structuring of urban power became more visible (Hall 1996, 7).

At the beginning of the twenty-first century – another critical moment in the history of globalization – cities at the core of the world economy are again becoming contested terrains, as medleys of 'anti-globalization' protesters (a disputed term, clarified below) converge on places where globalizing *élites* gather. In 1994, the fiftieth anniversary of Bretton Woods, institutions focused the attention of social movements and, for a while, The World Bank and the IMF became significant places of transnational politics, where gathered 'Fifty years is Enough' coalitions having in common their opposition to structural adjustment policies.[3] Most famously, 50,000 people met in Seattle on 30 November 1999 to force the closing of the second ministerial conference of the World Trade Organization. On 16 April 2000, 8,000 protested the annual meeting of The World Bank and IMF in Washington (Hahnel 2000). In September, 15,000 were in Prague to protest the Fifty-fifth Annual World Bank/IMF Summit – the first such event held in a former Eastern-bloc country. A few months later, a few hundred were in Davos to protest the opening of the Thirty-first World Economic Summit. In July 2001, upward of 200,000 people were in Genoa to protest the meeting of G-7/8 heads of states.

Brought together by organizations with an acute sense of the marvellous and the sensational (e.g. the Ruckus Society, the Direct Action Network, Reclaim the Streets, Mobilization for Global Justice), coloured wondrously (in Prague, yellows were 'ecolos', pinks reds of all sorts, blues anarchists and anti-fascists), their carnivalesque aesthetics and sense of happening contrasting markedly with the dutiful greys and decorous fêtes of world order (last year at Davos, Youssou N'Dour sang and danced for globalizing *élites*), often amplified by similar happenings elsewhere, summit protests are spectacular episodes that dramatize the evils of twentieth-century capitalism, and make them, for a while at least, matters of political contention.

In this chapter, we look at three moments in urban history, when the movement of social forces in cities highlighted very different modes of relation to space: the dockworkers' strike in London (August to September 1889), the election of the first reform mayor in the history of New York City (November 1894) and protests surrounding the 'Summit of the Americas' in Québec city (April 2001). To emphasize most clearly differences that will be useful later – when we look into emerging modes of social relation to the contemporary world economy – these episodes will be visited twice: first, to enquire into the unitary politics of place; second, to look at the civic organization of space – ostensibly apolitical, but in fact a strategic answer to situated politics.

Occupying places

A sense of place is a political construction, created from concrete, contingent practices, in particular circumstances.

London 1889

In the late 1880s, places in London became more politically charged than they had been since the collapse of Chartism. Key to the rise of an urban sense of place and, consequently, to politicizing urban issues, were fights over concrete locations. Between 1886 and 1888, the struggle for free speech in Trafalgar Square (a traditional forum for working-class agitators) rallied unskilled workers as never before (Webb and Webb 1989, 373). In the East End, Tower Hill was the 'Trafalgar Square of East London' (Smith and Nash 1984 [1890]). There as well, orators harangued crowds and outlined programmes and tactics. Crowds 'took in what was said through [their] eyes', sizing up the strength of their number and their unity, money was collected and means to organize crowds into movements were born that later sustained other struggles (Smith and Nash 1984 [1890], 79). From the struggle for Trafalgar Square, for instance, was born *The Link*, 'a little weekly newspaper' that, less than a year after its founding, played a key role in mobilizing public opinion and gathering funds on behalf of striking matchmakers at the Bryant & May match factory, a starting point point of the 'new unionism' (Thompson 1988, 240–241; Thompson 1967).

> [P]ublic opinion was aroused in a manner never before witnessed; £400 was subscribed by hundreds of sympathizers in all classes; and after a fortnight's obstinacy, the employers were compelled, by sheer pressure of public feeling, to make some concessions to their workers.
>
> (Webb and Webb 1989, 388)

Perhaps the best illustration of the importance of struggles over concrete locations in the emergence of a broader, more social and political sense of place in London is the dockworkers' strike, the most famous strike of the nineteenth century (Stedman Jones 1971, 315). The strike began as a dispute over the division of the 'plus' on the Lady Armstrong, tied at the West India dock.[4] By 12 August, the dispute had made the rounds of workers and was already being seen as an emblematic struggle. On 14 August 2,500 dockers from the South Basin (West India dock) stopped work. Dockers from the Royal and Albert docks came out on 16 August. A few days later, dockers at the Tilbury docks (twenty-four miles down river) followed suit, and then those working at the Surrey Commercial and Millwall docks. A week after the beginning of the dispute on the Lady Armstrong, dockworkers from all docks were on strikes.

On 22 August the strike entered a new phase, 'as it was no longer confined to dock workmen, but was being extended to general labourers in many places'.[5] By 27 August, 100,000 men were out.[6] On strike, of course, were dockworkers – for the most part unskilled casual labourers hired by dock companies themselves – who wanted a raise from 5d to 6d an hour (the docker's tanner, the symbolic heart of the strike), as well as an end to the 'plus' system, a minimum call of four hours, and wages of 8d an hour over-time for work done between 6 p.m. and 6 a.m. Also out were skilled workers of almost every branch of river work: wharfingers, stevedores, lightermen, bargemen, coal heavers, ship's artificers, painters, engineers, ballast heavers, shipwrights and so on. Although not of a single class, skilled workers generally had regular employment and good pay. As a group, they had neither dispute with their own employers nor direct quarrel with dock companies, but came out in support of dockers, for 'entirely unselfish motives' (Champion 1890).[7]

The story of the dockers' strike was written in places. The first site of struggle was the dock area itself, where were organized pickets to keep out the 'blacklegs' (replacement workers).[8] As a contemporary account put it: 'If the [dock] companies could, by hook or by crook, have got vessels loaded and discharged, the dockers would never have got their tanner' (Champion 1890). A key site of activity, pickets were challenged by dock companies (who argued unsuccessfully that dockers and their supporters had gone beyond their legal right to 'observe and persuade' blacklegs), and they were explained by *The Times* to its readers, whom it encouraged to garner for themselves, in the spirit of late Victorian sightseeing:

> A picket consists of two or more men on strike stationed at a given place to watch and to prevent, for the present it will be assumed only by moral suasion, any men from taking work where ordinary workers are 'out'. The curious may see a strong picket at any time at Paddington, Euston, or Liverpool street; but the best place to see them are opposite the Dock-House, and thence to Fenchurch-street station, or at any of the dock gates.[9]

For dockworkers, who feared that thousands of blacklegs would be hired from nearby counties, or from Amsterdam and Belgium, picketing was a central organizing issue (Oram 1964, 535; Smith and Nash 1984 [1890], 102). For the duration of the strike, round-the-clock pickets were organized at dock entrances to prevent strike-breakers from entering dock areas and to encourage those already inside – whom dock companies were feeding and housing in sheds – to come out (Oram 1964, 535). Under the leadership of stevedores and sailors – accustomed to the discipline of pickets – between 12,000 and 15,000 dockers were organized and manned pickets, for a daily strike wage of 2s (Champion 1890, 26; Oram 1964, 536). Through moral suasion, 'bombarding', undeniable intimidation and with visits paid by picket inspectors to vessels awaiting unloading, the number of blacklegs was kept to a minimum, and had a negligible effect on the outcome of the strike (in great contrast to earlier dockworker strikes).[10] On this first front, victory was clearly with the dockers, which left docks sorrowful sites worthy of pictur-esque gaze.[11]

Docks were also important as meeting places, where principals from the Strike Committee communicated information to dockworkers and their sup-porters (Smith and Nash likened mass gatherings during the strike to 'the dockers' morning newspaper' (Smith and Nash 1984 [1890]). Dock meetings were also events where the movement could gather new supporters: on 17 August, the first Sunday of the strike, a mass meeting was held at the gates of the East India docks that witnesses considered 'the real beginning of the great strike' (Smith and Nash 1984 [1890]). After the meeting, members of the 'Amalgamated and United Societies of Stevedores' stayed on site and voted in favour of the strike for the next day.

In addition, docks were starting points of processions to various centres of power, both symbolic and material: political clubs up Pall Mall, the Houses of Parliament, St James' Palace, Westminster Abbey, St Martin's Hall and, significantly, the financial City. There, dockers and their supporters visited, daily for the duration of the strike, the Dock House on Leadenhall Street, the Chamber of Commerce and the Lord Mayor's Mansion.

Figure 2.1 Dockers' picturesque: 'Aspect of the Riverside Wharves During the Strike'
Source: *Illustrated London News*, No. 2629, vol. xcv, Saturday, 7 September 1889,
p. 297. By permission of the British Library, slide 308–309 03091

Processions were grand affairs that grew grander as the strike progressed.
On 15 August, 15,000 men marched from the docks through London to Hyde
Park, accompanied by a single band (Oram 1964). The following day there were
60,000 marchers, 'with fifteen bands and two hundred banners' (Oram 1964,
539). On 21 August, a procession of 20,000 marched to the city that involved
'the regular dock labourers, permanent men, stevedores, carters, drivers, lightermen, wharfingers and others'.[12] On 23 August, the procession numbered over
70,000 men.[13] Three days later, an important procession marched to the rail-
way coal depots with the intent of rallying coal workers and of stopping the
supply of coal to the city. To move coal workers, the procession featured
coalies as well as 'flags and emblems of queer device – a basket of coal, a loaf of
bread . . . or a doll called "the Poor Docker's Baby", and a grotesque figure of
Father Neptune to signify that the cause was connected with shipping'.[14]
(Although it did not stop coal delivery, the procession of 26 August did have
an impact: the following day 3,000 men employed by coal merchants struck.)[15]
On 28 August, the procession was 90,000 marchers strong (Oram 1964).
Again there were banners, flags and bands, allegorical groups and *tableaux
vivants* representing all river trades. H. Llewellyn Smith and Vaughan Nash
provide an evocative account:

[Behind brass bands] streamed the multitude whose calling lay at the
dock and riverside. Such finery as they boasted in the way of flags and

banners had been lent by friendly and trade societies, and this gave the procession the appearance of a great church parade. . . . There were burly stevedores, lightermen, ship painters, sailors and firemen, riggers, scrapers, engineers, shipwrights . . . and unmistakable casuals with vari-coloured patches on their faded greenish garments . . . a stalwart battalion of watermen marching proudly in long scarlet coats, pink stockings, and velvet caps, with huge pewter badges on their breasts, like decorated amphibious huntsmen; coalies with bags tied to the end of poles, fishing aggressively for coppers with bags tied to the end of poles . . . skiffs mounted on wheels manned by stolid waterman; ballast heavers laboriously winding and tipping an empty basket, Father Neptune on his car in tinsel crown, and flowing locks. . . . Emblems quaint and pathetic were carried in the ranks, the docker's cat . . . the docker's dinner and . . . the docker's baby.

(Smith and Nash 1984 [1890], 85–86)

In the manner of their time, processions of dockers were urban 'performances in motion through space' (Goheen 1990) and, as such, they were privileged occasions to gather funding, take stock of the strength of the movement and of the resolve of the men, and target common enemies (a favourite was Mr Norwood, Chairman of the Joint Committee, whose effigy was carried daily).[16] As with pickets, processions were also occasions to discipline the residuum into a movement. Again, Smith and Nash provide a useful contemporary account:

The leaders [of dockworkers] could hardly have occupied themselves better than in organizing and leading the strike procession. It kept masses of men occupied and interested, a matter only second in importance to keeping them fed, and it was a grand opportunity for enforcing a respect for order and discipline amongst the heterogeneous dock populace, who had never known before what it was to fall into line, to follow their leaders, or, indeed, to have any leaders to follow.

(Smith and Nash 1984 [1890], 83)

So orderly were processions of dockers and their supporters that they secured the co-operation of the police, which helped to create 'an image of the docker as a responsible citizen worthy of help' (Oram 1964).[17] In contrast to previous periods of agitation by the residuum (the struggle for Trafalgar Square, for instance, marred by Bloody Sunday) the movement of dockers was not repressed by police, and the National Guardsmen were not called in, which increased sympathy for the strike outside the East End, and in the City in particular:

though there was little public sympathy shown in the earlier days of the strike, as soon as it became widely known that thousands of the strikers had marched through the City without a pocket being picked or a window being broken, and that at the head of the procession was a man whose public position was a guarantee that 'the mob' had a responsible leader, the British Citizen felt he might go back to his suburban villa when his day's work was done with full confidence that his warehouses would not be wrecked in the night, and that he could afford to follow his natural inclination and back the poor devils who were fighting with pluck, good humour and order against overwhelming odds.

(Champion 1890)

Other sites of note, great and small, were: Hyde Park, where crowds sometimes numbered 100,000; Tower Hill, where great gatherings were held '[d]ay after day, with the regularity of a cathedral service, for an entire month'; East End bakery shops, butchers, grocers and public houses, that were picketed to 'encourage' owners not to feed blacklegs. Less charged politically, but no less important to the outcome of the strike, was the Wade's Arm tavern on Jeremiah Road in the East End. There, the Strike and the Finance committees met. The latter was responsible for issuing and receiving collection boxes that had been circulated during daily processions, for tallying contributions and, most importantly from the point of view of the strikers, for stamping and distributing relief tickets. Altogether, some 440,000 tickets were issued during the strike, numbers increasing with need as the strike went on (in the last days of the strike, an incredible 100,000 tickets were issued and distributed).[18]

Struggles over these specific sites, as well as efforts to organize gatherings and movements, were key to socializing the struggle of the dockworkers. Building on intra-neighbourhoods links, support networks (especially between women) and a broad sense of community growing in East London (some wrote of the reinforcement of neighbourhood 'provincialism'), and made more resonant by the increase casualization of work in the East End, and by the general de-skilling of dock trades (Stedman Jones 1971), the dockers' strike became a social strike, indisputably linked with the broader 'condition-of-the-people' question (Buxton 1890, 7).[19] By *The Times'* reckoning, this happened on 24 August. On that date, *The Times* stopped writing of the 'Strikes of Dock Labourers', and referred instead to 'The Strikes at the East-End'.[20] In the wake of the dockworkers' strike, there was 'an unruly saturnalia' of protest, strikes, industrial and political action in the whole of the East End (Oram 1964, 539). Shipscrapers went on strikes, as did soapworkers, ropemakers, orange porters, tailors, cigar-makers, ironworkers and boot-finishers.

Women sometimes marched in processions (that customarily ended with 'three ringing cheers for the wives and children at home . . . bravely bearing up against the pangs of hunger') and they organized a rent strike in the East End, hanging banners from their windows that read:

No rent paid in the East End of London 'til the docker gets his tanner.[21]

Landord, please don't call for your rent. Our husbands are out on strike. We will pay when the strike is over.[22]

Or, more poetically:

Our husbands are on strike, to the wives it is not honey,
And we all think it right not to pay the landlords' money
Everyone is on strike so landlords do not be offended,
The rent that's due we'll pay to you when the strike is ended.[23]

In a period when the East End was being defined from the outside, as a *terra incognita* away from the respectable West End, the heart of London's darkness, Jack the Ripper's turf, 'the boldest blotch on the face of the capital of the civilized world', home to Jews (and thus, perhaps, to Jacob the Ripper), outcasts and the residuum, the dockworkers' strike provided a rare moment of self-definition for East Londoners.[24] It changed places with politics and provided the context for a social strike. That is why dockers got their tanner.

New York 1894

At the time of London's dockworkers' strike, places in New York also became charged with politics, though of a very different sort. Key here was the struggle between the machine politics of Tammany Hall and the burgeoning civic reform movement.

Before the civil war, gangs and ethnic associations had been 'basic units of social belonging' for working and idle poor men and their families (Sante 1992, 197–235). Ranging from fraternal organizations to criminal groups, gangs were firmly rooted in place: the 'Dutch Mob' dwelled on Houston Street east of the Bowery; the 'Mackerelville Crowd' stayed between Eleventh and Thirteenth Streets, First Avenue and Avenue C; the 'Hell's Kitchen Gang' hung near the Hudson River Depot on Thirtieth Street; the 'Stable Gang' stayed near the Washington Street barn, the 'Five Pointers', the 'Sixth Ward Gang', the 'Hudson Dusters' and the 'Shirt Tails' all hailed from the Sixth ward, as did the infamous 'Plug Uglies'. Other gangs and ethnic associations drew their *esprit de corps* from equally fixed loyalties to places in their countries of origin, transferred with immigration to what Herbert Gans termed 'urban villages' (Gans 1982). The 'Kerryonian', for instance, were rooted in memories of County Kerry in Ireland. The 'Order of Sons of Italy', the 'Polish National Alliance', the 'Pan Hellenic Union', the 'New York Hebrew Free Loan Society' were also rooted in places, real and imagined (Sante 1992, 199, 216, 217).

Fire-engine companies were also important units of social belonging. They too were tied to places that were keenly defended:

on February 23 [1863], Hook and Ladder Company Number 18 attacked

Engine Company Number 26. On March 9, Hose Companies Number 9 and Number 50 slugged it out, and on June 1 Hook and Ladder Company Number 4 took on both Hose Company Number 1 and Hook and Ladder Company Number 3. In the winter of 1864–1865, five policemen were shot while trying to separate skirmishing firemen. . . . Black Joke Engine Company Number 33 fortified their engine house with a howitzer to guard against raids by other companies.

(Cook 1974)

In neighbourhoods below Hudson street in particular, gangs, ethnic associations and fire-engine companies were part of a proto system of governance that structured allegiances and disciplined social relations (albeit in a manner as different as can be from the orderly picketing of London dockworkers): quotidian relationships were near-feudal pacts of protection and assistance, and small riots were common occurrences at election time, or during holidays and labour disputes (Myers 1968 [1917], 131). When, exceptionally, New York's residuum left the structured confines of neighbourhoods and urban villages, it did so in a manner that was generally undisciplined and disorderly, even by the rough standards of neighbourhood relationships. A good example is the 1863 anti-draft riot ('the most violent and destructive civil rebellion in the nation's history' (Czitrom 1991) that brought the largely Irish crowd out of the Lower East side, up Eighth and Ninth Avenues, to Central Park and then, down Third Avenue, to the draft office on Forty-sixth Street and back to the Lower East Side.[25]

After the civil war, the rough discipline of gangs, ethnic associations and fire-engine companies was folded into the machine politics of Tammany Hall. The politics of place grew more tightly structured, intra-neighbourhood riots stopped, as did riotous outbursts out of places, with very few exceptions (e.g. the Tompkins Square riot of January 1874 and the 1893 hunger riot for which Emma Goldman was sent to Blackwell's Island Penitentiary).

Founded in 1789 as an anti-English, anti-aristocratic, patriotic, 'social, fraternal and benevolent organization, based on democratic principles that . . . all might mingle on the basis of manhood rather than that of wealth or culture', the Tammany Society was named after a great chief of the Delaware indians, an icon of nativist spirit of independence, famed for 'his wisdom, benevolence and love of liberty' (Myers 1968 [1917]). In 1805, the Tammany Society grew a political wing, Tammany Hall, that later became indissociable from the Democratic Party of New York (founded in 1828). Through it, Tammany Hall ruled New York, with few interruptions and some limits, from the civil war to the First World War.

In a sense, Tammany Hall was a bigger, more hegemonic gang, distinguishable from smaller ones by its less violent (one would not say more peaceful) methods and broader turf. During Boss Tweed's regime (1863–1871) certainly, Tammany Hall ruled New York much like a gang would its turf, on a near-feudal system of personal allegiances and protection. The result was unimaginable corruption and system-wide graft and protection rackets (Allen 1993b). Boss Tweed was driven out of City Hall in the autumn of 1871, following a public campaign orchestrated by the *New York Times* and *Harper's Weekly*, financed by 'bankers and others who had become ... alarmed at New York's precarious credit standing in the international money markets' (Glaab and Brown 1967, 205), and backed by middle-class taxpayers worried that poor immigrants would drag the city into insolvency. After defeat in the mayoral election, Boss Tweed relinquished his position as 'Grand Sachem' of the Hall.[26] Under the leadership of 'Honest John Kelly' Tammany Hall was restructured on the ward basis which it kept until well into the twentieth century.

After John Kelly's death in 1886, Richard Croker (once leader of the 'Fourth Avenue Tunnel' gang) became 'Grand Sachem' of Tammany Hall. Under his leadership, Tammany Hall was at it most successful as a political machine and, arguably, at its most developed as a system of governance, providing constituents with a rough regime of social welfare, distributing employment and material aid, offering mediation with the law and so on (Lowi 1964, 82; Sante 1992, 251–277). Between 1886 and 1888, Abraham Hewitt was Tammany Hall's Mayor of New York City (Boss Croker himself did not stand for election). In 1888, Tammany's Hugh Grant fought and won an election against a 'brownstone front' assembled in 'good districts' north of Hudson, from 'assembly men and aldermen ... all gentlemen ... club men of Knickerbockers ancestry'.[27] In November 1894, Hugh Grant again stood as Tammany's candidate for mayor, but was defeated by William L. Strong, a reform candidate (on whose campaign more below). After defeat, Boss Croker went into voluntary retirement in Europe. He returned in 1897 to win the first mayoralty campaign of greater New York. He retired in 1901.

Key to machine governance was control of places that mattered to immigrants and newly enfranchised voters, its key constituents.

> The boss system took the immigrant fresh off the boat and made him an American citizen. It found him a place to live, kissed his babies, entertained his whole family on the district club's annual boat ride, picnic or clambake, which was the event of the year in a lower-class society of limited pleasures. It fixed traffic tickets and jury notices for the shopkeeper, winked at the building and sanitary-code violations by the landlord or sweatshop operator, reduced tax assessments for big property owners. The boss system made money for the boss and for the party organization, but it also made life more bearable for a lot of little people who had no access otherwise to government, who knew of its operations only through their contacts with the machine. Tammany and its counterparts were whipping boys for the editorial writers in their ivory towers, but they were friends to the man in the street.
>
> (Moscow 1971, 19)

The first sites of machine politics were arrival docks and related offices. To place immigrants and ensure the swift naturalization of would-be voters, Tammany Hall created naturalization bureaux and it installed its judges in appropriate chambers (Lowi 1964, 37). In the run-up to the 1866 elections, for instance, Tammany judge Albert Cardozo of the New York Supreme Court 'often grant[ed] naturalization papers to as many as eight hundred persons a day, most of them sight unseen'. When Judge Cardozo was promoted, Judge Georges C. Bernard took his place as Tammany's naturalization judge. In preparation for the November 1868 election, he devoted himself entirely for a month to naturalizing aliens. 'He held court daily from 6:00 pm to midnight to process applications . . . initializing each application without reading it.' By election day, he had provided citizenship papers to more than 10,000 men, the vast majority of whom voted a straight Tammany ticket (Allen 1993b, 104).

In neighbourhoods on the Lower East Side where immigrants settled, machine politics was rooted in many places. In contrast to '[c]ollege professors and reformers who go up in a balloon to think' and cannot distinguish one place from the other (as Tammany philosopher and ward heeler George Washington Plunkitt put it), the Hall was defined by its embeddedness in place (Riordon 1963, 17). Ward heelers, who were the linchpin of machine politics and embodied all the functions of governance ('the economic overlords, the social arbitrer, the unofficial agent of . . . government, and the patron of the community'[28]), were also place incarnate, in spite of Boss Kelly's desire to 'establish the principle that powers be attached to party roles and offices and not to individual party cadres' (Lui 1995). Ward heelers lived in, and were 'fitted to the district [they] ran', and there was no separation between their private lives and their public functions (Riordon 1963, 45; Salter 1935, 23). When the district changed, the ward heeler was either replaced or else he changed along with his assigned place, sometimes crossing what in other contexts would have been unbreachable social divides:

> when Tim Sullivan's heavily populated Irish district in New York gave way to invasions of Jews and Italians, he adjusted with grace and sagacity, gleefully donning a yarmulke for Bar Mitzvahs, learning enough Yiddish and the Neapolitan dialect for friendly chitchat, appearing prominently at all ethnic festivities.
>
> (Callow 1976a)[29]

Ward heelers all had a place where they could be found, whether a grog shop, a tavern, 'the corner cigar store, the drugstore or such place. He goes there every night. When the voter wants him, he knows where to find him' (Riordon 1963). The ward heeler's place was the hub of machine politics, in Theodore J. Lowi's words, 'the heart of neighborhood *gemeinschaft*' (Lowi 1964).[30] Big Tim Sullivan's spot (in an area that had 'the highest population density and percentage of immigrants in the city') was a clubroom on the

Bowery that could seat 250, and where, beginning in 1894, Christmas dinners were served to 'as many as 5,000 hungry diners' (Czitrom 1991, 539, 545; Zink 1968, 89). George Washington Plunkitt's famous office was a bootblack stand in the County Court off Foley Square, at the core of the fifteenth district.

Neighbourhood events also defined places of machine politics. Clambakes, summer outings, weddings, Bar Mitzvahs and torchlight parades were all occasions for Tammany Hall to grant favours and cement allegiances. Fires and funerals were also 'great vote-getting occasions', when ward heelers could demonstrate their usefulness and secure future votes (Riordon 1963). Myths of picnics were made that united wards and heelers:

> On July 30, 1902, Tammany Hall's William Devery and his club staged a bash that must set a record of its kind, by way of an outing for only the women and children of his district – ten thousand of them. He rented two steamboats, six barges, and one tugboat, for a joy ride up the Hudson. The fleet was equipped with six physicians and six nurses, forty-five musicians, and an opera troupe. Devery charmed the ladies and a few thousand screaming children with 6,000 pounds of candy, 1,500 quarts of ice cream, uncounted heaps of sandwiches and pies, rivers of soft drinks and, practical politician that he was, 1,5000 nursing bottles for the tiny ones.
>
> (Callow 1976a)

The quantified mythology of men's picnics also served to fuse machine and place:

Figure 2.2 The spectacle of place: 'May Party in Central Park, about 1890'
Source: The Museum of the City of New York

The ambition of the district leader on these occasions is to demonstrate that his men have broken all records in the matter of eating and drinking. He gives out the exact number of pounds of beef, poultry, butter, etc., that they have consumed and professes to know how many potatoes and ears of corn have been served. . . . According to his figures, the average eating record of each man at the outing is about ten pounds of beef, two or three chicken, a pound of butter, a half peck of potatoes, and two dozen ears of corn. The drinking records, as given out, are still more phenomenal.

(Riordon 1963)

Of course, the defining events of machine politics were elections, and the most important Tammany places were voting sites. To control voting, Tammany Hall mobilized all its officers and used all its power. Associated gangs (the 'Dead Rabbits' were the largest) controlled voting booths, preventing non-machine voters from reaching the poll, sometimes beating up recalcitrant citizens and stuffing boxes (O. Allen 1993). District captains, block and tenement helpers got the Tammany vote out, early and often when possible. In Big Tim Sullivan's district,

every saloon, pool room, and gambling house in the district served as an active center for vote-getting and afterwards payrolls were opened to reward faithful political workers. The Comanche Club, the association headquarters, and numerous lodging houses and saloons of the Bowery registered hundreds of 'mattress' voters at every election and thus helped to swell the Sullivan vote.

(Zink 1968)

When in office – which was much of the time between the civil war and the First World War – Tammany Hall made every place a place of politics: policing brothels and pool rooms provided opportunities for protection money, and so lucrative police captaincies were sold to Hall sympathizers, for money or the promise of future favours. So it was with various and sundry positions on municipal boards and commissions. The Central Park Commission, the Quarantine Commission, the Commissioner of Emigration, the Commissioner of Public Charities, were all nodal points of machine politics. Street corners were also sites of machine politics, as bailing out prostitutes was a good sideline for district captains, and provided money that could be used to curry electoral support. Control of construction sites also provided untold opportunities to reward urban villagers who had been faithful to the Hall with a job. The most famous building site associated with Tammany Hall was New York County's Courthouse, built in Tweed's years at a cost of $13 million, approximately four times what England had paid for the Houses of Parliament, and twice what the United States had paid for Alaska (Callow 1976a, 55).

Real estate deals were also occasions for Hall officers to pocket 'honest graft' and further oil the wheels of machine politics:

> Just let me explain by examples. My party's in power in the city, and it's going to undertake a lot of public improvements. Well, I'm tipped off, say, that they're going to lay out a park at a certain place. . . . I see my opportunity and I take it. I go to that place and I buy up all the land I can in the neighborhood. Then the board of this or that makes its plans public, and there is a rush to get my land, which nobody cared particularly for before. . . . Ain't it perfectly honest to charge a good price and make a profit on my investment and foresight? Of course, it is. Well, that's honest graft.
>
> (Riordon 1963, 3)

Tenements, too, were places of machine politics. In a period when they were being defined by 'Friendly Visitors' and moral reformers as a lesser place where dwelled 'a crowded, lower-status' lot, tenements became basic units of machine governance. There, food baskets and emergency coal were delivered in moments of crisis, ward heelers interceded with landlords on tenants' behalf, and politics was further entrenched.[31]

Under Tammany's rule, no place went unpoliticized, as Boss Croker explained to W.T. Stead of the *London Review of Reviews*: 'If we go down into the gutter it is because there are men in the gutter, and you have got to go down where they are if you are to do anything with them' (Allen 1993b, 194).

'The Boss and his machine, his ward system, his political clubs, his favors, his hi-jinks, his torchlight parades and picnics, bound the citizen to his neighborhood, the neighborhood to the machine, and the machine to a people's politics' (Callow 1976a). This, according to Daniel P. Moynihan, is what made New York at the end of the nineteenth century 'the first great city in history to be ruled by men of the people, not as an isolated phenomenon of the Gracchi or the Commune, but as a persisting, established pattern' (Moynihan 1976).

In 1894, Tammany Hall lost the mayoralty race to a civic coalition that argued, against the politics of place, for 'a clean, straight, city government, administered . . . on purely business principles' (Parkhurst 1970 [1895]). Then, a reformist coalition took power that was 'consciously directed at depoliticizing the political' (Lupsha 1976).

Québec city 2001

In Québec city, where this book was conceived and largely written, the 'Summit of the Americas' was held between 20 and 22 April 2001. After Miami (1994) and Santiago (1998), it was the third official gathering of heads of states of the hemisphere held since George Bush launched the 'Enterprise for the Americas Initiative' (EAI 1991) to 'unify the Americas from Anchorage to Tierra Del Fuego in the world's biggest free trade pact'.[32] In what is fast becoming tried fashion (but a few years old, anti-summit protests are already set in their ways), the 'Summit of the Americas' occasioned a saturnalia of protests, teach-ins, direct actions and street theatre, organized for the most part either by *Opération Québec Printemps 2001* (OQP 2001, a broad coalition of local community and student groups), or by the *Comité d'acceuil du Sommet des Amériques* working with the *Convergence des Luttes Anti-Capitalistes* (CASA/CLAC, both anarchist groups, the former from Québec city, the latter based in Montréal).[33]

Central to protests in Québec city was the tension between concretely located events, and a more diffused global sense of place.

The first sites of struggles appeared on Friday, 20 April, as was beginning a *Carnaval anti-capitaliste* organized by the CASA/CLAC. At 1 p.m., a crowd of some 5,000 gathered at Laval University in the suburbs where people assigned themselves to either a green bloc (peaceful and festive), a yellow bloc (obstructive and defensive) or a red bloc (intent on disturbance and direct action). Greens went either to Lower Town to the *Ilôt Fleuri* (a wasteland in Lower Town beneath a highway, remade into a post-industrial happening place: think Blade Runner meets travellers' festivals), or to the *Faubourg Saint-Jean Baptiste* uptown where the local *Comité populaire* had organized a peaceful occupation of the neighbourhood.[34] Yellows and reds (along with a small 'black bloc' gathered by the *ad hoc* Autonomous Organizing Collective of Anti-Authoritarians from the Mid-West, Northeast, Montréal and Québec), marched to the 'security perimeter', surrounding the heads of state meeting (a 3.5-kilometre-long, 3-metre-high fence, defended by a united front of municipal, provincial and federal police – in all more than 6,000 policemen and women, aided by more than 1,200 soldiers and student volunteers from local police colleges, who worked as stools among protesters).[35]

The yellows, the reds and the blacks arrived at the security perimeter in mid-afternoon. A catapult brought from the Ottawa region by the Deconstructionist Institute for Surreal Topology (self-described Lanarkists) tried to launch stuffed toys into the security perimeter while those who had received training in civil disobedience tried to organize a sit-in. Both were swiftly overtaken by events: a segment of the fence was brought down, police invaded the green zone and shot tear-gas, and the already familiar to-and-fro of anti-summit protest began. For the next two days, the security perimeter was challenged by mostly peaceful protesters, met by virtually incessant firing of tear-gas.[36]

Well removed from the security perimeter surrounding the heads-of-state gathering, some teach-ins and conferences were held in what was termed the 'solidarity perimeter' in the Limoilou neighbourhood. Drawing on militants and experts from such nodes of anti-globalization activity as the International Forum on Globalization, the Third World Network, or *L'Observatoire sur la Mondialisation*, they focused on a wide variety of political issues related to globalization in general and to the Free Trade Area of the

Figure 2.3 Defending the security perimeter, Québec 2001
Source: Lanctôt and Brulé 2001

Americas (FTAA) in particular: the privatization of water, the clear-cutting of forests, union history, human rights, healthcare, art and activism, education, the Tobin tax and so on. Workshops on interacting with the media, legal rights, direct actions and ways of conducting civil disobedience were also held inside the solidarity perimeter.

Giving colour and context to events were theatre groups – some linked to OQP, others to the CASA/CLAC, or from outside Québec – working to foster what the historical avant-garde (Futurists, Dada, the surrealists) would have recognized as a radically creative ambience. The best, most derisive action was in the Saint-Jean Baptiste neighbourhood, where a section of the fence was decorated with bras and girdles, some inscribed with slogans ('My mother is not for sale'), others with bilingual anti-FTAA/anti-ZLÉA slogans (English on one cup, French on the other, with more equanimity than is usually found in the politics of language in Québec).

Feeding mainstream and alternative newspapers and working to facilitate links with other events elsewhere in the hemisphere was the *Centre des Médias Alternatifs-Québec 2001* (the CMAQ), Québec's link to the IndyMedia family. Set up in the autumn of 2000 by Alternatives (a DFAIT-funded NGO), officially launched at parties in Québec city (on 25 January) and in Montréal (on 1 February), the CMAQ was headquartered in the *Méduse* art complex, on *côte d'Abraham*, a short walk – but more than a stone's throw – away from the security perimeter, but within range of policemen's gas. There were also housed medics who helped those harmed by tear-gas and rubber bullets.

These places, of course, did not just happen; they were constructed, sometimes in the most literal sense of the term. Between June 2000 and the beginning of the Summit, some fifty *formations* (training courses, from prepared kits) were given near and around the city by *formateurs* and *formatrices*, to a medley of groups (union locales, community groups, nuns, students and women's groups), on a variety of issues relating to neoliberal globalization (and, in the case of CMAQ's *Ateliers de formations*, on the manufacturing and dissemination of dissenting news).[37] In that period, there were also teach-ins and *formations* in Montréal, two CLAC/CASA *consultas* in Québec city, several meetings of the *Université populaire* and *Alternative*-linked radio shows (on CKIA, *Radio Basse-ville*); truly innumerable conferences on globalization-related issues (organized by such diverse groups as the *Table de concertation contre la pauvreté de Sainte Foy-Sillery*, the Ontario Coalition Against Poverty, *Droit de Parole, Communication Basse-ville*, the Shakti women of colour collective, the Immigrant Workers' Centre); at least one workshop on legal rights (organized by the *Ligue des Droits et Libertés*); as well as numerous anti-capitalist activities and spectacles (in Québec city anti-capitalist music was becoming a genre unto itself). Between mid-January and March, a CASA/CLAC caravan reached two dozen cities in the Canadian Maritimes and in the northeast United States, holding several meetings wherever they stopped. During protests, OQP and CASA committees, in collaboration with others, organized food, housing as well as medical assistance and legal aid for those who were injured or arrested.[38]

Beyond what was constructed in the most voluntarist sense of the term, protests in Québec city were also charged by a more abstract – but no less determining – sense of context. A good measure of the significance of a global sense of place to the making of protests in Québec city is how groups and people involved were 'practically conscious' (to borrow Anthony Giddens' term) of happenings elsewhere on the terrain of the world economy, and how their politics were being defined not only locally, but also in answer to what was done elsewhere, in other circumstances (Giddens 1984). Here we have a good example of the manner in which 'global reflexivity' is animated politically.

Especially revealing here is how issues inherited from the very short history of summit protests became structuring concerns in preparation for Québec's Summit of the Americas.[39] Early summit protests were events unto themselves. Sure of their contrapuntal unity, radically defiant of political intent and instrumental thinking, participants subsumed political differences under strategic concerns: how to block that street or climb that pole, what to do to be seen and heard, where to converge, 'how to climb trees, block roads, lock down on doors, eat and shit in extreme situations, scale buildings, deal with cops, minister to the injured, show solidarity and survive in jail', how to 'hold ... the space, wait ... [and] make ... the point that we have a right to be here'.[40] When the 'Peoples' Global Action Against Free Trade and the World Trade Organisation' (PGA) held what was arguably the first contemporary anti-summit protests in Geneva in May 1998, diversity of politics and tactics reigned, with radically little concern for common programmes:

> the people came with the banners of all kinds of struggles against some aspect of globalization: local unions fighting privatizations or austerity, groups of solidarity with the south, squatters, plus many personal banners, musicians, and the caravan tractors towing a huge sound system.[41]

A year later in Prague, a simple colour scheme sufficed to articulate different positions and, 'despite tactical and strategic differences between protesters, most agreed that their action had been effective in . . . shutting down the summit and bringing the destructive policies of the World Bank and IMF to the attention of the world'.[42] But in Seattle – the first significant anti-globalization protest held in the USA and a crucial moment in many respects – the nature of protest changed. Although there were moments of broad collaboration ('Teamsters and Turtles Together at Last'), Seattle protests are most remembered – most significantly by militants involved in making protests in Québec – for a sharp division between street protests and the orderly politics of trade unions wanting to get 'labour a seat at the table' to make globalization work for workers.[43] Tellingly, twenty city blocks separated union workers gathered in a football stadium at the foot of the Space Needle to hear speeches and wave banners 'under the indulgent eyes of the Seattle constabulary' and the convention centre where 'protesters on the front line were taking their stand'. When the divide could have been breached (as the union crowd left the stadium), 'the marshals for the union march steered the big crowds away from the action' (A. Cockburn 2000).

In this context, the subjective sense of totality that had prevailed in Geneva and Prague disintegrated into the political settling of scores: *in situ* no more, protests became objectivized and politicized. In what must be one of the more curious moments of anti-summit protest, Medea Benjamin and her colleagues from the San Francisco-based Global Exchange, who had waged a four-year campaign against Nike, stood on the steps of Nike Town and other sweatshop outlets in downtown Seattle to defend them against anarchists and other trouble-makers, calling on the police to identify and arrest them (A. Cockburn 2000).

After Seattle, anti-summit protests became remarkably less about themselves, more reflective and politically deliberate, and more divided. This was evident, for instance, on 16 April 2000, when 8,000 demonstrators met in Washington for the annual meeting of the World Bank and IMF (unsupported by organized labour), and in Nice in December when thousands of activists gathered against the summit of European Union heads of state. In both cases, anti-summit protesters were cut off from local political issues and there were sharp conflicts between political affiliations and tendencies (Hahnel 2000).

More explicitly political than Geneva's PGA or Prague's Initiative Against

Economic Globalization (INPERG), Québec's OQP was, from the beginning, a more intent host. While the former groups were lithe organizations that functioned as technical links between movements rather than centres of political power in themselves (more like corresponding societies than the Comintern), OQP made itself into something that resembled an executive committee and it spent almost the whole year preceding the Summit of the Americas wading through broad ideological debates (Are 'we' to define ourselves as 'citizens', 'the people' or 'the proletariat'? Are 'we' against 'capitalism', 'neoliberalism', 'globalization' or 'capital'? Are 'we' for 'reform' or 'revolution'?). It also tried to settle on a correct plan of action to match its political aims and to draw up an 'invincible, credible, legitimate' political programme that would be 'understandable by all and absolutely realist'.[44] Not before its *Manifeste* was finally drawn up in February 2001 did OQP put aside political differences with the CASA/CLAC to co-ordinate housing and food distribution initiatives.[45] Three weeks before the Summit, the immense task of finding housing for out-of-city militants had barely begun, teach-ins and demonstrations due to take place in the 'solidarity perimeter' had not yet been planned and medical and legal assistance services were still divided along broad political lines. The CMAQ was still working on ways to reconcile the IndyMedia 'open publishing' tradition with its desire for politically relevant reporting.

In the weeks, days and hours before the Summit, amazing energy was expended and protests did emerge from having been nearly buried in globally reflective politics. Then, the global sense of place was translated into politics. Protesters were fed and housed (some at Laval University or in local colleges, a few in private homes), an indisputable sense of place and event was created and, *in situ* again, protesters did create a radical presence that challenged both the will-to-order of the heads-of-state summit and the apolitical reformism of the people's summit (analysed below). However, so animated were protests by global reflectivity (and by the anticipation of tourists, in majority everywhere, including among the police) that the patient politics of civil disobedience and the fragile ambience of anti-summit protests were rapidly overtaken by more animated and confrontational ways of politics, especially near the security perimeter. In spite of considerable efforts invested in civil disobedience (by one estimate, a third of the people who participated in Friday's CASA/CLAC march had received some form of legal or political training), protests did not shape up at all as planned. Reacting to events from Seattle and elsewhere, dynamized by a globally-inflated sense of predetermination, all those involved were looking for a more definite and quicker resolution than they would otherwise have had. Thus did cosmopolitan ghosts come back into the picture, carried by global reflectivity: spectres confronting spectres, everyone in Québec acted with more abandon, fighting what *The Economist* had called – before Seattle – the 'fight for globalization'.[46]

In the end, police ran out of tear-gas and took to using rubber bullets more offensively than they had planned. Carnivalesque happenings – the most fragile indicators of a sense of place and event – were swept away: the Funk Fighting Unaccountable Naughty Korporations were gassed out of their efforts to reclaim the streets, the Lanarkists were not given much time to catapult stuffed animals into the security perimeter, carefully constituted 'affinity groups' never did get set up, the *Ilôt Fleuri* was charged by police and the *Faubourg Saint-Jean Baptiste*, a green zone no more, was inundated with tear-gas.

Four hundred and sixty people were arrested in Québec city during the Summit of the Americas and charged with the habitual menu of offences against the State: assault of a policeman, unlawful assembly, causing a disturbance, rioting. Crimes of presence, they give us a clear indication of what globally made civility cannot tolerate.[47]

Civic ordering

When places in London and New York became charged with politics, civic coalitions assembled themselves that were characteristically made up of social forces rooted outside places where political situations were made. For the most part, they argued against the politics of place, for the city to be seen as a whole functionally divided, a space of right angles, flowing goods and circulating people, freed of irritants and resistance.

To protect and entertain globalizing *élites* attending the Summit of the Americas (thirty-four national delegations, 9,000 delegates in all), Canada's Department of Foreign Affairs and International Trade (DFAIT) erected a 'security perimeter', and it organized perfectly apolitical contests, festivals and colloquia. The DFAIT also reserved space for, and helped finance, the second People's Summit of the Americas, held in a circus tent in the old harbour in Lower Town, beside picturesque old Québec, well away from the security perimeter. Although they did not agree about much else regarding negotiations surrounding the Free Trade Area of the Americas (FTAA), participants in all DFAIT events did share an abstract understanding of the world economy (and of the Americas in particular), and all worked to define a consensual, sustainable, path for capitalist accumulation.

London 1889

As rooted in their place as were dockworkers in London's East End were dock companies, represented during the 1889 strike by the London and India Docks Joint Committee, headquartered at Dock House on Leadenhall Street in the financial City.[48] Over-extended, under-capitalized, facing increasing competition (from one another, from other docks and ports in Britain and on the Continent), their revenues falling (as steamshipping, railroad and telegraph favoured just-in-time practices that reduced revenues from wharehousing[49]), dock companies dug in their heels, defending a regime of work that gave them power over hiring, but was too inefficient for shipowners and City financiers for whom the Port of London was a not place unto itself, but a nodal point in worldly circuits of capital and merchandises.[50]

When the London docks opened at the beginning of the nineteenth century, companies favoured the professionalization of work, and they developed what George Pattison called an 'active and well-intentioned welfare policy' that included

> provident societies for the permanent men, an institute with a library and a museum, cottages and gardens, tea parties . . . compassionate allowances for men injured in the service, shelters for men wanting for work.
> (Pattison 1966, 269)[51]

The trend towards professionalization and decasualization continued through the 1850s and 1860s. By the 1870s however, dock companies had opted – for reasons already mentioned and to counter the increased militancy of dockworkers (who had already formed the Labour Protection League) – for a regime of work that banked on 'casual labour with high rates of pay and low earnings rather than permanent or preferable labour with low rates and high earnings' (Pattison 1966, 274). The resulting casualization did increase the political power of dock companies over the workers they hired, but it made the organization of work less efficient, and it slowed down mechanization (Lovell 1969). The result was 'inefficient and discontent labour' (Pattison 1966, 274), and the political marginalization of dock companies. When the 1889 strike came, they could neither make allies with wharf and granary owners, their closest competitors, nor with shipowners, their principal clients.

More generally, the fact that they were entrenched in a defensive position put dock companies at odds with civic reformism just as it was becoming a hegemonic perspective in the 1870s and 1880s.

Before then, the triumph of economic individualism over common civic purpose had been evident aesthetically, in what Lewis Mumford called the 'collapse of form' of mid-Victorian cities (Mumford 1961, 202), as well as politically, in the breakdown of governing structures. In the age of *laissez-faire* utilitarianism, when 'without design' was a laudatory term (Mumford 1961, 515), London was 'a veritable jungle of areas and authorities and a nightmare of inefficiency'.[52]

> There were upwards of 120 local Acts for the denser portions of the metropolis, and 80 distinct local jurisdictions, many of which coincided neither with parish, nor union, nor police district, nor any other recognized divisions. Even single streets were divided, often longitudinally, and paved and cleaned at different times under different jurisdictions. In the Parish of St Pancras, there were no less than 16 separate paving boards, acting under 29 Acts of Parliament.
> (Hall 1998, 700)[53]

What reform had taken place had been piecemeal initiatives born of specific circumstances that did not rise above the rooted power of vestries and remained, on the whole, politically ineffectual. A year after the cholera panic of 1854, for instance, a Metropolitan Board of Works was created that undertook the massive task of upgrading the ancient sewage system of London (Hall 1998, 691–693). Equipped with 'rather limited powers largely of a civil engineering nature' (street improvement, paving, cleansing, lighting, sewage and drainage), the Board of Works was mired in self-interested wrangling; it 'completely failed to awaken any civic spirit in the minds of London's inhabitants' and became increasingly corrupt (Robson 1948; Young and Garside 1982).

However, in the 1860s and 1870s a wide variety of social forces with interests beyond London itself began to underwrite the movement for civic reform. For them, London was less a place unto itself than 'the Mother-city of the Kingdom and of the Empire' (to quote Charles Booth[54]), a home to the imperial race (as Lord Rosenbery, the imperial foreign secretary who later became the first Chairman of the London County Council, put it). Most notables were titular aristocrats and rentier bourgeois, the principal financial backers of suburban expansion around London, globally oriented manufacturers and industrialists, 'who were . . . prepared to countenance public spending to improve the standing of "their" city' (Savage and Miles 1994, 60); and, importantly, colonial clerk and administrators, City managers and insurers, financiers, stockbrokers and jobbers, middle- and lower-middle-class workers, residents of the suburb, who were beginning to 'abdicate from the urban realm' (Garside 1984). In the movement for civic reform, these social forces were joined by other outsiders to places of trouble: middle-class social scientists anxious 'to maintain the stability of institutions by connecting the measured costs and inefficiencies of social wastage', journalists and Grub Street novelists exoticizing the dark continent of one-room harlots, philanthropists, Oxbridge reformers of the Settlement Movement, preachers and proselytizers wanting to fix 'floating' secularists to their parish.

The view of the city they defended was perhaps most clearly rendered in new constructions: between 1870 and 1910, London was a *grand chantier* of imperialist and world empire construction: the stock exchange was expanded, buildings in Whitehall were added to house the Foreign Office; the Colonial Office, the India Office, the Royal Colonial Institute and the Admiralty building were reconstructed. In South Kensington, the massive Imperial Institute of the United Kingdom, the Colonies, and India was erected. Between 1880 and 1910, more than a hundred clubs were built, principally around Whitehall, to cater for the fast-growing class of rentiers, soldiers, imperial administrators. Among principals were: the East India Club, the Empire Club, the Naval and Military Club, the Oriental Club, the United Services Club, the St James, the Travellers', the Imperial Colonial Club, the United Empire Club and the Overseas Club. In political terms, the 1888 Local Government Act established the London County Council, the 'first elected municipal council in London's history that possessed some degree of unity and a semblance of civic life' (Robson 1948).[55]

This is the sentiment that was mobilized by dockworkers during their marches, which made them more agreeable to the city in general, and to the City in particular, than dock companies were:

> There have been few strikes in British history which have been helped by subscriptions from the City, cheered on by stock-brokers, and won in an atmosphere of carnival. But all this was true of the dock strike of 1889.
>
> (Stedman Jones 1971, 315)

On Friday, 30 August, three weeks after the beginning of the strike, the Strike Committee issued a 'no-work manifesto' that called for a general strike for the following Monday.[56] Unmoved, the Joint Committee refused even to meet with the Strike Committee, still arguing that granting dockers their tanner would lead them to bankruptcy.[57] Although withdrawn on Sunday morning, the manifesto did crystallize widespread worries in London that a city-wide social strike was imminent. At this point, when it became obvious that dock companies would not defeat the dockers, social forces rooted outside both the East End and the docks began gathering to find a way out of the stalemate.

At the heart of the movement were shipowners and City financiers, whose interests were neither tied to the docks nor, of course, to the East End. Shipowners had met once before during the strike, on 23 August, at the offices of the Peninsular and Oriental Steam Navigation Company on Leadenhall Street, adjacent to the Dock House. At that meeting, 'between 60 and 70 gentlemen, representing most of the great shipping firms in the United Kingdom' had decided, 'after a long discussion, that [they] would at present take no direct action in reference to the agitation'.[58] On 30 August, the very Friday of the 'no-work manifesto', Cardinal Manning ('well known in the East End for his unorthodox temperance campaigning, mainly among the London Irish'[59]), Aldermen Sir Andrew Lusk (acting Lord Mayor of the City) and Colonel Henry Smith (acting Commissioner of the City Police) went over to the Dock House, 'with the purpose of asking the Joint Committee to terminate the strike', but they were not received favourably by the Joint Committee.[60] Neither was the appeal issued on that day by 'great employers of labour' (mostly shipping companies) who feared that the strike 'if continued will have a disastrous effect upon the interests of the nation at large; upon the interests directly of the port of London, and will permanently injure the business by which working men have hitherto earned their livelihood'.[61]

On the Monday after the spectre of a social strike had been raised, a *nébuleuse* of committees began meeting to find a way out of the stalemate. On 2 September, a deputation of shipowners presented dock companies with a detailed plan of resolution.[62] On 3 September, 'mysterious deliberations of ... gentlemen' began 'in the Board-room of the London Chamber of Commerce'.[63] On 4 September, Mr Lafone, leader of about half of the wharfingers, entered into negotiations with the Strike Committee, quickly reaching an agreement that allowed work to resume at warehouses, wharves and granaries that agreed to pay dockers their tanner and abide by a more modern regime of work. On 6 September, *The Times* reported 'private meetings of gentlemen interested in the trade of the port of London from which salvation might come'.[64] By then, committees of liberals, conservatives and radicals had all met and presented settlement plans.[65] Also on 6 September, Master Lightermen and Bargeowners met at the London Corn Exchange in the City, and sent a missive to the Surrey Dock Company, the Millwall Dock Company and the Joint Committee of the London and India Docks that left no doubt about their grievances with dock companies:

> We the undersigned, corn merchants and factors and persons otherwise interested, beg to give you notice that the dispute between the dock companies and their men has caused a general deadlock of stoppage to our business. The direct and indirect loss is extremely heavy, and we beg to say that we shall hold you responsible for any loss or damage may accrue to us therefore. We shall protest against the payments of charges on goods lying at your docks, for which under ordinary circumstances we should have been liable.[66]

Still on 6 September – by which date shipowners were in 'a state of something very near akin to revolt against the dock companies'[67] – Lord Mayor Alderman Whitehead returned from vacation in Scotland:

> to intercede first of all with the dock committee to come to a settlement with the labourers, and [to serve notice that] he will, if need be, convene a public meeting of the citizens of London to bring further influence to bear on the parties of the strike.[68]

Immediately, he assembled a Committee of Conciliation (later named the Mansion House Committee) of Cardinal Manning, Lord Brassey, Sir John Lubbock (MP and President of the London Chamber of Commerce), Sir Andrew Lusk and Mr Sydney Buxton, MP.

As soon as it was assembled, the Committee of Conciliation met with principals of the Strike Committee, and it adopted the position that dockers should be paid 6d an hour for regular work hours and 8d for overtime hours between 6 p.m. and 6 a.m., that contract work be abolished, the 'plus' divided equally between dockers and foremen and that work days should be at least four hours in duration.[69] All the dockers' demands, then, were to be met (this, plus the fact that he had served as bagman for funds raised by Australian trade unionists for dockworkers, raised accusations in the press that Lord Mayor Whitehead favoured a general strike for the East End).

With the full weight of the City behind strikers, dock companies were forced to abide by the recommendations of the Committee. There remained only questions related to the fate of blacklegs (they were to be retained as part of the regular workforce and protected from harassment by the dockers), to establish how much time dock companies would be given to put the new work regime in place, and when dockers would get their tanner. Another week of haggling, during which both parties to the stalemate were considerably weakened (the dockers demobilized *en masse* and the companies were further ostracized by other interests in the port), and the strike was settled on the aforementioned conditions.

On Monday, 16 September, work resumed and 'cheerful scenes of industry were again witnessed at the docks'.[70]

A year after the strike, dockworking had become an 'organized and regular industry' (Buxton 1890). By 1900, 'the docks [were] no longer privately owned but under the . . . more effective policing of the Port of London Authority', a centrepiece of civic reformism in London (Schneer 1994).

New York 1894

The 1880s and 1890s were also years of civic gatherings in New York. Until then, 'social reformism' had remained principally a moral and public hygiene movement, led by Friendly visitors, 'charity organisations and such "flawed saints" as the New York Female Moral Reform Society' (Todd 1993, 245):

> their major flaw being that, in their innocence from sin, they were also innocent of it; that is, while they saw sin behind every bush, they

Figure 2.4 Cheerful scenes of industry: 'Dockers at Work: Unloading a Cargo of Tea'
Source: Illustrated London News, No. 2632, vol. xcv, Saturday, 28 September 1889, p. 393. By permission of the British Library, slide 393 03085

had little imagination for the forms it might take. Anything foreign might be wrong, any error might be deliberate, anything fleshy was undoubtedly bad.

(Sante 1992, 278)[71]

Outsiders of places of trouble, moral reformers also operated from the margins of politics (in some cases self-consciously, and deliberately, so).[72] Only in extraordinary circumstances could they bring about some changes that took away key sites of machine politics. After Tammany's Fernando Wood ran New York's police too much like a private gang, the reformist Metropolitan Police Bill was adopted in 1857 and a Board of Commissioner of Police was established in 1860 that did limit some possibilities for graft. Following the anti-draft riots of 1863, 'the Council of Hygiene conducted the first city-wide survey of housing conditions', and it began agitating for reform of zoning laws concerning 'slaughterhouses, milk-cow stables and fat-boiling and gut-cleaning establishments', all place of Tammany politics. 'As well they pointed to the conditions of the streets, whose gutters were running with blood or overflowing with garbage and refuse. Preventive action had to be taken, they warned, if epidemics and social discord were to be averted. . . . It was only the fear of a cholera epidemic in 1865 that finally pushed through the passage of a law creating the Metropolitan Board of Health' (Boyer 1994, 30).

But in ordinary circumstances, social reformism did not amount to a political movement that could, as Jacob Riis wished, use politics as a weapon 'to cut straight and true'.[73] This is principally because it did not rally New York's ruling *élites*, comprised primarily of wealthy merchants and manufacturers who either accommodated themselves to Tammany's control of place (and took advantage of its ability to deliver services and provide opportunities to business), or fought the Hall on social and moral grounds, arguing that proper places beget respectable working classes (Havard 1964; Merton 1976). Control over place, then, was sometimes disputed (mayoral politics in particular was increasingly a matter of Tammany Hall versus *élite* clubs), but the politics of place itself was not challenged. As a result, municipal government in New York remained, as elsewhere in the USA, 'a thicket of little governments, fragmented, overlapping, and dispersed' (Callow 1976a). In the 1880s, machine politics grew into a full-fledged governing system in the Lower East Side, and it even threatened to spill over into the gridded part of the city, through control of an expanding transport infrastructure. This threat became particularly important with the opening of the Ninth Avenue 'El' in 1880, that opened the Upper West Side to expansion and made it a matter of serious political contention whether it would indeed become, as wished for by the very civic and anti-Tammany 'Municipal Arts Society' (a key proponent of the 'City Beautiful Movement'), a neighbourhood of a mix of upper-class mansions, single family homes, fashionable apartment buildings and residential hotels, or an annex to Tammany's territory.[74]

Then, vested interests rooted outside places of trouble fused together into a 'structural reformists'' movement that argued for the affairs of the city to be managed entirely on business principles, efficiently, professionally, with as little politics as possible (Boyer 1994; Holli 1976; Miller and Melvin 1987). This was not the moral movement of fallen angels, but a political movement working for the restructuring of New York governance 'in the interest of efficiency, economy, public health, comfort, and safety'.[75]

Of central importance to the gathering of civic forces in New York was a broad shift among ruling *élites*. In the 1880s, New York had established itself as the centre of an American economy that was expanding by manifest destiny and foreign conquest, arguably becoming the world metropolis *par excellence* in the process (Sutcliffe 1984, 11). In the transition a new ruling coalition of commercial and investment bankers, railroad and utility entrepreneurs, insurance executives, industrialists, lawyers and other professional and technical experts came to power (Hammack 1982). This new financial *élite* filled 'skyscrapers . . . with the offices of corporations which conduct . . . business in other parts of the country . . . and Fifth Avenue with the residences of capitalists who made their money in the West', and they financed what Robert Stern termed the 'Cosmopolitan Era' in New York's architecture.[76] Completed in 1865, the Stock Exchange building was enlarged in 1870, and again in 1881 and 1887. In 1901, it was demolished to make way for the building that still stands, which opened in 1903 (Lockwood 1976, 269). In a little more than a decade, the Metropolitan Museum of Art (1880), Carnegie Hall (1891), the Brooklyn Bridge (finally completed on 24 May 1883), the Metropolitan Opera (1893), the Washington Bridge (1889), and the American Museum of Natural History ('the largest building on the continent', 1892–1898) were built, and a theatre district began growing in the 1940s and 1950s west of Seventh Avenue, in what was formerly Hell's kitchen (Schlesinger 1983; White and Willensky 1978).

For all their differences, members of this new *élite* either 'look[ed] outward rather than at the metropolis itself' or they regarded New York as a terrain of speculation, where money transited for a while (Hammack 1982). In all cases, the new *élite* saw New York not as a place unto itself, but as a location in the world economy: 'Today, there are no new worlds to find. Upon us is the responsibility never laid before on a people – building the world's capital for all time to come.'[77]

From that point of view, machine politics was an archaic regime that could no longer be tolerated:

> the personalism of the boss, his antipathy to systematization and bureaucratization and his capacity for intermingling private and public spheres . . . belonged to the days of frontier politics but were ill-suited to the exigencies of modern business.
>
> (Havard 1964, 86)

In March 1894, the Senate Committee on the Police Department of the City of New York began hearings into police corruption. Called for by Revd Charles Parkhurst, chaired by Republican State Senator Clarence Lexow and financed by the Chamber of Commerce of the State of New York (a recently formed organization that aspired to become 'the parliament of the region's business interest'), the hearings brought together all branches of the reformist movement (Hammack 1982).[78] Throughout the summer, the Lexow hearings continued, adding empirical evidence to Revd Parkhurst's crusade against 'the slimy, oozy soil of Tammany Hall' that had begun two years previously, with a Valentine's Day sermon that emphasized the link between sexual immorality ('New York is a very hot bed of knavery, debauchery and bestiality') and political corruption ('the polluted harpies that, under the pretense of governing this city, are feeding day and night on its quivering vitals').[79]

On 6 September 1894, dignitaries of Good Government Clubs ('goo-goo clubs' in popular parlance), county republicans, members of the Municipal League and other select citizens invited by the 'Committee of Seventy' assembled at Madison Square Garden to call for 'the affairs of the city [to be] . . . conducted as a well-ordered, efficient and economical household, in the interest of the health, comfort, and safety of the people' (Todd 1993, 249). Mr Larocque chaired the meeting and concluded his opening address with a striking keynote, 'saying that party politics have no part in city government and that what was needed was an economical administration of what ought to be a business enterprise'.[80] On 19 September 1894, the 'Citizens' Committee of Seventy' first gathered at the Chamber of Commerce. Present were such prominent New Yorkers as J.P. Morgan, William Bayard Cutting, Morris K. Jesup, William E. Dodge Jr., Cornelius Vanderbilt, former mayor William F. Havemeyer, Judge James Emott, Robert Roosevelt, and, of course, not a single resident of the Lower East Side (Boyer 1978, 165; Callow 1976b). Immediately, it called on Good Government Clubs and other anti-Tammany organizations to 'redeem our city at the next election from the shame and misrule that have been so long imposed upon it by the Tammany organization'.[81]

In preparation for the upcoming mayoral election, William L. Strong (formerly a dry goods merchant turned banker and president of the Businessmen's Republican Club) was chosen to lead a united reform ticket (Todd 1993). On the strength of votes concentrated in the Upper West Side and central Manhattan, away from working-class downtown and riverside districts, Strong beat Tammany's Hugh Grant by 50,000 votes to become the first 'structural reformist' mayor of New York City (Hammack 1982). The following morning, the *New York Times* celebrated:

> The triumph of those who believe in decency and honesty against corruption in all forms in municipal affairs, and Rev. Charles Parkhurst spoke of the triumph of a 'movement to purify the atmosphere of the city.'[82]

Not surprisingly, Strong's first gesture for reform was the appointment of Theodore Roosevelt as police commissioner. 'He became a terror to pinochle players in the back rooms of saloons. The small joys began to disappear from daily life, and their place was taken by the abstract ghost, the Law, which could neither see, taste, nor touch' (Callow 1976a).

After a period of flutter (in 1897, the reform coalition split and Tammany's Robert Van Wyck was elected, to be replaced in 1901 by Seth Low, a reunited reform candidate), civic reformism installed itself as a hegemonic mode of governance in New York and in other American cities. Everywhere, 'city comptroller' governance was installed (Boyer 1994; Kaplan 1983). The American mayor became chairman of the board and citizens 'stockholders' (Holli 1976). In addition, a professional civil service and expert-based structures of authority were put in place to solve problems (Glaab and Brown 1967, 193–194). Grand, monumental plans were drawn up. (In 1904, for instance, the New York City Improvement Commission presented a grand plan to let 'New York take its place as one of the great Metropolitan Cities of the World'. Key to it was the co-ordinated 'laying out of parks, streets and highways, the location of city buildings [and] improvement of water fronts' to 'form a homogeneous whole'.)[83]

Between cities, urban observatories and 'urban policy planning networks' (e.g. the National Municipal league, the International City Managers Association) were set up, often by the wealthiest families in the country: the Rockefellers, the Rosenwalds, the Harrimans (Domhoff 1978).

Québec city 2001

More than a gathering of 'anti-globalization' protesters, Québec's 'Summit of the Americas' was a meeting of globalizing *élites* intent on defining further the terms of what Ricardo Grinspun and Robert Kreklewich appropriately recognized (in relation to the Free Trade Agreement and the North American Free Trade Agreement) as a 'neoliberal conditioning framework' in the Americas (Grinspun and Cameron 1993).

At the centre of happenings in Québec city was a meeting of heads of states of the hemisphere that took place at the *Centre des Congrès*, in the middle of the 'security perimeter' (which also protected much of the touristy old city, where the spouses of globalizing *élites* spent days sightseeing, undisturbed by the usual commotion of the tourist trade).

Also organized by the DFAIT were song-and-dance celebrations of hemispheric peoples and cultures. Starting in the autumn, *Voix des Amériques* concerts were held at *Le Capitole*, the permanent venue for *The Elvis Story* (in English on the marquise), a hyper-real revue (a 'real copy' in Umberto Eco's term, a perfect substitute for reality) that draws much of its clientele from the tourist trade and the suburbs, whose producers have spearheaded attempts to commodify *Place d'Youville*, a former marketplace that serves as a gathering place for youths and, sometimes, a starting point for urban riots (Eco 1986).

The last concert in the *Voix* series, held days before the Summit, was the Tropicalia review, that promised 'all the *joie de vivre*, all the colours of Brazil ... a trip south through the samba and the bossa nova'. At the end of the Summit, DFAIT sponsored an extravaganza of 600 artists, later televised by the Canadian Broadcasting Corporation, the official broadcaster of the Summit.

Other DFAIT-sponsored events included: a Summit school (to encourage young reporters to enquire into 'the realities of Americas'); a Youth Forum ('Emotion, authenticity and cultural diversity') that produced a 'practical, realistic, report', later circulated among official delegations; a picture-drawing contest; a cooking festival ('Savouring the Americas'); a 'Writers of the Americas' Summit; a film festival; a book fair (the 'Library of the Americas'); and an 'Inter-American Cooperation Beyond Free Trade' colloquium focusing on the 'wealth and complexity of inter-American co-operation', hosted by Laval University's *Institut Québécois des Hautes Études Internationales* (a privileged partner of both DFAIT and Canada's Department of Defense), that ended on Friday, 20 April, as the heads of states Summit began, by making policy recommendations that were, conveniently, a faithful match for the 'Summit of the Americas Declaration and Plan of Action', released as the Summit ended on Sunday, 22 April.[84]

Further removed from the security perimeter was the second 'People's Summit of the Americas' that had as its theme 'Resisting. Proposing. Together'. Organized by the *Réseau Québécois d'intégration continentale* (RQIC) and Common Frontiers – respectively Québec's and Canada's link to the Hemispheric Social Alliance (HSA) – the People's Summit was largely funded and, literally, placed by Canada's DFAIT and Québec's Ministry of International Relations.[85]

In keeping with the heads of states' Summit, the People's Summit was a mix of the purposeful and the festive. From Monday through Thursday, policy forums involving registered representatives of 'civil society' dealt with issues outlined in the latest draft of the 'People's Hemispheric Agreement' (PHA) on 'women and globalization', 'education', 'labour', 'agriculture', 'communications', 'human rights', the 'environment' and so on. In the evenings, plenary sessions were held to find ways to aggregate demands and reach consensus that could later be incorporated into the next draft of the PHA.

On the Saturday, the People's work was done and a People's March was held. A first group – about 10,000 – gathered on the Plains of Abraham (in Upper Town, near the security perimeter); another, larger group – estimates vary from 30,000 to 50,000 – gathered in Lower Town near the People's tent. When they met – at the corner of Charest Boulevard and *rue de la Couronne* in Lower Town, a short walk away from the security perimeter – they formed one of the largest crowd ever assembled in Québec history (comparable even to that which heard young Céline Dion sing for Pope John-Paul II in 1984). But immediately, the march split into two, very unequal, groups. Aggressively shepherded by 1,500 marshalls from the *Fédération des Travailleurs du*

Québec, upward of 60,000 people walked away from the official Summit to the *Parc de l'exposition*, where they were assembled in a parking lot, between a shopping centre and the Pepsi coliseum, to listen to speeches from their representatives.[86] A much smaller group – perhaps 1,000 – broke away from the People's March and walked back uptown to support direct actions against the security perimeter.

For all their differences, participants in heads of states' and People's summits did share a common relation to the emerging space of the Americas. In contrast to protesters, for whom the hemisphere is a life milieu, they both looked to the Americas as a place of abstract politics, to be gridded for efficiency's sake. This, as we will see in Chapter 4, goes to the very heart of neoliberal governance.

Conclusion

In the 1880s and 1890s, two cities at the core of the world economy were loci of political struggles. Picketing dock gates, fighting off blacklegs or listening to Ben Tillet or Tom Mann deliver the 'morning newspaper', dockers occupied places where they were usually most vulnerable to the arbitrary power of companies' foremen hired to select the day's labour. Gathering in parks or around pubs, organizing rent strikes, dockers and their supporters and their sweethearts and wives also gained political energy in quotidian places. Moving about from docks to the East End and then to the City, they traversed functionally separate zones to create a political geography markedly different from that of civic reformers, for whom the docks and the City were sites of the empire and of the world economy, and the East End was the *terra incognita* of the residuum – 'those vast miserable, unmanageable masses of sunken people'.[87] When East was East and West was West and each 'knew his place' dockers drifted everywhere and in between, making a situation and a collective subject as they went.[88] For five weeks in the autumn of 1889, London dockers fought placed fights that structured their movement and helped socialize their struggle, not by organizational fiat, but through the dialectics of place. There were pickets at dock sites, gatherings in Hyde Park, Tower Hill and elsewhere, and processions to clubs up Pall Mall, to the Houses of Parliament, St James' Palace, Westminster Abbey and to Dock House on Leadenhall Street. Territory became context, and, *in situ*, the struggle of the dockworkers gained amplitude, resonance and social significance. Links were made with other struggles that nullified attempts by employers to fragment the residuum and play one group off against another (the employed against the unemployed, skilled against unskilled, the 'royals' and the casuals, the unionized against the un-unionized, men against women). Against efforts to cadaster workers, the dockers' strike created an irreclaimable 'unitary ambiance' (IS 1958b) that companies could not quell quickly enough for City financiers and shipping companies. That is why the dockworkers' strike ended in victory for the dockers.

By contrast, Tammany's balls, clambakes, picnics and torchlight parades were not sites of *dérives* at all, but spectacular diversions. What makes these moments essentially different from events related to the pluri-sited and move-able struggles of dockworkers is not their relative immobility (IS scions did, after all, invent 'still *dérives*'), but how they were made. Above all, *dérives* are conjunctural moments, when social forces are moved by immediate needs and opportunities and make places for themselves in a manner sovereignly defiant of broader schemes and constructed rationales. It is this immediacy that the IS sought to emphasize by answering to the immediate 'solicitation' of architecture rather than the spectacular designs of urbanists. In contrast, Tammany's events answered to the broad ordering logic of machine politics; they were devices through which machine politics inscribed itself in new places. They were about control of place. Spectacular products of an alienat-ing division of labour, they went against radical moments of recapturing, when serialized individuals and groups gel into a collective subject, for better (the dockers' strike) or for worst (the 1863 draft riots, for instance, which provided occasions for racist attacks on black institutions). Certainly, Tim Sullivan's clubroom, George Washington Plunkitt's bootblack stand and gang-controlled voting stations were significant places of politics, but as con-trol spots where no collective subject could assemble itself. Rather than 'places' in Yi-Fu Tuan's sense of the term, they were anchoring points for bossism. Machine politics ruled by removing the radical possibilities of place and making an alienating spectacle of neighbourhood unity.

Against placed politics, moral and structural reformists argued for the city to be seen as a levelled, absolute space, an 'object before the subject' (Tschumi 1998, 29) and for the affairs of the city to be managed entirely on business principles: efficiently, professionally, with as little politics as possible (Boyer 1994; Holli 1976; Miller and Melvin 1987).

For three days in April 2001, provincial, bourgeois Québec city was charged with more politics than it usually is, as protesters took to the streets against globalizing *élites*. Whether such events are constitutive of a trans-national subject that can hold off attempts to grid the world economy is the subject matter of the remainder of this book.

3 Occupying places in the world economy

> When space feels thoroughly familiar to us, it has become place. Abstract knowledge about a place can be acquired in short order if one is diligent. . . .
>
> But the 'feel' of a place takes longer. . . . It is made up of experiences, mostly fleeting and undramatic.
>
> (Tuan 1977, 6, 183–184)

To capture what is distinct about the contemporary flight of social forces to the world economy, some have written of a more modest internationalism (Lipietz 1993), others of grass-roots (Waterman 1988; 1992a) or demodernizing (Friberg and Hettne 1988) internationalism. In many works (including my own), Foucault's idea of 'resistance communities' guides the appraisal of what is being born of current movements (Amoure 1997; Cunningham 1988; Drainville 1995a; 1997; Mittleman 1998; Munck 1992; NEFAC 2001; Ong 1987; Pile and Keith 1997; Schwartz 1997).

Looking at concrete practices, this literature often offers great insights into transnational social movements and organizations. However, lacking a more general theory of global order and change, it frequently says little about their political importance, for now or for the future. To built on its findings, we need concepts that are both germane to contextualized practices (outside which only ghosts live) and can highlight the fundamentals of broader processes of order and change in the world economy. This is what 'modes of relation to the world economy' hope to do.

Here, we begin our investigation into contemporary modes of social relations to the world economy, by looking at social forces struggling against the ways and consequences of globalization. This work will inform a political argument that will be made in Chapter 5, after we have looked at neoliberal ordering in the world economy.

This chapter is divided into two sections. The first presents a short historical review of oppositional politics in the world economy from the 1840s (when began the 'classical age' of left internationalism) to the Bretton Woods crisis (when global 'anti-systemic movements' began surfacing).[1] In the second section, we take our first measure of contemporary happenings.

From classical Left internationalism to anti-systemic movements: abstract subjects out of place

Before the Bretton Woods crisis, the predominant challenge to world orders came not from social forces in movement in the world economy, but from internationalist and cosmopolitan programmes drawn on behalf of inferred, imagined or theorized planetary subjects. These were, then, to recall Marx, 'perfectly political' challenges, that spoke of 'Man's specied-life, as opposed to his material life' and appealed to 'an unreal universality' (Marx 1975).

In the era of *Pax Britannica*, there were certainly attempts to organize what Marx called 'guerrilla battles' against capital and to get workers of different countries 'not only [to] *feel* but [to] *act* as brethren and comrades in the army of emancipation'.[2] During the great European strike movement of 1866 to 1868, for instance, workers of different countries did come together for meaningful transnational campaigns, or in support of local strikes (Braunthal 1967).[3] Workers of different countries also met at universal exhibits where they 'chatted a while' (to borrow Victor Hugo's expression) and learned from one another (Hugo 1985). At the 1851 Great Exhibition in London, for instance, 1,000 French workers met with their British counterparts to discuss ways to organize strikes, and to compare salaries and work hours. Lessons learned in London had a significant influence on the development of French *sociétés de résistance*, and on the fight for workers' rights in France: In 1863 French workers gained the right to form co-operatives and in 1864, the right to form associations for the purpose of negotiating collective agreements (Fougère 1905).

Born out of the support of English and French workers for Polish autonomy, the International Working Men's Association (1864–1876) did call for 'the immediate combination' of the still-disconnected working-class movements of European countries, and it did attempt to organize circumstantial and purposeful struggles: 'One of the best means of demonstrating the beneficent influence of international combination is the assistance rendered by the IWMA in the daily occurring trades' disputes.'[4] This strategy of active resistance led the IWMA, for instance, to fight concrete fights: for the regulation of the international supply of labour ('to counteract the intrigues of capitalists always ready, in cases of strikes and lockouts, to misuse the foreign workman as a tool against the native workman'), the extension of the ten-hour days, and the defence of national autonomy. It also brought the First International to give its 'complete and emphatic allegiance' to the Geneva International Peace Congress,[5] and Marx to write that, at the moment of Lincoln's re-election as President of the United States pledging to abolish slavery, 'the star-spangled banner carried the destiny of the working class'.[6]

But strategic presence on the terrain of the world economy remained an exceptional event. For all their differences, the many internationals that met in the classical age of Left internationalism (the Democratic Friends of All Nations, the Fraternal Democrats, the First and the Second internationals and so on) were all occasional gatherings of out-of-place subjects. In political terms, they were akin to cosmopolitan *salons*, distinct in their intent from philosophical gatherings of the previous century, but not in their relationship to the world economy.

So it was with the international women's movement (Rupp 1997). In the nineteenth century, the movement was concerned principally with putting forth an alternative cosmopolitanism based on the universalization of what were assumed to be innately female values. The International Council for Women, for instance, was founded (in 1889) on the basis that 'the cause of women is the cause of religion and morality all the world over', and proposed to represent, as founding member Lady Aberdeen put it, the 'mothers of the world'.[7] It was on behalf of this abstract subject that it lobbied for a higher moral order. In the same period, the International Women Suffrage Alliance (1904) fought for equal citizenship rights for women on the bases both of the need for equity and the moral contribution of women to the cause of justice the world over. More immediate concerns, closer to the material experience of women, were of course also part of the early phase of women's internationalism. The *Congrès International de la Condition et des Droits des Femmes* that met at the Paris world fair, for example, demanded that women's domestic work be regulated, and that fair wages be paid by the state.[8] Women also fought for international conventions on the regulation of night work and childbirth (adopted respectively in 1906 in Bern and in 1919 at the first session of the *Conférence Internationale du Travail*[9]). In both cases, however, struggles were not waged by a global movement of women fighting concrete, situated struggles, but by nationally grounded institutions arguing for an abstract political subject on whose behalf was drawn a universalist agenda (concerned in this case with the protection of women's motherly duties and the preservation of women's reproductive labour). For the women's movement as for workers, the world economy was not a field of practice.

Until the First World War, global gay politics was also rooted in *salons* where would-be representatives of an imagined global subject gathered. In that period, the *Cercle Hermaphroditos* (1895) and the Scientific Humanitarian Committee (1897–1942) organized largely scientific campaigns and petitions that addressed themselves to doctors and other 'prominent figures' who had roles to play in constructing, and treating, homosexuality (Adam 1987, 18; Lauritsen and Thorstad 1974, 29). That 6,000 'prominent figures' signed a petition of the Scientific Humanitarian Committee against Paragraph 175 of the 1871 Second Reich's Penal Code (which criminalized homosexual acts), 'of whom half were doctors', was, of course, crucially important, but it did not indicate a global social movement in the making (Lauritsen and Thorstad 1974, 14).

In the inter-war period, cosmopolitan institutions fighting programmatic battles on behalf of imagined global subjects easily over-determined attempts to organize concrete, situated struggles on the terrain of the world economy.

Again, global politics was severed from contextualized experiences, and ghostly proxies were invented on whose behalf struggles were waged.

A key development here was the split between rival internationals that began at the Zimmerwald Peace Conference of 1915, when pacifists and social democrats wishing to end the First World War clashed with Spartakists and others who wanted to radicalize it. This split was institutionalized with the creation of the Third International (1919) and fully consumed by the thesis adopted at the 6th Congress (Moscow 1928), that turned, as Julius Braunthal put it, 'the Communist International into an organ of the Soviet state' (Braunthal 1967, 255). From then on, there was little room to man-oeuvre for global movements, campaigns or actions not allied with one of many competing internationals: the Socialist Workers International (1923–1940), the Second International (1889–1914, 1945–), the Second-and-a-Half (1921), the Third (1919–1943) or the Fourth (1938–).

The tragic history of anti-fascist brigades during the Spanish civil war ('the most impressive example of *internationalist practice* according to Michael Löwy) illustrates well the over-determining of transnational praxis in this period (Löwy 1990). Started as somewhat fragmented, 'primitive, unprepared and leaderless' units of anarcho-syndicalist, communist and Trotskyist work-ers, the brigades became stakes in fractional struggles between the Comintern and Trotskyists, and, as Franco's phallanges were winning the war, the control of internationalist brigades became more important than the defeat of the fascists (Braunthal 1967, 457). Similarly, many efforts to assemble a global labour movement that would represent all workers and organize effective campaigns were recuperated and distorted by cosmopolitan chicaneries. In the inter-war period, the Amsterdam International and the Red Trade Union International, for instance, competed, according to Zinoviev, to, 'win them [workers] over to our side . . . [and] bring them under [our] control' (Braunthal 1967, 175). Again, Left internationalism was severed from experience.

After the Second World War, state-centred modes of regulation prevailed throughout the world economy (Keynesianism and Fordism in the centre, state socialism in the East, 'peripheral Fordism', 'bloody Taylorism' and 'over-developed statism' elsewhere), and the national level remained the priv-ileged place for social forces to meet. Occupying the terrain of the world economy were, again, imagined subjects easily bent out of shape by cosmo-politan agendas.

To take but one example: in countries at the centre of the world economy, the women's movement was principally defined by issues and institutions close to the heart of the Keynesian state, and sometimes sponsored by the state itself. In the USA, for instance, the National Organization of Women (1966) was created by the Kennedy Commission on the Status of Women. In England, the state was the privileged terrain of socialist feminists (Rowbotham 1996). In Canada, the National Action Committee on the Status of Women was, and is still, a state-funded and state-bound group. In socialist countries as well, state agencies structured the women's movement (Howell 1997). On the terrain of the world economy, women were represented by ghostly institutions that hosted occasional gatherings and drew cosmopolitan blueprints, but did not organize a meaningful political movement. As late as 1984, Robin Morgan's *Sisterhood is Global*, intended as a survey of 'women as a world political force', found little that was transnational about the women's movement and presented, instead, a collage in sixty-nine chapters concerned with nationally centred movements (Morgan 1984).

In addition, the cold war and related peripheral conflicts (e.g. in Algeria, Korea, Indo-China, Egypt, Yemen) turned – as Emma Goldman had said of the First World War – 'the whole world into a collection of national penitentiaries', and they submitted the global movement of social forces to the discipline of competing cosmopolitan blueprints.[10] The world of labour, for instance, was colonized by the World Federation of Trade Unions (WFTU) and the International Confederation of Free Trade Unions (ICFTU), both cold war creatures. Again, the global movement of social forces was distorted out of shape and participants were impressed into global regiments.

Some global movements, of course, did have a measure of relative autonomy from inter-state relations, but only in exceptional circumstances, and only for a while (Breyman 1994; Galtung 1988). Most notable in this respect were the student movement, the anti-apartheid movement and the anti-nuclear movements. Like the anti-slavery movement – that began with Quakers in Pennsylvania in the 1680s, two centuries before internationalism had installed itself as an organizing strategy – it was a focused, circumscribed struggle.[11]

Thus it was that, between *Pax Britannica* and the crisis of *Pax Americana*, in a period when transnational capital was moving beyond an 'international' understanding of its activities towards a 'world' perspective (Michalet 1976; van der Pijl 1989; 1997), Left internationalism installed ghosts on the terrain of the world economy.

Contemporary happenings: concrete fights over locations

In the past twenty years or so many of the dynamics that had kept social movements grounded to the national level have lost their structuring power. First, the East–West axis has ceased to be a conditioning framework, and room to manoeuvre has opened up for transnational movements that do not explain themselves in terms of grand plans for the ordering or the reordering of the world. Arguably for the first time since the end of the Napoleonic wars, the structuring of state-to-state relations does not now wholly over-determine social and political relations in the world economy.

The crisis of Fordism in countries at the core of the world economy and the accelerating transnational segmentation of production have also had a considerable impact on social movements in the world economy. Starting in the mid-1970s, the accelerating globalization of production and finance precipitated a crisis of state-centred modes of regulation everywhere in the world economy that both reduced the political benefits of state-centredness for social movements and made it more urgent for them to build what Baldemar Velasquez, president of the US Farm Labour Organizing Committee, called 'organizing' rather than 'political' alliances with counterparts elsewhere in the world economy.[12]

More generally, the acceleration of globalization and what Alberto Melucci called the 'planetarization of human experience' (Melucci 1995) has precipitated a veritable flight of social forces to the world economy. Although a hastily assembled and disorderly movement, involving a bewildering variety of groups and social forces often coalescing in short-lived alliances that left few traces, enduring programmes or convenient synthesis, this flight can generally be said to be made up of (1) campaign-centred movements that are both (2) linked to one another increasingly by transnational institutions, and (3) grounded by, and constitutive of, a sense of place. Through them, the world economy is becoming a field of practice.

Campaign-centred movements

In the world of labour, a many-fronted struggle is being waged against neo-liberal restructuring of the world economy. A first front is made up of local strikes projected transnationally. A well-known but revealing story comes from local 5668 of the United Steelworkers of America's (USWA), which organized a model transnational campaign on behalf of 1,700 locked out workers of the Ravenswood Aluminum Corporation's (RAC) metal-smelting facility in Ravenswood, West Virginia. In 1991, the Kaiser Aluminum and Chemical Corporation (KACC) was purchased by RAC, a company formed for that purpose by Charles Bradley of Stanwich Partners Inc, a group of international investors headed by global commodities trader March Rich. At that time, Rich had been living for several years in Zug, Switzerland, where he had sought refuge from prosecution by the US Department of Justice on '65 counts of tax fraud and racketeering' (Herod 1995a, 350). Within months of the sale, jobs and wages were cut, the pension plan was altered, working cadences were increased and workplace safety became a central concern of workers. Union activity increased and a walkout appeared imminent when workers were summarily locked out by RAC. In the following eighteen months, USWA's local 5668 organized a transnational campaign with help from the Industrial Union Department of the AFL-CIO, the International Metalworkers' Federation, the International Union of Food and Allied Workers' Association (IUF), the International Federation of Chemical and Energy Workers' Union (ICEF) and the International Confederation of Free Trade Unions (ICFTU). For the most part, the campaign focused on anti-Rich activities. It involved lobbying Jamaican politicians (up to, and including, Prime Minister Michael Manley), Swiss and Dutch Bankers (financial backers of Rich), developing contacts with a Czechoslovakian metalworkers' union (that led to President Vaclav Havel personally intervening to prevent the purchase of a Czechoslovakian aluminium company by a Rich-controlled group), and organizing an international campaign, in collaboration with the IUF and the ICEF, to protest the acquisition of the 'Athenee Palace' Hotel in Bucharest by a group also controlled by Rich. All in all, the Steelworkers organized sustained anti-Rich activities in twenty-eight countries on five continents (Allen 1993a; Herod 1995a, 353).

Another significant transnational labour campaign was organized by Bridgestone Firestone (BS/FS) workers in the USA, 'one of the longest and toughest disputes in recent US industrial history'.[13] During the 1994 round of negotiations, Bridgestone – BS/FS's parent company – demanded several crucial concessions from the union, including wage and benefits reductions, mandatory twelve-hour-shifts, the abolition of seniority rights, the gutting of safety protection, the elimination of labour-management co-operation schemes, a reduction of holidays and, significantly, greater freedom to outsource (Fumiaki 1995). On 12 July 1994 a strike began that involved 4,200 workers at five BS/FS plants (in Oklahoma City; Akron, Ohio; Decatur, Illinois; Des Moines Indiana; Noblesville, Indiana). In January 1995, 2,300 striking workers were discharged and 'permanently' replaced by non-unionized workers – the largest such replacement in US history. On 22 May, the United Rubber Workers (URW) changed strategy and strikers offered to return to work under BS/FS's conditions. Some workers did go back to work, but the company forced more than 1,000 men and women on to a waiting list, in violation of the back-to-work agreement. On 1 July 1995, URW merged with the United Steelworkers of America (USWA), which launched its biggest corporate campaign ever. The scope of the campaign was truly extraordinary: 3.6 million handbills, nearly a million 'Don't Buy Bridgestone/ Firestone' stickers and bumper stickers, 250,000 campaign buttons, 115,000 black flags (on which more later) and 15,000 'Don't Buy' T-shirts were distributed, and 63,000 yard signs were displayed. Thousands of separate campaign events were organized that involved over 60,000 USWA participants and volunteers, and 1,100 separate USWA locals were actively involved. The campaign reached eighty-six countries including sixteen that were visited personally by replaced Bridgestone/Firestone workers. Forty-three delegations of foreign workers visited the USA to lend support.[14]

The first results from the campaign were felt in the autumn of 1996, when BS/FS started recalling illegally 'replaced' workers who were still without work.[15] In early December an agreement was reached between USWA and Bridgestone that included wage increases (40 cents per hour on basic pay), signing bonuses ($750 for all employees), gains on holidays, increased pension provisions and, most importantly, an extension of the 'pattern bargaining' system.[16] On 12 and 18 December, BS/FS workers voted by a three-to-one margin to approve the new contract.

As well as specific strikes, a host of work and safety issues have also kindled significant transnational labour campaigns: work conditions in export zones, living wages for apparel workers, redundancy firings, increased work cadences, systematic overwork and so on. (Brecher and Costello 1991a; 1991b; Hecker and Hallock 1991; Herod 1995b; Kidder and McGinn 1995). On the last subject, a significant campaign was mounted in Asia against *karoshi* – death by overwork.[17]

Where the push for regional integration has been the strongest, transnational campaigns have also become regional affairs (Drainville 1997; 1999). In the Americas, for instance, projects for regional or hemispheric integration have been at the forefront of the political agenda for a decade. In this context, a veritable saturnalia of transnational strikes, social movements and 'cross-border coalitions' has been organized that has involved 'agro-industrial workers, rubber tappers, papermakers, milk producers, building and wood workers, steelworkers, automobile workers, metalworkers, professionals, government workers and bank workers' as well as women's groups, indigenous organizations and environmental groups (Drainville 1999; Moody 1995; Smith and Healy 1994). Most remarkable have been campaigns waged by the Amalgamated Clothing and Textile Workers' Union (ACTWU), the International Ladies Garment Workers' Union (ILGWU), the Teamsters and the United Auto Workers (UAW) on behalf of *Lunafil* workers in Amatitlán, Guatemala (Hogness 1989; Interhemispheric Resource Center 1996c[18]); the UAW's campaign in support of Ford workers in *Cuautitlán*, Mexico, following the murder of labour activist Cleto Nigmo in January 1990; and the cross-border campaign organized by the AFL-CIO, the International Longshoremen's Union, the United Farm Workers (UFW) and the International Union of Electrical Workers, on behalf of Mexico's independent bus drivers' union (that became a *cause célèbre* when film-maker Oliver Stone began supporting it (Akira 1995a; Brecher and Costello 1991a; Hays 1996; Interhemispheric Resource Center 1996b; McLaughlin 1996a; Moody 1995). At the time of writing, the Federation of Textile Union Workers (FTUW), the US Guatemala Labour Education Project (US/GLEP) and the Campaign for Labour Right were still involved in a significant hemisphere-wide campaign against the Phillips-Van Heusen Company (PVH) that began in December 1998, when PVH locked out workers at the *Camisas Modernas* factory, less than a year after they had won a six-year battle for union recognition (to become the only export factory workers in Guatemala to be both unionized and represented by a collective agreement (McClain 1992).[19]

Resonant symbols of global integration, corporate brand names have also served as starting points of numerous transnational campaigns.[20] In the past decade alone, General Electric, Guess, Mitsubishi, Monsanto, Nestlé, Nike, Reebok, Suzuki and GAP have been targeted by significant transnational campaigns, especially in East Asia and in the USA.[21] (In the USA, 'the ZAP the GAP' campaign is credited with bringing back streaking[22]). In the San Francisco Bay Area – a nodal point of transnational activism – Global Exchange, Sweatshop Watch, UNITE (the Union of Needletrades, Industrial and Textile Employees) and the Asian Law Caucus have campaigned against

Tommy Hilfiger and sixteen other clothing manufacturers on behalf of workers in Saipan, in the Pacific Northern Marianas Islands. They organized a public awareness campaign, called for a boycott and filed a lawsuit ('the first legal attempt to hold US retailers accountable for the abuse of workers by subcontractors').[23]

Transnational labour campaigns have also concerned themselves with prominent labour activists. After the oil strike of 1994, for instance, the UAW, The International Federation of Chemical, Energy, Mine and General Workers' Unions (ICEM) and the AFL-CIO's Solidarity Center (SC) involved themselves in important campaigns for the release of imprisoned Nigerian labour leaders from Nupeng and Pengassan, the two principal unions of oil and gas workers. In January 1996, they secured the release of four leaders of oil workers, detained without trial since the summer of 1994: Wariebi K. Agamene (Nupeng president), A. Aidelomon and Mr Eleregha, (Pengassan branch chairmen) and F. Addo (Pengassan's third vice-chairman). Another key imprisoned union leader (Frank O. Kokori, Nupeng General Secretary) was freed later in 1996.[24] Still about Nigeria, an important transnational campaign for the release of Ogoni activist Ken Saro-Wiwa ended with his hanging on 10 November 1995.

Recently, the global women's movement has also been an increasingly campaign-centred affair, concerned for the most part with concrete and situated struggles: abortion rights, teleworking, excision and female sexual mutilation, household consumption, wages for housework, the rights of immigrant workers, control over reproductive technologies, homeworking and the putting-out system in the garment industry, and gender exploitation in export-processing zones (Cottenier and Hertogen 1991; Ecumenical Coalition for Economic Justice 1992; Enloe 1989; Luijken and Mitter 1987; Shrage 1994; Truong 1990; Waterman 1992b). This last struggle has involved principally groups in the Americas (*Mujer Obrera, Mujer a Mujer*, the Coalition for Justice in the Maquilladora, the Maquila Solidarity Network, the Support Committee for Maquilladora Workers, the *Centro de Orientacion de la Mujer Obrera, Despacho Obrero*) and in Southeast Asia (the Philippine Workers' Assistance Center, the Asian Pacific Workers' Solidarity Links). In Europe and South Asia there have been significant women's campaigns against sexual tourism and to defend the rights and freedom of sex workers (Lap-Chew 1996).[25] In Southeast Asia, the Asian Women Workers' Center has organized a modest campaign to bridge the gap between Japan's extensive daycare system (established in the 1960s) and daycare arrangements elsewhere (Nitta 1995). In Muslim countries, the International Solidarity Network of Women Living Under Muslim Laws (WLUML) documents cases and issues action calls on behalf of:

> three feminists arrested and jailed without trials, kept incommunicado for seven months in Algeria for having discussed . . . the project of law known as 'Family Code', which was highly unfavorable to women '. . . an

Indian Sunni woman who filed a petition in the Supreme Court arguing that the Muslim minority law applied to her in her divorce denied her the rights otherwise guaranteed by the Constitution of India to all citizens . . .' '. . . a woman in Abu Dhabi, charged with adultery and sentenced to be stoned to death'.

(Miles 1996, 123)

Although by and large still nationally bound and structured by cosmopolitan agencies – the International Gay and Lesbian Association (ILGA, 1978) and the International Gay and Lesbian Human Rights Commission (1991) – that lobby on behalf of an absentee subject, global gay and lesbian politics has also shown signs of moving towards more punctual, campaign-centred actions at the global level, organized by more radical organizations such as Lesbian Avengers, Act-UP, Radical Faeries and Queer Nation, that favour direct contact between activists. The AIDS crisis, of course, has focused political energies, and made organizing more urgent, as have the imprisonment and torture of gays and lesbians (LaViolette and Withworth 1994), and the rise of 'family-values' politics in the USA. On this last subject, US-based organizations (Lesbian Avengers, Act-UP, the Radical Faeries and Queer Nation) have acted globally in a strategic manner quite in contrast with the abstract, policy-minded ways of the ILGA.

We have declared war on heterosexism and homophobia. This of course means the [heterosexuals], but also the mainstream, nicey-nicey, assimilationist, '[w]e're just like you nice straight folks except for who we sleep with' Gay and Lesbian bowel movement. This movement needs to be flushed, and we are the tidy bowel Queers! We will target many with our random, unpredictable, terrorist attack who are deserving punishment. hateful breeders who bash us and assimilationist scum that water down our angry voices and channel our effort into a system that oppresses us are both cause to pull out the ammu[nition] and come out shootin'.

(BRATS Manifesto, Queer Nation)[26]

Frequent subjects of *realpolitik* reckoning – about who stood or fought with whom, did what when, won or lost which battle, or what was won or lost in it – transnational campaigns are also significant in terms of the relation they establish to the world economy. This is something we will discuss below, when we consider emerging modes of relation to the world economy.

Transnational institutions and horizontal linkages

In a note to Paul Lafargue written in answer to anarchist concerns, Marx referred to the International Working Men's Association as 'a link . . . not a center of power'.[27] However fair Marx may have been in his assessment of the First International, he certainly did not foretell future developments: without exception, internationalist agencies born in the century that followed the demise of the IWMA in 1876 did attempt to install themselves as centres of power.

In the past two decades, however, established centres of power have either been supplanted as locus of global political organizing, or they have been re-centred to play a more modest role in support of transnational campaigns. The last internationals (the second and the fourth) have become debating societies, trailing the transnational movement of social forces rather than initiating it. In the world of labour, what remains of the WFTU acts as a lobby, playing a negligible role in the global movement of social forces. For its part, the International Confederation of Free Trade Unions (ICFTU) – once a star chamber of cold war cosmopolitanism – has re-invented itself to support transnational campaigns organized by affiliated federations, unions or even locals (Herod 1995b, 356). While still a centre of business unionism, the ICFTU has become more of a link, in an effort to catch up with transnational campaigning (Interhemispheric Resource Center 1996a). This has encouraged national federations that had hitherto pursue a more independent path to international solidarity (Quebec's *Confédération des syndicats nationaux*, for instance) to join, or rejoin, it (Güntzel 1993).

Alongside re-engineered and recentred institutions now also exists a group of relatively new research institutes, think-tanks, TSMOs and information clearing-houses that document, assist and inform transnational campaigns.[28] Table 3.1 and Table 3.2 list some members of this group.

Facilities listed, of course, vary enormously in terms of resources and membership, and in their relationship with governing agencies. For instance, the consumer politics of the Women's Environmental Network (WEN, which has organized consumer campaigns for organic chocolate, cotton nappies and sanitary towels) contrasts sharply with PARC's 'People's Plan for the 21st century' (PP21), *Mujer Obrera*'s work to assist displaced workers in the Maquilladora of El Paso (López 1991), or with the ICCSASW's efforts to organize solidarity campaigns among sugar workers of the world.[29]

What institutions listed in Table 3.1 and Table 3.2 do share is a rootedness in concrete, situated, struggles. Many were born directly of transnational campaigns and have remained intimately connected to concrete struggles. The US/Guatemala Labor Education Project (US/GLEP), for instance, was born in the *Lunafil* campaign and has played an important role in organizing other labour protests in Guatemala, most notably for workers at Petrosteel, *Confecciones Transcontinentales* and Phillips-Van Heusen (Hogness 1989; McClain 1992). In similar fashion, the *Cuautitlán* campaign led to the creation of MEXUSCAN, the North American Ford Workers' Solidarity Network, that later played a key role in co-ordinating activities from other labour groups involved in cross-border solidarity movements: the Canadian Auto Workers (CAW), the UAW, Labor Notes, the Coalition for Justice in the Maquilladora (CJM), *Alianza Civica* and so on (Carr 1994; Interhemispheric

Table 3.1 Transnational institutions

Name	Established	Mandate
Pacific-Asia Resource Center (PARC)	1973 (Tokyo)	'A secular, non-profit, multifunctional organization working with the various people's movements in Japan to facilitate development of solidarity links with people in struggle in Asian, Pacific and other countries.'
The Caribbean Association for Research and Action (CARFA)	1985	'An autonomous umbrella organization for active women in the region and Caribbean women living outside the region "committed to understanding the relationship between the oppression of women and other form of exploitation in the society and to work actively for change".'
Association of African Women for Research and Development (AAWORD)	1977	'To undertake research which calls for the participation of women and emphasizes their presence in all cultural, social, economic and political processes of change . . . to create networks among African women researchers.'
Women's International Information and Communication Service (WICCE)	1974	'Among the many issues and strategies ISIS/WICCE deals with are the organizing of women's groups against economic development policies that marginalize and exploit women workers.'
International Commission for the Coordination of Solidarity Among Sugar Workers (ICC-SASW) *and* the Sugar Workers & Industry Education Resource Library	1983	'To carry on the work of assembling information for research and education on the sugar industry . . . within the framework of solidarity among workers in the sugar industry worldwide, in field and factory, in cane and beet, in underdeveloped and in industrialized countries.'
International Women's Tribune Center	1976	'A communication and technical assistance support service for more than 16,000 women and women's groups in 160 countries.'

Organization	Year (location)	Description
Transnational Information Exchange (TIE)	1979 (Amsterdam)	'To enable the exchange of information and experience between action and research groups working on transnational corporations . . . to develop a dialogue between such groups and trade unions and other workers' organizations . . . to encourage positive and practical alternatives within the labour movement.'
International Labour Research and information Group (ILRIG)	1983 (Cape Town)	'To assist organizations of workers in South Africa to learn from the experiences of their counterparts in other countries, and to encourage the development of international links of labour solidarity.'
Asia Pacific Workers Solidarity Links (APWSL)	1982 (Tokyo)	'To promote education for grassroots workers, to issue action alerts on workers' and human rights issues in labour disputes, to expand . . . people's network . . . to guarantee women's equal participation.'
Asian Women Workers' Center (AWWC)	1983 (Tokyo)	'Works to help Asian's female labourers and promote exchanges among workers in the region.'
People's Action Network to Monitor Japanese Transnational Corporations (PAN)	1987	'Tracks various Japanese TNCs and has been involved in campaigns including against Mitsubishi Kasei Company for the pollution caused by its joint venture partner in Malaysia. PAN publishes Japan TNC's News.'
Maquila Solidarity Network	1995	'A Canadian network promoting solidarity with groups in Mexico, Central America and Asia organizing in maquilladora factories and export-processing zones to improve conditions and win a living wage'; fights for collaboration between 'groups in the North and South' meant to promote 'employment with dignity, fair wages and working conditions, and healthy workplaces and communities.'
Workers' Center	1996 (Ciudad Juárez, Mexico)	Offers 'ongoing education in workers' rights and in how to organize a union . . . provide[s] contacts with qualified and sympathetic lawyers . . . when . . . labour rights are violated . . . offer[s] classes in other areas of direct usefulness.'

Name	Established	Mandate
International Forum on Globalization	1996 (San Francisco)	'To stimulate new thinking, joint activity and public education in response to the rapidly emerging economic and political arrangement called the global economy.'
Inter-Hemispheric Resource Center	1979 (Albuquerque, New Mexico)	'Since 1979, the IHRC has monitored, researched and analysed worldwide events and provided people with the information they need to make informed decisions, to direct policy and to be instruments for social change.'
Asia Monitor Resources Center	(Hong Kong)	'To support democratic and independent labour movements in Asia ... undertakes research, publishing and educational activities on labour and development in the Asia-Pacific region.'
Center for Transnational Labor Studies		'Intends to monitor the activities of Japanese transnational corporations and to discuss the strategies necessary for strengthening workers' international solidarity. Our ambition is to explore new transnational labour studies by deepening international communication among workers and researchers. Hopefully, we will make a small contribution towards the revival of an active labour and social movement.'
Center for Women's Resources	1973 (Vancouver)	'To make resources, information and analysis available that supports work against oppression based on gender, race, class, sexual orientation, ability and other forms of discrimination.'

Organization	Founded	Description
International information centre and archives for the women's movement	1935 (Amsterdam)	'The source, the intermediary and the supplier of information and documentation for all those who occupy themselves with the position of women, whether it concerns books, periodicals, data, addresses, archives, visual materials, current or historical, national or international.'
Transnational Institute (TNI)	1974 (Amsterdam)	'A worldwide fellowship of committed scholar-activists. It was one of the first research institutes established to be transnational in name, composition, orientation and focus. In the spirit of public scholarship, and aligned to no political party, TNI seeks to create and promote international co-operation in analysing and finding possible solutions to such global problems as militarism and conflict, poverty and marginalization, social injustice and environmental degradation.'
International Institute of Social History	1935 (Amsterdam)	'One of the world's largest documentary and research institutions in the field of social history in general and the history of the labour movement in particular.'
Global Exchange	1988 (San Francisco)	'A non-profit, non-governmental organization that seeks to build people-to-people ties between the developed and developing world.'
Asian Migrant Center (AMC)	(Hong Kong)	'Working with various networks – migrant, labour, religious, and women's organization – at grassroots, regional and international levels, AMC advocates for human and labour rights of migrants at regional and national levels by: organizing consciousness-raising and educational forums to empower migrant associations to advocate for migrants' rights; facilitating local and regional lobbying to fully utilize national and international conventions/instruments to protect and advance rights and standards; disseminating action alerts for quick international responses on urgent cases of violations of

Name	Established	Mandate
		migrants' rights; helping migrants prepare for their return by promoting collective savings and building community projects and enterprises.'
Global Reach	1981 (San Francisco)	'To promote a more efficient use of the potential of the Internet, offering to find new clients by adapting the commercial promotion on the Web to different target countries and cultures.'
Labor Notes	1979 (Detroit)	'The voice of union activists who want to put the movement back in the labour movement since 1979'; tries to restore 'the power that the labour movement has lost in the past decades.'
Third World Network		'Works to bring about greater attention to the needs and rights of people in Asia and the Pacific, Latin America and Africa as well as to environmental problems in those regions, . . . integrating discussion of these social and ecological issues with a focus on general and specific economic trends relating to TNCs, free trade and multilateral development banks.'
Center for Labor Education and Research	1976 Hawaii	'To provide labour education, research and labour-related programmes to workers, their organizations and the general public.'
Australia Asia Workers' Links		'A network of several state-level Australian unions seeking to promote international solidarity through the exchange of information; has connections with progressive trade unions and worker support groups in Indonesia, Fiji, Sri Lanka and South Korea.'

Center for Labor Research and Education	UC Berkeley	'An outreach unit of the Institute of Industrial Relations at the University of California at Berkeley. Its research, education and service programmes activities address the intellectual and policy issues of the California labour community, and emphasize critical thinking about issues of current concern.'
US Guatemala Labor Education Project	1991	'An independent non-profit organization that has led US efforts to support Guatemala workers.'
Global Trade Watch	1993	'The Public Citizen division that fights for international trade and investment policies promoting government and corporate accountability, consumer health and safety, and environmental protection through research, lobbying, public education and the media.'
RAINBO	New York	'A clearing house of materials ... on FGM and related topics ... especially interested in collecting materials on in-country studies, surveys and other research, and educational and training materials ... compiled bibliographies on medical facts about FGM and health and human rights aspects of FGM.'
The Center for World Indigenous Studies	1984	'Dedicated to wider understanding and appreciation of the ideas and knowledge of indigenous peoples and the social, economic and political realities of indigenous nations.'

Table 3.2 Transnational links online

Name	Address online (est.) date	Mandate
Sweatshop Watch (1995)	http://www.sweatshopwatch.org	'A coalition of labour, community, civil rights, immigrant rights, women's and religious organizations, and individuals committed to eliminating the exploitation that occurs in sweatshops . . . with a focus on garment workers. . . . Our decisions, projects, and organizing efforts are informed by their voices, their needs and their life experiences.'
Fourth World Documentation Project	http://www.cwis.org	'To present the online community with the greatest possible access to Fourth World documents and resources.'
Corporate Watch Web Site Online	http://www.corpwatch.org	'Counters corporate-led globalization through education and activism. We work to foster democratic control over corporations by building grassroots globalization – a diverse movement for human rights, labour rights and environmental justice.'
Modemmujer	modemmujer@laneta.apc.org	'Apropiarnos del espacio público que ofrece el Internet y estar a la vanguardia en el uso de las nuevas tecnologías de comunicación para la articulación a nivel internacional del movimiento amplio de mujeres.'
Virtual Sisterhood	http://www.igc.apc.org/vsister/	'A global women's electronic support network dedicated to strengthening and magnifying the impact of feminist organizing through promotion of electronic communications use within the global women's

Organization	Address	Description
Institute for Global Communications (IGC)	http://www.igc.org/igc/gateway/about.html (1987)	'movement . . . to make a dent in the language barrier that inhibits women's electronic communication across language groups.'
Campaign for Labor Rights	www.summersault.com/~agj/clr	'To actively promote change towards a healthy society, one which is founded on principles of social justice, broadly shared economic opportunity, a robust democratic process and sustainable environmental practices.' 'A programme of the Labor Defense Network (LDN) which, for more than fifteen years, has been turning the slogans of international labour solidarity into concrete action; offers an effective tool for concerned individuals, unions and community/faith/student organizations to support each other in common struggle.'
The National Organization of Circumcision Information Resource Centers	www.nocirc.org (San Anselmo, CA) 1986	A 'clearing house for information about circumcision . . . an organization of diverse individuals committed through research, education and advocacy to securing the birthright of male and female infants and children to keep their sex organs intact.'
The Female Genital Mutilation Education and Networking Project	http://www.fgmnetwork.org/eradication/advocacy.html	'Offers informational supports for education about the female genital mutilation around the world.'
Global Trade Watch (Public Citizen)	1971 (Public Citizen)	'Fights for international trade and investment policies promoting government and corporate accountability, consumer health and safety, and environmental protection.'

Name	Address online (est.) date	Mandate
International Centre for Trade and Sustainable Development (Resource Centre Online)	http://www.ictsd.org	'Designed to support the integration of sustainable development and the international trade system through building bridges, capacities and knowledge . . . provides a regularly updated online document search service.'
Cyber Picket Line	http://www.cf.ac.uk/socsi/union	'Comprehensive directory of labour on the Internet.'
International Center for Research on Women (ICRW)	http://www.icrw.org/	'To improve the lives of women in poverty, advance womens' equality and human rights, and contribute to the broader economic and social well-being. ICRW accomplishes this, in partnership with others, through research, capacity building and advocacy on issues affecting women's economic, health and social status in low- and middle-income countries'
Asian Migrant Center Online	www.hk.super.net/~mrhr	'To provide readily accessible information and resources related to our work with migrants via the Internet. To this end we are trying to develop a site that offers both a comprehensive online resource centre and a user-friendly interface.'
Instituto Laboral De Educacion Sindical (Labor Studies Institute)	cquiros@igc.apc.org (Puerto Rico)	'To facilitate communication . . . through the exchange of documents and experiences that can help the struggle of . . . labour movements . . . to share strategies, develop solidarity work, co-ordinate international activities and foment investigations on labour issues.'

Resource Center 1996c). Likewise, the 1992 'Strategic Organizing Alliance' (SOA) between the United Electrical, Radio and Machine Workers of America (UE) in the USA and the Mexican *Frente Auténtico de Trabajadores* – a model of the genre – led to the creation of the North American Worker-to-Worker Network (NAWWN), a gathering of over 700 local unions and activists. Besides organizing other transnational campaigns, the NAWWN has also formed a core of 'committed activists [capable of organizing] rapid-response solidarity action to support workers and organizers who are victims of firing, threats, violence'.[30] These activists later played a key role in the transnational campaign to reinstate workers fired during a union organizing drive at General Electric's *Armadora* Plant in *Ciudad Juarez* in November 1993 (Correspondencia 1994). In this campaign, the UE/FAT alliance obtained 'the first secret ballot election in Mexican labor history'.[31] In environmental politics, Greenpeace's campaign against the 1989 Basel 'Convention on the Control of Transboundary Movements in Hazardous Wastes' gave birth to the International Toxic Waste Action Network, now in its tenth year (Smith 1999).

In the same manner, the Asia Pacific Workers Solidarity Links (APWSL), the International Labour Research Center (ILRC) or Southerners for Economic Justice, for instance, are all rooted in labour organizing, and all have explicit mandates to support ongoing struggles (Seiichi 1995; Southerners for Economic Justice 1993; Waterman 1996).

Also in Asia, the Asian Women Workers' Center (AWWC) has worked to document the transnational experiences of women of the region, emphasizing what is personal in the transnational, following what Le Corbusier would have dismissed as a donkey's path to the world economy. In the early 1990s, for instance, the AWWC documented and compared three murder cases involving Thai women pressed into prostitution in Japan, who had stabbed bar owners to death. In the same period, the AWWC launched an information and documentation campaign on behalf of nine women who had filed suit against Hitachi, claiming gender discrimination in wages, job posting and job training (Hiroko 1992). With the Hitachi 9, the AWWC took on 'the twin-career track system' now replacing wage discrimination as the principal form of gender discipline in Japanese transnational corporations (Keiko 1992). In taking these paths, the AWWC did not rise above lived contexts, or reset placed experiences, but rather worked horizontally to link hitherto unconnected cases.

Similarly, PARC is not a centre of power but rather acts as a 'switchboard for Asia's peoples movements'. PAN also gathers information and links union workers and NGOs in countries where Japanese transnational corporations are active (PAN 1997; 1998). The Asian Migrant Center and the Asian Migrants Forum both work to document and link transnational experiences, as do the Center for Transnational Labor Studies, the Transnational Institute and the Asia Monitor Resources Center (Petrat 1994). In a similar manner, the Korea Labour Society Institute (KLSI) works on call from trade union federations and national centres to document labour/management relations, labour policies and labour problems. Having gathered the necessary information, the KLSI then distributes it to labour activists through its Professional Research Center, where labour activists from abroad also gather. In the same spirit, the ICCSASW informs sugar workers of living and working conditions, strikes and wage settlements elsewhere, interpellating them not as part of a generic whole (the would-be united 'Sugar Workers of the World'), but as workers brought together by their involvement in the sugar industries, and differently contextualized, through a variety of factors: home country dependence on export crops, working conditions in other industries and so on.

In the world of labour, International Trade Secretariats (ITS), World Industry Councils (WIC) and World Corporation Councils (WCC) have put themselves increasingly in the service of transnational labour campaigns.[32] ITSs in particular (and among them most notably the International Metalworkers' Federation, the International Federation of Chemical, Energy and General Workers' Union, the International Textile Garment and Leather Workers' Federation and the International Union of Food and Allied Workers' Associations) have played a key role in support of transnational campaigns, and they have served as key links between locally rooted strikes and struggles (Herod 1995b; Kidder and McGinn 1995; Spooner 1989). During the Ravenswood campaign, for instance, the International Metalworkers' Federation (IMF) worked alongside the AFL-CIO's Industrial Union Department to provide key research facilities that allowed for the transnationalization of the campaign (Allen 1993a). In addition, the International Union of Food and Allied Workers' Associations (IUF) and the ICFTU 'organized [an anti-Rich] rally of some 20,000 trade unionists in Romania' that was a key moment in the struggle (Herod 1995b, 352). Created in the mid-1960s as co-ordinating bodies for national unions, and long enfettered in international politics, World Corporation Councils have lately grown to play a key role in organizing transnational labour campaigns.[33]

In the women's movement, the Women's International Information and Communication Service (ISIS/WICCE, 1974), has 'connected more than 10,000 women's groups in 130 countries' working 'against economic development policies that marginalize and exploit women workers' (Peterson and Runyan 1993). In the same spirit, the International Feminist Network (1976) has worked 'to facilitate the mobilization of the women's liberation movements on an international scale when needed', the 'Feminist International Networks of Resistance to Reproductive Technologies and Genetic Engineering' (FINR-Rage, 1984) has worked 'to stimulate and link worldwide feminist research on, analysis of, and resistance to the use, abuse, and control of women in reproductive and genetic research and technologies', and the 'Women and Global Corporations Project' of the American Friends Service Committee links 'workers, activists and researchers worldwide who are promoting legislation to stop TNC practices that are reducing jobs and wages for women workers in the North and exploiting women's cheap labor in the South' (Miles 1996; Peterson and Runyan 1993). In the struggle against sexual slavery, Human Rights Watch's 'Women's Rights Projects' has completed a key work of documentation (Human Rights Watch 1993; 1995).

Recently, Web-based institutions (Table 3.2) have also served as clearinghouses for placed information, and has linked between placed experiences. In the world or labour, for instance, the Campaign for Labor Rights is the principal site-based information centre. Sweatshop Watch and the Corporate Watch Web Site Online are both 'watchdog websites' designed to provide activists (as well as academics and journalists) with up-to-date information and analysis on specific transnational corporations. In the women's movement, notable links include: 'Virtual Sisterhood', an electronic support network committed to encouraging exchange of information and strategies between women's movements; *Modemmujer*, an electronic link founded by five Mexican NGOs, and the 'Directory of Information' of the Women's Environmental Network, which provides 'instant accurate information on consumer product' to link women of different countries (The Women's Environmental Network 1994). Against the MIA, such groups as the People's Global Action Against Free Trade (PGA), Global Trade Watch, The Third World International Network Forum on Globalisation and the Polaris Institute (Canada) used Wed-based resources to link movements around the world, and the world's largest, searchable, anti-globalization archive was assembled.

As well as documenting specific struggles and linking them with one another, transnational institutions have also been involved in what I have called elsewhere 'solidarity tourism' (Drainville 1999, p. 237). Since the beginning of the 1990s, for instance, Global Exchange has offered 'Reality Tours' that 'allow people to go past what they read in the media and travel beyond hotels and beaches'. Destinations offered in 2000 included Cuba ('Explore the many faces of Cuba. . . . Learn about our island neighbor and the warmth of the Cuban people while experiencing their dramatic history and culture reflected in their daily lives'); Haiti/Dominican Republic ('Explore the depths of Haiti's rich history and culture. . . . Learn about Haiti's long struggle for democracy and see how Haiti offers the open-minded visitor an opportunity to understand vibrancy and hope in the midst of challenge); India ('Learn how Gandhian solutions are still being applied'), Mexico (¡Bienvenidos!. . . . Visit . . . Chiapas and learn more about the history and culture of indigenous communities. Speak with representatives of a variety of local organizations and gain a better understanding of popular movements and modern day social struggles in Mexico').[34]

In the world of labour, solidarity tours have become frequent events. In the Americas, the UE/FAT alliance is an important broker of worker-to-worker exchanges. In a typical visit, a rank-and-file delegation of UE women visited Mexico in August 1996 and toured plants, meeting with workers and leaders of the union and co-operative sectors to discuss problems facing women workers. In 1997, FAT representatives made three trips to the USA; in exchange, three groups of UE workers travelled to Mexico, 'becoming familiar with the work of the FAT . . . in the interior and in *Ciudad Juarez*. During their stay, they toured plants where workers are represented by FAT-affiliated unions, participated in organizing sessions, meetings of the Mexican Action Network Against Free Trade, a FAT national meeting, and other activities.[35] Between 23 July and 1 August 1999 CISPES (Committee In Solidarity with the People of El Salvador) sent 'labour rights' delegates/clients (costing US $1,300) on a one-week tour of El Salvador to help strengthen the international labour movement and build cross-border solidarity. In a spirit reminiscent of *The Times*, enjoinder to visit pickets of dockworkers, 'curious' solidarity tourists were encouraged to:

> meet organizers of the Salvadoran labor movement. . . . Witness the harsh effects of neoliberal policy. . . . Hear testimony from workers. . . . See how workers are fighting for their right. . . . Discuss youth organizing with FMLN juventud. . . . Visit FMLN-governed municipalities. . . . Help build cross-border solidarity.

In the same spirit, the Canadian Auto Workers' 'Southeast Asian Campaign Tour Against Globalization' (24 February to 10 March 1999) took thirteen Canadian women workers and organizers to five Southeast Asian countries (Indonesia, Thailand, Malaysia, The Philippines, Singapore) to 'share their experiences and views on the recent Economic Crisis and Globalisation . . . how they have affected their lives and what they are doing to cope as well as resist'. Four days of leadership training workshop in Malaysia, hosted by the Women Development Collective, were followed by tours of Manila and Zamboanga, a free trade zone where the tour joined in a picket. The 'Tour Against Globalization' then went on to Korea, 'to share with the movement there and exchange our experiences [and] to forge genuine international solidarity'. On 8 March the tour arrived in Seoul, and met with representatives of the women's committee from KWWAU, the Korean Confederation of Trade Unions.

In East Asia, the APWSL's co-organized – with the Hotel Employees and Restaurant Employees' Union (HERE) – the first Japanese–American solidarity tour, in support of striking workers at the Japanese-owned 'New Otani' hotel in the Little Tokyo district in Los Angeles (Seiichi 1996; 1997; Toshiko 1996). In the same period, the APWSL was organizing 'alternative tours' of export zones in New Zealand, to study the effect of deregulation (McLaughlin 1996b; Maynard 1999; Seiichi 1997; 1999). In like spirit, the AWWC organized 'grass-roots exchanges' between women workers and activists (Hiroko 1993; Yukie 1998); and the GAATW 'Comparative Workshop' with invited representatives from Cambodia, Vietnam and Laos.[36]

Ways for transnational institutions to gather money solidarity tours are also means through which local struggles are transnationalized and enduring links established. As I have documented elsewhere, solidarity visits were key to the building of cross-border solidarity movements during anti-NAFTA campaigning in the Americas (Drainville 1999). Similarly, SHF's 'mining exchange project' opened up channels of communication between mineworkers in Canada, South America and Southern Africa that have had a structuring impact on transnational campaigns (Hays 1996, 2). During the BS/FS campaigns, replaced workers went to Izmit and Istanbul in Turkey, and to Tokyo, where they met with ICEM affiliates and, as if to emphasize that global politics, like all politics, is local politics, with Revd Jesse Jackson, who was in Tokyo to meet high-ranking Bridgestone officials (Fumiaki 1995).[37] Demonstrations in Argentina and Brazil during an 'International Day of Action and Outrage', for instance, were organized by replaced workers touring South American Bridgestone plants. During the *Camisas* struggle, the AFL-CIO, UNITE and the US/GLEP organized tours where workers' representatives met with university students, investors, union members and religious groups.[38]

Although often negligible in terms of *realpolitik* influence, solidarity tours are significant in that they highlight well the position of transnational institutions *vis-à-vis* the global movement of social forces. This too we must keep in mind when we consider emerging modes of relation to the world economy.

Transnational campaigns as placed events

In marked contrast to neoliberal governance – that begins and ends outside all political and social contexts – transnational campaigns are rooted in both concrete and situated struggles, and they are constitutive of a broader, more political sense of place.

The Ravenswood campaign, for instance, was rooted in 'a powerful sense of place' growing out of long-standing ties between workers and the community (the average striking worker had twenty-four years' experience at the plant). Strengthened by community support, local pickets endured long enough for the transnational campaign to be effective (Herod 1995b, 355). In turn, the transnational campaign strengthened community resolve and broadened the local social basis of the strike. In the end, the connection between the local strike and the transnational campaign strengthened both, and the Ravenswood struggle became more than the sum of its parts. That is why Ravenswood strikers won their struggle.

In the BS/FS campaign, the first sites of struggle were BS/FS plants themselves, where pickets were held daily until 22 May 1995, when the URW made its unconditional offer to return to work. Once removed from BS/FS plants was 'Camp Justice', a tent city set up in front of the BS/FS headquarters in Nashville, Tennessee, following the ICEM/USWA/AFL-CIO 'World Conference on Bridgestone/Firestone' (13–14 March 1996). There, replaced workers and their supporters gathered for events that Benjamin Tillet and London dockers would have easily recognized. On 12 July 1996 (the second anniversary of the strike and an 'International Day of Action and Outrage' against BS/FS), a rally was held at 'Camp Justice' which was attended by more than 600 USWA members and community supporters:

> they heard fiery speeches by USWA Secretary-Treasurer, Leo Gerard and John Sellers, Executive Vice-President of the USWA-RPIC who has led negotiations with the company. . . . [Afterwards] the crowd gathered around a circle of miniature black-flags. On each was written the name of one of the 400 workers who were illegally fired and have not yet been called back to their jobs. . . . The crowd then marched the short distance from Camp Justice to the BS/FS headquarters, led by Leo Gerard and three local religious ministers. . . . Previous marches had stopped in the roadway facing the building. This one took a different route . . . the angry workers invaded the building's parking lot and swept to the front door where they were met by security guards and police. . . . After the chanting crowd withdrew, the ministers were admitted to present a petition and a scroll citing the names of all the replaced workers. They later reported that . . . management had received their message but appeared unaffected by their requests. . . . With that message the crowd returned to Camp Justice to continue the fight.[39]

For the duration of the campaign, 'Camp Justice' was occupied twenty-four hours a day, seven days a week, by replaced workers and their supporters. 'We're going to sit in their face one day longer than it takes to win this battle, and get a fair contract' said Ron Holder, of USWA Local 1055, representing workers at the Bridgestone plant in LaVergne, Tennessee.[40]

Indy car races were also sites of note during the BS/FS struggle. Taking advantage of Bridgestone's efforts to publicize its products and build a base of American customers, 1,000 replaced workers carried black 'Bridgestone/ Firestone Flags' to the Indy 500 on Memorial Day weekend in May 1996. On the weekend of 29–30 June 1996, 500 members of USWA locals from throughout Ohio converged on Cleveland to demonstrate at the Cleveland Medic Drug Grand Prix and promote the 'Don't Buy' campaign. Again, workers displayed black flags, distributed leaflets and gave away miniature black flags. In Toronto (12–14 July 1996), 500 USWA members converged on the Molson Indy, again carrying black flags.

Still further removed from BS/FS plants were 'cyberpickets' (invented then), and real-life processions that took place in Europe and South America, especially during 'International Days of Outrage': on 10 July 1996, 2,000 Bridgestone workers in Argentina stopped production and held a two-hour-long General Assembly in front of their plant.[41] On 12 July Brazil Bridgestone workers in São Paulo stopped work for one hour at shift changes at 5:30 a.m. 7:30 a.m. and 1:30 p.m. Three days later, several thousand rallied outside the Pirelli tire plant (where workers are also ICEM members). The following day, a procession of several thousand workers (also ICEM members)

Figure 3.1 Places of struggle: BS/FS flags at Camp Justice, Nashville, Tennessee, March 1996
Source: Photo taken by Jim Catterson, International Federation of Chemical, Energy, Mine and General Workers' Union

gathered outside the Goodyear tyre plant.[42] In Tokyo, where BS/FS's world headquarters are situated, Zenroyo organized a 'Solidarity group to support BS/FS Workers in Dispute' (Fumiaki 1995).

Brand-name campaigns have also drawn from community-based alliances between labour organizations and others, and have also been constitutive of community. The PVH campaign, for instance, brought together grass-roots and religious groups, human rights advocates, AFL-CIO workers and UNITE members, students and CISPES and STITCH activists in a wide variety of sites hitherto barren in terms of politics. At the Valley West Mall in West Des Moines, Iowa, PVH campaigners distributed several hundred leaflets and marched in procession, carrying signs that read: 'Support Workers in Guatemala' and 'Van Heusen Shirts Made in Sweatshops'. In Salt Lake City, eight activists 'spent a few hours spreading the word about how PVH fired all 500 unionized workers at its Guatemala factory when they came to work expecting to receive their Christmas bonuses'.[43] During the second week of June 1999 alone, the PVH campaign brought local activists together in Canoga Park, Long Beach, San Francisco, Trumbull, Washington DC, Chicago, Boston, Detroit, Minneapolis, St Louis, Buffalo, New York, Portland, Philadelphia, Pittsburgh, and elsewhere in the USA.[44] To further local mobilization, US/GLEP and CLR distributed leaflets and 'Activist Packets'.

The GAP campaign that began on 18 June 1999 (the 'International Day of Action Against Economic Globalization') has also been rooted in places and constitutive of it. In San Francisco, it has been an important factor of mobilization (Global Reach and Global Exchange report almost weekly leafleting activities).[45] On 1 May 1999, during a rally to 'Stop Saipan Sweatshops' and 'Celebrate International Workers' Day', a large crowd of protesters gathered outside GAP's flagship store at Powell and Market Street, holding signs, banners and handing out leaflets. A quartet sang 'The Sweatshop Hokey Pokey' and the protest culminated with the 'pieing' of an eighteen-foot effigy of GAP Chairman Donald Fisher, 'whose face was splattered with a whipped cream pie by a lovely stilt walker'.[46] After the pieing, a procession left for the GAP store on Duboce and Market. There,

> a sea of people stopped traffic on Market Street and cheered while Donald Fisher, Gap Sweatshop CEO, again got a pie right in the kisser! Redwood forest activists, protesting the Fisher family's clear cutting of the last old growth redwoods in Mendecino County, led the chant 'Mr. Fisher – you've got a store, what do you need the redwoods for?'[47]

Six weeks later, a GAP crowd again gathered at the Justin Herman Plaza for a 'street takeover' of the financial district.

In a similar manner, the Nike campaign has brought activists together and charged new places with politics, singing songs as social as the dockworkers':

> *Just Don't do it*
> *Just Don't*
> *Justice, Do it, Nike*
> *The Swooshtika*
> *Just Boycott It*

(Klein 2000a, 366)

Particularly interesting here have been efforts to charge nodal points in Nike's marketing scheme with political significance (basketball and golf tournaments), sporting goods and shoe stores, university campuses). To further mobilization there, CLR compiled a list of universities that have contracted purchase agreements with Nike, and it assembled a network of speakers 'to come to your campus to talk about the campaign to win justice for Nike's production workers'.[48]

Brand-name campaigns have also encouraged national gatherings of social forces. In Japan, for instance, APWSL's 'New Otani' and 'Don't Buy Reebok' campaigns were both privileged occasions for the strengthening and broadening of coalitions between hitherto dispersed social movements. Support pickets were organized, political action committees set up and organizations linked. In the case of the 'New Otani' dispute, the hub of activity was HERE's Local 11, where was headquartered the 'New Otani Workers'

Support Committee'. There, rank-and-file members from Osaka Zenrokyo, the Union Network (an independent union group), members of the Hanaoka Support Committee, RINK (Right of Immigrants Kansai Network), and a variety of citizens groups met and worked together, on a terrain that was, at once, local, national and transnational (Flynn 1997; Seiichi 1996).

Still in Japan, APWSL's campaign for the rights of migrant workers spawned a 'National Network in Solidarity with Migrant Workers' (1997) that brought together representatives of documented and undocumented migrant workers in Japan, union representatives (from Zenrokyo, the National Union of General Workers, Tokyo South, the Foreign Laborers' Union, the All-United Workers' Union) as well as various citizens' groups (the Japan Association for the Study of Chinese Forced Labor, the Hanaoka Victim Support Group) (Akira 1995a; Akira 1995b; APSWL-Japan 1994; Hideo 1994; McLaughlin 1996a; 1996c). At its June 1999 meeting, the Network gathered more than 500 Japanese activists, as well as foreign workers from a dozen countries (McLaughlin 1999). In the same spirit, the AMRC and the Committee to Support Kader Workers organized a transnational campaign on behalf of the families of 189 victims of the May 1993 fire at the Kader Toy factory (in the export-processing zone of Buddhamonthorn in Thailand) which received much external support (in Hong Kong, for instance). Significantly, the Kader campaign brought together all major unions and social movements in Thailand in an unprecedented coalition that remained united until a compensation agreement was signed (Chua and Wai-Ling 1993).

In the summers of 1988 and 1989, the PP21 campaign brought together more than 120,000 Japanese and foreign activists in nineteen different regional gatherings. Importantly, each gathering had a different theme, linked with the ambient community. The Sapporo meeting, for instance, focused on deindustrialization and the crisis of dairy farming, salient local issues (Pacific-Asia Resource Center 1988).[49]

Transnational campaigns against the politics of global regulatory institutions have also spawned placed events. Launched in February 1998, the loosely gathered 'People's Global Action Against Free Trade and the World Trade Organisation' (PGA), for instance, has inspired innumerable local events. The first WTO ministerial conference in Geneva (May 1998) occasioned PGA-style 'global street parties' on all five continents. In Geneva (not a habitual location for street parties) a 'beautiful gypsy circus' of 200 tractors and bicycles was met with 1,000 police officers, customs officials and army volunteers. In New York, 10,000 people gathered at the United Nations – the largest such gathering since the Reagan–Gorbachov Summit (1984). Again, the protest brought together social forces with little in common besides their opposition to the ways of the WTO.

> The people came with the banners of all kinds of struggles against some
> aspect of globalization: local unions fighting privatizations or austerity,

groups of solidarity with the south, squatters, plus many personal banners, musicians, and the caravan tractors towing a huge sound system. Everyone there agreed: stupendous, unbelievable demo. In front, holding the PGA banner (with a four meters high banner from India behind them) were some members of the international Convenor's Committee and some other representatives of peoples' movements that participated in the First PGA conference.

In Hyderabad (the symbolic heart of peasant struggle in India), the 'Joint Action Forum of Indian People against the WTO and Anti-People Policies' (JAFIP) organized a procession that gathered tens of thousands of peasants, agricultural labourers and industrial workers. In Tel Aviv there was a street party: 'over 500 people walked and danced from Dizengoff Square to the beach, while a van with DJ was driving in front doing the music. . . . The party ended in a pleasant sunset rave.' In Leuven (Belgium), a 'Reclaim the Streets' party took place. In Prague, 3,000 people joined the street party. 'They blocked the city's main road with thirty drums, a puppet show, fire performances, four sound systems and twenty DJs.' In Lyon, the PGA street party attracted 200 people, and 'lots of crazy anti-corporate costumes and signs, a few dogs and bikes, several drums and whistles, and even a float'. In Seville, the 'Network of Struggles against Neoliberalism' distributed a manifesto 'For Humanity, against the Dictatorship of Money'. In Brasilia, an anti-WTO march brought together 50,000 people. In Brisbane, 'a small but effervescent crowd partied 'til dark and then went home'.[50]

In Montréal, *Opération SalAMI* held a street party outside the Montréal Stock Exchange, and a *Teach-In Citoyen* on 'The Globalization of Injustice: Resistance and Alternatives'. Echoing the PGA's call for non-violent civil disobedience, sit-ins and blockades were organized. 'Today' said *SalAMI's* Philippe Duhamel,

> Montreal has done its part for the globalization of resistance. We're proud of what we've done. 'The promoters of the globalization of injustice cannot say that their programme of huge profits, the destruction of social programs and the impoverishment of ordinary people has any longer a consensus in Quebec.[51]

In the United States and Mexico, border communities have been both the starting point for a wide variety of transnational campaigns (that have for the most part focused on working conditions in Maquilladora industries) and have been transformed by transnational campaigning. As Elaine Burns suggested, this is perhaps explained by the central role played by women's groups in cross-border activism (e.g. *la Mujer Obrera* in El Paso, *Fuerza Unidas* in San Antonio, the Support Committee for Maquilladora Workers in San Diego/Tijuana, the Coalition for Justice in the Maquilladora in San Antonio Texas). Shaped by concerns about the relationships between work and community, transnational campaigns have been built as community projects, and they have reinforced a local sense of place (Burns 1991, 7–8).[52]

In the Americas, the hemisphere-wide struggle against neoliberal integration has not only transcended national locality; it has also been constitutive of it (Drainville 1999). The effect has been felt especially in Canada and in Mexico. By virtue of their proximity to the USA, these two countries are at the centre of the movement for continental integration into the Americas; by their national political mythology as well as by the self-interest of social groups most urgently interpellated by regionalism, they are rebuffed by it. In a word, social movements, especially in Canada and Mexico, are at once driven by the emerging regional context to forge inter- and transnational strategic links of the sorts discussed above, as they are pushed inward and encouraged to broaden the social basis of opposition to integration. This latter effort has brought such networks as the *Red Mexicana de Acción Frente Libre Comercio* (RMLAC) and the Action Canada Network (ACN), that were the principal driving forces behind the creation of inter- and transnational coalitions of social movements in the Americas, to the forefront of national-centred struggles to broaden the democratic process.

In Canada, the ACN positioned itself as handmaiden to 'coalition politics', and the national case against integration adopted a broader, and somewhat idealized, notion of 'community sovereignty', defined by the Canadian Center for Policy Alternatives as 'our ability as a nation to determine our own destiny', as a necessary barrier to transnational neoliberalism (CCPA 1992a). What Tony Clarke called a 'new nationalism' spoke of 'Canadian workers . . . reclaim[ing] the sovereignty of the[ir] country,' of the refusal to 'give up on Canada, [and] abandon the rich legacy of rights and benefits . . . our forebearers fought so hard to give us' and of 'holding the country together'. It prompted such initiatives as the Council of Canadians' 'Citizens' Agenda', the *Commission populaire itinérante* of *Solidarité populaire Québec*, and the 'People's Agenda', launched by the Canadian Labour Congress in December 1991 after two years of consultation with other groups opposed to the North American Free Trade Agreement (Barlow 1993; CCPA 1992b; Griffin Cohen 1992, 16; Poirier 1992, 3; Roy n.d.; Valin and Sinclair 1992, 170). If, as Alain Touraine put it, political struggles are struggles over historicity – that is to say, struggles over 'the set of cultural, cognitive, economic, and ethical models by means of which a collectivity sets up relations with its environment' – Canadian opposition to integration in the Americas looked to have been as much about constructing a national collectivity as it has been about assembling inter- and transnational coalitions of social movements (Canel 1992, 28).

In Mexico as well, there has been an intimate connection between the growth of regional and hemispheric coalitions and networks of social movements and the transformation of national political relationships (Arroyo and Monroy 1996; Osorio 1996). Indeed, campaigns against NAFTA, the Enterprise for the Americas Initiative and, more broadly, against the

Maquilladorization of Central America, have served as anchoring points of sorts for democratization, alongside other crucial episodes such as the 1988 and 1991 elections, the 1994 devaluation of the peso, the Chiapas uprising and subsequent peace process (Heredia 1994; Luján 1996; Monroy 1994). In such landmark episodes in the development of grass-roots democratic politics in Mexico as the *Referéndum de la Libertad* (Liberty referendum, 24 September to 23 October 1995), the *Consulta Ciudadana* (the citizen's consultation, 26 February 1995) and the *Primera Jordana Nacional de Condena a la Política Económica del Gobierno* (the first day of condemnation of the economic policy of the government: 8 September 1996), the RMLAC played a central co-ordinating role, alongside other newly formed social groups and networks of social movements: the *Pacto de Grupos Écologistas, La Convergencia de Organismos Civiles por la Democracia, El Foro de Apoyo Mutuo, Ganando Espacio, Mujeres Punto, Entre Mujeres*, the *Red Nacional de Organismos Civiles de Derechos Humanos* (Chalmers *et al.* 1995; Cook 1995; Encuentro Nacional de Organizaciones Ciudadanas 1995; Red Mexicana de Acción Frente al Libre Comercio 1995, 1996).

Even in the USA, where coalition politics has not been stimulated by nationalist sentiments energizing popular coalitions in Canada and Mexico, the struggle against regional and hemispheric integration has also spawned unprecedented coalitions of unions, environmental and women's groups. In MERCOSUR countries as well, schemes for hemispheric and regional integration have created a context which appears favourable to the widening and broadening of links between different segments of national social movements. In Chile, most obviously, this broadening has brought the *Red Chile Para una Iniciativa de los Pueblos* (RECHIP) to the forefront of a broad coalition of social movements – of unions, women, peasants and human rights groups – which has argued for a *Carta de Derechos Económico, Sociales, Culturales y Ambientales y de Derechos Ciudadanas* (Red Chile de Acción por una Iniciativa de los Pueblos 1996). To a lesser extent, Paraguayan social forces have also broadened links in response to MERCOSUR (Céspedes 1994).

These fragments suggest that transnational campaigns are situated events which begin and end in contexts. Borrowing Jane Jacob's terminology, they may be thought of as 'hop-and-skip' events that force 'working relationships [on to] people . . . who enlarge their local public life beyond the neighborhoods of streets and specific organizations or institutions and form relationships with people whose roots and background are in entirely different constituencies' (Jacobs 1993 [1961], 175). When such campaigns unite people of distinct backgrounds and preoccupations into a working relationship, neighbourhoods become successful, that is to say capable of self-government 'in its broadest sense, meaning both the informal and formal self-management of society' (Jacobs 1993 [1961], 149). This too is something we must keep in mind as we try to theorize the movement of social forces in the world economy.

Conclusion

For score sheets: Ravenswood and BS/FS workers won, partisans of Ken Saro-Wiwa and opponents of NAFTA did not, and the campaigns for the rights of Saipan, Nike and Reebok workers, for abortion rights, wages for housework, against excision, sexual tourism and gender exploitation continue.

More broadly, these campaigns offer us glimpses of a new political subject creating itself in the world economy, and, perhaps, of a new mode of relation to the world economy. In marked contrast to grand absentee subjects (e.g. the proletariat, global sisterhood, global civil society, humanity) this is not a syncretic, totalizing (and easily recuperable) subject, but a conjunctural subject, 'present in the now' as Walter Benjamin wrote of surrealists (Benjamin 1973, 261). Neither just 'here' in the local or parochial sense of the term, nor simply 'out there' in the world economy, this subject is both 'deterritorialized' and 'reterritorialized' – to borrow Michael P. Smith's expressions for the dual belonging of transnational migrants (Smith 1994).

Already, times and places exist where this new subject may be seen. The curious may want to visit Nike towns during 'Nike Days of Action', or when visits from sales representatives give CLR activists occasion to talk about its global campaign; GAP stores in San Francisco during an 'International Day of Action Against Economic Globalization'; Bangkok brothels being picketed by GAATW activists; and Maquilladora communities in El Paso and San Antonio (probably the most enduring meeting points between placed struggles and the global context).

4 The civic ordering of global social relations

> In the space of power, power does appear as such ... it hides under the organization of space.
>
> (Henri Lefebvre)[1]

> So, what I have had to do with the comprehensive framework is to try and engage civil society.
>
> John Wolfensohn (The World Bank 2000)

In the years immediately following the collapse of the Bretton Woods system, a transnational response to the crisis was articulated in regulatory agencies of the world economy, both public and semi-public (e.g. the International Monetary Fund, The World Bank, the Organisation for Economic Cooperation and Development, the Transnational Commission, the Bank for International Settlements) and private (debt securities and bond rating agencies).

For the most part, these agencies had been part of the nationally centred edifice of *Pax Americana*. In the context of a worldwide crisis, they became increasingly autonomous from individual nation-states (including those at the core of the world economy) and from the dynamics of inter-state relations in general. Working as members of a common concern, they defined what J.M. Fleming of the International Monetary Fund called a 'system of guidance' for the whole of the world economy (Fleming 1975).

From a narrowly economic point of view, neoliberal concepts of control were not efficient. To take but two salient examples, global monetarism – the first instance of transnational neoliberalism – did not anchor an effective monetary regime for the post-Bretton Woods world, and was abandoned at the beginning of the 1980s when the IMF, the BIS and the G7 called for the re-establishment of pluralist and discretionary monetary policies.[2] Also ineffective were special credit and compensatory facilities introduced by the IMF and The World Bank to deal with the debt crises, that neglected everything political about adjustment. Piecemeal initiatives born of specific circumstances, they did not rise above the rooted power of nation-states, even in debtor countries, where corruption and weak financial surveillance made up a financial regime archaic by the emerging standards of *Pax Planeta*.

From a political point of view, what is remarkable about neoliberal concepts of control born in the immediate wake of the Bretton Woods crisis, is how much they relied on coercion, how little they worked on consensus and, in governance parlance, how 'inefficient' they were. It was to remedy this problem that global agencies brought the ordering spirit of civic reformism to the world economy.

As civic reformism in the nineteenth century took 'the evils of nineteenth-century cities' as its starting point, global governance began with circumscribed problems:

> in the global neighborhood, citizens have to co-operate for many purposes: to maintain peace and order, expand economic activity, tackle pollution, halt or minimize climate change, combat pandemic diseases, curb the spread of weapons, prevent desertification, preserve genetic and species diversities, deter terrorism, ward off famine, defeat economic recession, share scare resources, arrest drug traffickers, and so on.
>
> (Commission on Global Governance 1995)

As a problem-solving enterprise, global governance is shaped by two simultaneous and mutually reinforcing policy processes. First is the gelling of scattered policy ideas into an increasingly comprehensive blueprint. Over the past decade or so, this process has fused together ideas about the relationship between human and military security, human rights, the protection of biodiversity, the role of non-state actors in the international system, proper relationships between inter-state bodies and non-governmental organizations, political, economic and ecological sustainability and so on. Second is the movement of this increasingly coherent blueprint from organizations and policy bodies of a consultative, indeed almost experimental, nature (e.g. the Brandt, Palme, Brundltand and Nyerere Commissions, the McBride Report, ECLA, UNCTAD, UNCLOS, UNESCO) towards core regulatory agencies of the world economy (e.g. The World Bank, the OECD, the Bank for International Settlements, the International Monetary Fund).

The combined action of these two processes has made governance a policy paradigm of considerable influence at the global level. Already, governance's ideas have framed a remarkable variety of participatory programmes and funding mechanisms that have engaged substantial political and material resources from regulatory agencies. From The World Bank and the IMF, for instance, have come new grants programmes, lending windows and important efforts to 'mainstream' and 'upstream' NGO participation (to use dedicated vernacular). The OECD as well has operationalized governance into concrete policy objectives, aiming, for example, to 'reduc[e] by one-half in the proportion of people living in extreme poverty by 2015', or for 'universal primary education in all countries by 2015'.[3]

Beyond specific policy initiatives, governance is also a broad ordering strategy for the world economy that attempts to construct a perfectly apolitical civic space. To occupy it, regulatory agencies of the world economy are gathering civic-minded interlocutors with whom they hope to negotiate what IMF Managing Director Michel Camdessus called 'the widespread acceptance of a set of general propositions about the most effective way of achieving sustainable growth'.[4]

In this chapter, we enquire into governance's civic gathering from the point of view of 'modes of social relation to the world economy'. Our examination is divided into three parts. First, we look at the global level proper, where we begin with a relatively brief visit to the self-styled 'global conferences' of the United Nations. As a group, these conferences are useful monads of a new order that lend themselves well to a physiognomic reading.[5]

Were Walter Benjamin alive, and were he to attempt doing for the 'global city' of governance at the close of the twentieth century what he did for Paris of the nineteenth century, he would undoubtedly saunter about in UN conferences, as we are about to do.

Our critical faculties awakened by a tour of global conferences, we will proceed with a more systematic and sober analysis of less conspicuous sites where are tentatively defined the terms of global civility, from the periphery of power (e.g. the United Nations Department of Public Information's 'NGO Resource Center', ECOSOC's 'Committee on Non-Governmental Organizations', the UN's Environmental Liaison Center) to the centre (e.g. The World Bank Inter-agency Group on Participation, the 'NGO-World Bank Committee,' IMF-sponsored 'town hall meetings').

Below the global level, governance has also served as a blueprint for the re-invention of social relations within regions and cities of the world economy. In the second and third parts of this chapter, we will look briefly at these lesser sites of governance. Thus, from global *salons* to actually existing cities, we will visit sites most telling of governance's civic gathering.

The global level

Although claims surrounding the gelling of 'global civil society' are questionable on both empirical and political grounds, suggestions that a 'third sector' has only now begun to gather in the vicinity of international organizations are not without foundation.[6] When the League of Nations (LoN) first met, NGO representatives were so marginalized that they struggled with ordinary tourists to get but a view of proceedings (Kreimer *et al.* 1995, 2). Although the LoN's 'International Bureau Section' did monitor NGO activities and maintained informal contacts with a select few, only on rare occasions were delegates from 'private associations' (as NGOs were known then) even included on the list of consultative agencies. The 1932 Disarmament Conference was such an occasion, as were meetings of the LoN's 'Committee on Child Welfare and Traffic in Women and Children'

(Interim Committee to Consultative Non-Governmental Organizations (1948) 1978, 12–13).

Before the outbreak of the Second World War, the LoN broadened its still-irregular relationship with private associations, going so far as thinking in more formal, even operational terms. In the words of the LoN's last *Handbook of International Organizations*, published in 1938:

> As the years have gone on, the League's relations with international associations have increased in scope and variety. With some of them, it works in close and permanent co-operation. . . .

> Official league bodies lend an attentive ear to the wishes and suggestions of private associations, as witness the reception of their delegations by the President of the Assembly and by the Conference for the Reduction and Limitation of Armaments. The League's administrative services are in constant touch with the international organizations, the Secretariat sends representatives to their congresses and conferences and keeps up a continuous correspondence with them besides frequent personal contacts.[7]

In 1945, more than 1,200 non-governmental organizations attended the founding conference of the UN in San Francisco, that mandated the Economic and Social Council (ECOSOC) to make 'suitable arrangements for consultation with non-governmental organisations which are concerned with matters within its competence'.[8] These arrangements began to take shape with the first ECOSOC meeting in London in early 1946, and with the Report of the 'Committee on Arrangements for Consultation with Non-Governmental Organizations' of June 1946. This report found a role for NGOs as a source of expert advice and as a bridge between UN agencies and the 'world's public opinion' (Interim Committee to Consultative Non-Governmental Organizations (1948) 1978, 19). Later 'Notes for Representatives of Non-Governmental Organizations' confirmed the political importance of maintaining contact with NGO representatives, who were encouraged to 'keep . . . [their] membership fully informed of the economic and social work of the United Nations in detail' (Brock 1955, 4).

This recognition of NGOs' political role was exceptional for the post-war period. More generally, NGOs were considered apolitical providers of expert information and not appointed representatives of humanity (Chiang 1981; Lador-Lederer 1963; White 1951). ECOSOC guidelines, for example, divided NGOs according to functional capabilities and gave them policy functions commensurate with their competence, not their political representativity (Brock 1955; Interim Committee to Consultative Non-Governmental Organizations (1948) 1978).

In the post-war period, NGOs were for the most part anchored in specialized agencies of the United Nations: the International Refugee Organization,

the International Maritime Consultative Organization, the World Meteoro-
logical Organization, the World Health Organization, the International
Telecommunication Union, the United Nations Educational Scientific and
Cultural Organization, the Office of the UN High Commission for Refugees,
the UN Fund for Population Activities, the United Nations Children's Fund
(Interim Committee to Consultative Non-Governmental Organizations
(1948) 1978, 33–35; Salmen and Eaves 1991). There, expert NGOs were given
well-defined, often explicitly non-political, mandates.[9] Even such politically
minded organizations as the International Socialist Assistance (ISA, 1950),
for instance, was transformed by its association with UN agencies into a
virtually non-political relief agency.[10]

During this period, contacts between NGOs and regulatory institutions at
the centre of the world economy were sporadic at best, and sometimes simply
non-existent. At their inception, for instance, the IMF, The World Bank and
the International Bank for Reconstruction and Development made no provision at all for consultation with NGOs (Interim Committee to Consultative
Non-Governmental Organizations (1948) 1978, 33–34). Although the
OECD's Development Assistance Committee granted consultative status to
NGOs in 1962, its 1966 'Guidelines for the Co-Ordination of Technical
Assistance' took the exclusion of local NGOs so much for granted that its
efforts to respond more sensitively to the particular problem of recipient
countries were limited to increasing co-ordination between the local represen-
tatives of donor countries (Beigbeder 1992, 41; Thorp 1985, 48).

The relationship between NGOs and inter-state organizations remained
minimal until the beginning of the 1970s, when the agenda for a New International Economic Order (NIEO) began to take shape in specialized agencies
and conferences of the United Nations: the UNESCO, the United Nations
Conference on Trade and Development (UNCTAD), the third United
Nations Conference on the Law of the Sea (UNCLOS III) and so on.

Starting with the second development decade (1970–1979), the development discourse shifted away from technical/quantifiable objectives towards a
broader, and more political, goal of satisfying 'basic human needs', and a
planetary subject appeared on whose behalf were presented NIEO demands
for a more equitable world order. The Montego Bay convention that sealed
UNCLOS III (1973–1982) provides a useful reminder of the cosmopolitan
politics of the NIEO:

> All rights in the deep sea bed are vested in mankind as a whole, and . . .
> no states shall claim or exercise sovereignty or sovereign rights over any
> parts of the area or its resources. Activities in the Areas should be carried
> out for the benefits of mankind as a whole.[11]

In more concrete terms, would-be representatives of the NIEO's generic (and
gender-blind) mankind were increasingly invited to gather at sites where the
NIEO agenda was taking shape. At the 1972 Conference on the Human

Environment in Stockholm (that drew unprecedented attention to the idea of sustainable development), an important NGO contingent was involved, both to official proceedings and to 'protests, networking, consciousness-raising and other "unofficial" activities linked to the conference' (Conca 1995). In similar manner, the 1974 World Population Conference in Bucharest, the 1974 World Food Conference in Rome, Habitat I in Vancouver (1976), UN conferences on desertification (Nairobi, 1977) and on science and technology (Vienna, 1979) all brought NGOs to the heart of the NIEO (NGO Forum on the World Economic Order 1975; Ritchie 1996). The 1975 NGO Forum (a direct descendant of the 1948 'General Conference of NGOs') gathered in support of the NIEO programme (NGO Forum on the World Economic Order 1975). Over 6,000 women participated in the NGO Forum of the First World Conference on Women (Mexico City, 1975) which adopted a 'World Plan of Action' 'covering all possible aspects of their lives from food, health and education to family planning and political participation' (Chen 1996; Pietilä and Vickers 1994). Over 7,000 women attended the NGO forum at the second WCW in Copenhagen in 1980, and 14,000 were present at the third WCW in Nairobi in 1985 (Chen 1996, 141)

Within their appointed domains, gathering NGOs helped bolster the NIEO agenda, and they did have some influence over policy-making by transnational regulatory agencies. In the defence of human rights, for instance, and especially of the rights of 'disappeared' persons in Argentina and Chile, the reporting work of international NGOs was absolutely crucial (Cook 1996; Gaer 1996). In addition Amnesty International and the International Commission of Jurists (ICJ) were key to the drafting of the UN Declaration on Torture (1975) and the (1984) Convention on Torture (Pagnucco and Atwood 1994, 414). In part as a result of NGO work, DAC countries of the OECD increased official development aid substantially, and multilateral agencies increased concessional assistance to low-income developing countries. New crisis-management programmes were also introduced that focused more on satisfying basic human needs (the IMF 1976 'International Fund for Agricultural Development', for instance).

In terms of our enquiry, though, demands for a NIEO did not bring transnational subjects closer to the centre of political processes in the world economy. Indeed, the gap between the two widened during this period. The humanity on whose behalf NEIO plans were presented was an oppositional subject invented in peripheral fora by marginal states against 'unilateral transnationalism' stemming from the centre of political processes.[12] In this adversarial context, there were few resources for NGOs (in 1970, fewer than 1.5 per cent of all development assistance was filtered through NGOs[13]), and no room to manoeuvre, and thus little was accomplished in terms of the structuring of the relationship between would-be representatives of 'mankind' and regulatory agencies of the world economy. Not surprisingly, the 1975 NGO Forum which met in the Auditorium of the Dag Hammarskjold Library in New York during the seventh special session of the General Assembly (1–12

September 1975) received only brief visits from officials of the UN's Office of Public Information, the 'Center for Economic and Social Information (CESI), the UNDP and the Under-Secretary-general for General Assembly Affairs' (NGO Forum on the World Economic Order 1975, ix). There were no contacts at all with core regulatory agencies.

From the mid-1970s until the mid-1980s, the gap between the global subjects widened to justify and support the NIEO, emerging neoliberal 'concepts of control' continued to grow, and NGOs were pushed further towards the periphery of transnational politics. After 1975, ECOSOC's NGO Committee, for instance, began meeting only every two years, and in 1976, the ECOSOC session even opened 'without there being any provision for participation by NGOs' (Willetts 1982, 14). NGOs present at the 1980 UN Conference on Women were given, between them, only fifteen minutes to address delegates (Willetts 1982, 15).

So marginal was NIEO's 'mankind' to regulatory agencies of the world economy in the 1970s that when The World Bank conducted a broad review of its operation-evaluation procedures, it made no mention at all of NGOs. Programme performance was defined quite explicitly in non-political terms, and programme monitoring was deemed a wholly self-referential and internal affair:

> The operating efficiency of the World Bank is assessed regularly by the Programming and Budgeting Department . . . by the Organization Planning Department . . . by the Internal Auditing Department . . . and by individual departments themselves.
>
> (The World Bank 1979, 13)

No room was left for external imput, apart from that of senior bureaucrats of host countries (The World Bank 1979, 21).

In this period, of course, the Davos Forum (1971), the Trilateral Commission (1973) and the G7 summits (1975) were founded as *élite* gatherings, excluding – sometimes explicitly – NGOs and other would-be representatives of global civil society. Events thus remained until the mid-1980s, when governance's 'Global Civil Society' began supplanting NIEO's 'mankind' as the planetary subject of reference.

Global conferences

Perhaps the most visible sign of the new, selective inclusiveness of global policy-making was the 'explosive growth in the scale and scope of NGO participation in UN-sponsored global conferences' (Conca 1995, 111). Of the many global gatherings held in the 1990s, six United Nations conferences are usually recognized as emblematic events of global governance: the United Nations Conference on Environment and Development (UNED) (Rio de Janeiro, June 1992); the World Conference on Human Rights (Vienna, June

1993); the International Conference on Population and Development (ICPD) (Cairo, September 1994); the World Summit for Social Development (Copenhagen, March 1995); the Fourth World Conference on Women (WCW) (Beijing, September 1995) and the United Nations Conference on Human Settlements (Habitat II) (Istanbul, June 1996). Although some of these conferences have roots in earlier sequences (the WCW was the fourth UN global conference on women, the ICPD the third on population and development, and Habitat II the second of a series that had begun ten years earlier in Vancouver), they are usually grouped together as 'United Nations global conferences' (Schilen *et al.* 1997, 25). In governance's lore, they stand as the first policy-minded gatherings of global civil society.

The sheer number of participants certainly warrants attention: upward of 30,000 people attended the Global Forum of the Rio UNCED, among whom were 1,400 accredited NGO representatives. At the Vienna World Conference on Human Rights, the NGO Forum gathered '2721 representatives of 1529 organisations' (Gaer 1996, 58).[14] The ICPD in Cairo drew between 18,000 and 20,000 individual participants, and at least as many NGO representatives as Vienna. The Beijing WCW, the largest global conference in terms of NGO participation, attracted more than 50,000 participants to both the main conference and the parallel forum in Huairou. More than 8,500 representatives of 2,266 NGOs were accredited to Habitat II in Istanbul. Among non-state groups which met, made formal presentations to the 'Partnership Committee' or participated in the drafting of the 'Vision Statement' and the 'Global Plan of Action' were fifteen NGO caucuses, representatives from more than 300 private sector corporations, six regional networks of youth groups and 290 representatives from 210 private foundations of fifty-four countries. In parallel, the Human Solidarity Forum 'met to discuss the capacity of the human spirit to cope with rapid urbanization and its implications' (UNCHS 1997a, 10).[15]

More significant than gross numbers of participants is the manner in which global conferences framed participation and structured the relationship between transnational policy-making ventures and would-be GSC representatives. Here are found most revealing fragments of governance's civic-gathering.

Ahead of conferences, accreditation and sponsorship programmes began the process whereby would-be representatives of global civil society were selected and their participation in the affairs of the global city structured. Together, The World Bank's 'Special Grant' programme, the 'NGO' or 'Small' grant programmes from the UNDPs, the Global Environment Facility's 'Small Grants programme' (which began in 1992) made up part of a selection regime that grew to structure and discipline governance's inclusiveness (Participation and NGO Group 1996). Also part of this emerging regime were various and sundry preparatory conferences and pre-meeting gatherings. After the Rio UNED, these grew in size and importance to such an extent that they became events unto themselves. In preparation for Vienna, for instance, the 'Center for Women's Global Leadership' organized a strategic planning meeting of grass-roots activists from twenty countries that called for 'Sixteen Days of Activism Against Gender Violence' and later set a global women's agenda on gender violence (Bunch 1993). In September 1992, women's health advocates from Asia, Africa, Latin America, the Caribbean, the USA and Western Europe formed the 'Women's Voices '94 Alliance' and drafted the 'Women's Declaration on Population Policies' that later served to guide the work of an *ad hoc* coalition called 'Women Watching ICPD' (Chen 1996). The Third Preparatory Committee for the Fourth World Conference on Women in Beijing, which was held from 15 March to 6 April 1995 at UN Headquarters in New York, gathered between 1,400 and 1,500 NGO representatives from all over the world, as many, indeed, as the first UN Global Conference in Rio. Among them were representatives of such women's networks as 'GROOTS Internationals' (Grassroots Organizations Operating Together in Sisterhood), 'Habitat International Coalition-Women' and the 'International Council of Women' (Correspondencia 1995; Masumi 1995).

Whether convened by core regulatory agencies of the world economy or by relatively autonomous coalitions of NGOs, pre-conference gatherings also worked to establish relevance and set the limits of possibilities. Problems were selected, circumscribed and classified, policy priorities established and interlocutors gathered together on the basis of their problem-solving relevance. As we shall see below, this assembling of problem-minded interlocutors is at the very heart of governance, both at the level of the world economy itself, and in regions and cities of the world economy.

Once global conferences proper began, patented representatives of GCS were invited to convene in enclosed areas situated on the margins of inter-states gatherings, at varying distances from policy-making ventures. At the Rio UNCED and the Vienna World Conference on Human Rights, the NGOs' forum and the 'upstairs' realm of transnational policy-making were close to one another and the movement of persons and ideas between the two was relatively informal (Chen 1996; Conca 1995; Fisher 1993; Johnson 1993). In contrast, Beijing's NGO forum took place in Huairou, 50 kilometres from the site of the official heads-of-state summit.

In allotted sites, NGOs, CONGOs DONGOs and other would-be representatives of global civil society furthered contact with one another and drafted synthesized policy agendas, which were then brought to governing agencies and their content merged with that of official programmes. In terms of policy-making, negotiations surrounding this merging were the high point of summits, when participants fulfilled governance's defining obligation to 'learn together what [is] possible and not possible, what they really want . . . and how they have to behave to get what they want' (The World Bank 1996b). Repeatedly, NGO delegates to global conferences assessed their successes and failures by their influence at this point in negotiations. This account by Sandy Schilen of GROOTS International is characteristic:

the dominant [anti-poverty] strategies failed to reflect grassroots women's focus on participating in sustainable development. To ensure this focus was maintained, a core group of . . . women . . . met for ten days . . . in Beijing to develop a joint policy statement on these issues and to agree to continue organizing with other like-minded women through to . . . Habitat II.

. .

One reward for this initiative was a visit by Dr. Wally N'Dow, Secretary-General of Habitat II, to the final day of the grassroots tent to hear our plans and recommendations. Impressed by the hard work, he offered to help place gender issues and women's leadership at the center of Habitat II Conference.

(Schilen *et al.* 1997, 25)

At the end of summit politics were global declarations, statements of purposes, blueprints, plans and programmes of varying degrees of policy details, all bearing the seal of cosmopolitan concord. Rio's UNED, for instance, begat 'Agenda 21'; Cairo's ICPD a 'Programme of Action'; Copenhagen's World Summit a 'World Social Charter' and the '20/20 development compact'; Habitat II the 'Istanbul Declaration' and 'Habitat Agenda', and so on. Appended to these blueprints were forward-looking programmes and plans of action: Rio's UNED, for example, produced the 'Localizing Agenda 21 Programme', and Habitat II 'the Global Urban Observatory Programme', the 'Indicators' programme, the 'Best Practices Initiative', and so on. These later served to define the agenda of further co-governance gatherings, that were also events in themselves.

Already, we begin to have a sense of the politics involved in the making of a global citizenry. Now is a good time to conclude our brief visit to global conferences. As evocative as they may be as artefacts of global governance, global conferences give but a limited idea of the complex processes they represent. They are maquettes freezing what is dynamic and presenting as a tidy, finished product what is still in the making. To get a truer, more complex, sense of the civic politics of global governance, we need to move beyond scale models to actual *chantiers* of the global city.[16]

Beyond global conferences: the making of global civil society

Were governance to be limited to global conferences, it could be dismissed as a window-dressing exercise of little importance to the structuring of social relations in the world economy. Beyond conferences, however, ideas of governance have already begun to shape the political practice of regulatory agencies at the core of the world economy.

Cosmopolitan rhetoric aside, there is no ready pool of 'global civil society representatives' from which governing agencies can draw credible interlocutors with a vertical perspective unto the world economy and ready ideas leading to sustainable transnational policies. Indeed, a central task of governance has been to create such an interlocutor. Sometimes this has meant supporting already-existing organizations, and at other times, necessary interlocutors have been, quite literally, invented.

For organizations sitting at the periphery of centres of power, the structuring of global civil society is being done in relative continuity with pre-governance practices. At the UNDP, for example, the new 'Civil Society Organizations and Participation' and 'Partners in Development' programmes are extensions of pre-existing efforts to rationalize and expand NGO networking activities, particularly in Africa and Asia. Similarly, governance-inspired initiatives, such as the 'Local Initiative Facility for Urban Development' (LIFE, 1992) and the 'Sustainable Agricultural Network' (SANE, 1993), were grafted on to existing UNDP programmes. In the early 1990s, the UNHCR launched a 'Partners in Action' programme that enhanced the kind of expertise-based collaboration with NGOs already in place well before governance (with the result that NGOs now handle the better part of the UNCHR caseload).[17] In the same period, an 'Open-Ended Group on the Review of Arrangements for Consultations with Non-Governmental Organizations' was appointed that broadened ECOSOC's traditional mandate (Clark 1995). After Rio, the UNEP – traditionally close to NGOs – set up an 'Environmental Liaison Center' to serve as a NGO liaison unit. The Nairobi-based ELC now serves over 6,000 environment and development-minded NGOs (Conca 1995).[18] In similar manner, the UN Division for Economic and Social Information and the NGO Resource Center have broadened their links with NGOs. Again, these build on pre-existing relationships with NGOs.

At the centre of global power, however, attempts to link up and structure what Thomas Princen and Matthias Finger called the 'NGO phenomenon' have brought about much more drastic changes (Princen and Finger 1994, 6). As we saw, core regulatory agencies of the world economy traditionally shunned NGOs, especially in the period where neoliberal concepts of control were taking shape. In the age of governance, those same agencies now emphasize inclusivity, participation, consensus-building and the weaving of partnerships with would-be GCS representatives.

As I wrote elsewhere, the move to governance has to be understood in relationship to a broad shift away from harsh conditionality towards more civic and sustainable strategies of structural adjustment (Drainville 1995b). In the early years of global neoliberalism – when 'neoliberal concepts of control' first appeared – regulatory agencies of the world economy were concerned principally with safeguarding existing mechanisms of market-based regulation, and their policies were intent on forcing adjustments. This was evident, for instance, in the first phase of the debt crisis, when the IMF and The World Bank acted very much as debt collectors would, and conditionality was applied coercively, with little regard for national circumstances or the politics of adjustment (Drainville 1995b).

As the growth of private international credit created a lax credit context, debtor countries became generally less dependent on multilateral concessional funding (exceptions, of course, were sub-Saharan countries at the epicentre of the latter phase of the debt crisis). In this context, regulatory agencies faced an important crisis of authority, which they attempted to resolve by increasing the political leverage gained from concessionary funding.[19] In contemporary language, they sought more 'efficiency', both in terms of solving social and economic problems and, more broadly, in terms of furthering social and political adjustments to the global context (Poats 1985a, 62). The way to efficiency was to fold concessionary funding within broad adjustment plans that also concerned themselves with the political and social dimensions of structural adjustments, in the name of efficiency.[20] Here, we arrive at governance's doorstep.

In quantitative terms, there has been a veritable explosion in NGO funding. Most visible have been new 'capacity-building' programmes and funding windows targeted specifically at NGOs. At The World Bank, for instance, the proportion of projects involving NGO participation grew from less than 6 per cent in the period 1973 to 1988 to almost 50 per cent in 1995 (Marc and Schmidt 1995). A 'Special Grants Programme', a 'Fund for Innovative Approaches in Human and Social Development' and a 'Project Preparation Facility' were created at the beginning of the 1980s to support networking activities of NGOs and to facilitate dissemination of special publications (Fox 1996, 10; Participation and NGO Group 1996; The World Bank 1994b; 1996b). In 1983, a small Grants programme was created, 'to finance regional and global NGO activities and programs' (The World Bank 2000). In 1986 (with the 'Bolivia Emergency Social Fund'), The World Bank also opened a 'Social Funds' window to support short-term community-generated projects and to increase participation (The World Bank 1996b, 165). Since its opening, this lending window has been used for purposes of 'social reconstruction' and for the rehabilitation of 'social service infrastructure' from Albania (the 'Albania Rural Poverty Alleviation Fund') to Zambia (the 'Zambia Social Recovery Fund').[21] Likewise, the Global Environment Facility (GEF, 1991) has provided 'grants and concessional funding to recipient countries for projects and programs that protect the global environment and promote sustainable economic growth'. In governance's inclusive fashion, the GEF has brought core regulatory agencies together with peripheral ones (GEF projects and programmes are managed collegially by the UNDP, the UNEP and The World Bank) and it is inclusive: 'GEF projects must be country driven, incorporate consultation with local communities and, where appropriate, involve non-governmental organizations in project implementation.'[22]

Beyond multiplying funding windows and special grant programmes, regulatory agencies also began involving NGOs more closely in policy-making. At The World Bank, this was termed the 'mainstreaming' and 'upstreaming' of

NGOs. 'Mainstreaming' NGOs means involving them earlier in the policy cycle (Participation and NGO Group 1996). 'Upstreaming' means involving NGOs not only in policy-making, but also in promoting participation, so that socially acceptable policy ideas can flow from the ground up as well as from The World Bank down (The World Bank 1996b, 243).

In the institutional history of The World Bank, 'mainstreaming' and 'upstreaming' began in the early 1980s, when the Bank shifted away from 'physical project objectives' (e.g. the building of export-oriented infra- structures linked with 'harsh conditionality') towards 'sustainable policy reform' and 'soft conditionality' (The World Bank 1991, 5). The World Bank began official co-operation with NGOs in 1982 when the 'NGO–World Bank Committee' was created as an arena for policy discussions between senior World Bank staff and NGO leaders. At its inception, the Committee regrouped twenty-six 'NGO leaders' representing five continents, and its sec- retariat was located at the Costa Rica headquarters of ALOP, the Latin American Association of Development Organizations (Beckmann 1991; Paul and Israel 1991). In August 1988, the 'NGO–World Bank Committee' pub- lished the first World Bank operational statement on the relationship between the Bank and NGOs. Exceptionally, OMS 5.30 was not treated as an internal Bank document – the usual practice with operational statements – but made available to a wide circle of civic partner NGOs (Cernea 1988, 42). Still in 1988, Michael Cernea published 'one of the first . . . attempts to deal system- atically with NGOs as development institutions'; The World Bank introduced the 'Social Dimension of Adjustment Program', and it began gathering an 'NGO Profile Database' containing preliminary information on more than 8,000 NGOs (Cernea 1988; Participation and NGO Group 1996; Salmen and Eaves 1991, 95).

In August 1989, the Bank issued Operational Directive 14.70 on collabor- ation with NGOs. Its purpose was to set out a framework for involving NGOs as early as possible in the project cycle (Salmen and Eaves 1991, 95). Later in fiscal year 1989, the Bank began its first 'free-standing' NGO project:

> the TOGO Grass-roots Initiative Project . . . provides $3 million to com- munity-based projects designed and carried out by NGOs and project beneficiaries.
>
> (Beckmann 1991; SDA Unit (The World Bank) 1990)

In December 1990, The World Bank established a Bank-wide 'Learning Group on Participatory Development' that presented the Board with *The World Bank and Participation* report in September 1994. Within a year, the Bank had established an 'Interagency Group on Participation' (IGP) and a 'Task Force on Operational Collaboration' (TOC). Both involved key oper- ational managers of The World Bank and both further detailed the terms of NGO–World Bank collaboration. In parallel, World Bank action plans designed in the early 1990s emphasized the benefits of a 'country-by-country approach', and of involving local NGOs directly in all phases of Bank projects (SDA Unit (World Bank) 1990). Increasingly, the Bank defined its social targets more precisely (The World Bank 2000), and it made its aid more contingent still on the ability of recipient states to secure broad popular coalitions in favour of reform (Boorman 1992).

For efficiency's sake, the IMF also began working alongside NGOs and host countries, to improve 'performance, accountability and transparency of economic management', and to secure sustainable adjustments (English and Mule 1996, 167). In terms of public relations, the managing director, deputy managing directors and members of the Executive Board made themselves available for discussions with civic groups, and the External Relations Department (created in 1981) arranged media training for IMF officials and conducted information missions to a number of countries. In addition, the IMF made sustained overtures to organized labour. In 1989, a Public Affairs Division was formed within the External Relations Department. Throughout the 1990s, the managing director and deputy managing directors increased their public activities, and they 'made themselves more available for discussions with civic groups' (Scholte 1998, 43). 'In 1995, IMF management issued special instructions that the IMF's resident representatives should nurture contacts with trade unions in their countries of assignment' (Scholte 1998). In 1996, the IMF's managing director addressed, for the first time, a World Congress of the ICFTU. The following year he addressed the World Confederation of Labor (Scholte 1998). At the staff level, operational departments of the IMF briefed increasing numbers of interested representatives of civil society on policy developments. In Washington and on the field, the IMF organized numerous seminars for civic associations, attended by academics, labour unions, environmental groups, development NGOs and other would-be denizens of global civil society.

More operationally, the IMF opened the 'Structural Adjustment Facility' in 1986. This was the first Fund window opened exclusively to low-income developing countries, and it was designed explicitly to facilitate politically sustainable adjustment (Drainville 1995b; Kenen 1989). In 1987, Michel Camdessus became Managing Director and immediately launched a systematic effort to expand NGO involvement in Fund operations. That same year, the 'Enhanced Structural Adjustment Facility' emphasized the IMF's new preoccupation with 'soft conditionality' designed to 'bring some of the poor (and the not so poor) into coalitions . . . broad enough to provide sustained support for adjustment policies' (Polak 1991).[23]

At the OECD as well, concerns over the efficiency of concessionary funding provided the impetus for a move to participatory development (Cernea 1988; Lewis 1985). At the beginning of the 1980s already, the DAC had 'its first meeting devoted to collaboration with non-governmental organisations' (Lewis 1985, 58). In 1985, the 'Review of Twenty-Five Years of [DAC] Development Cooperation' was published following a wide-ranging study of the effectiveness of official development aid (Poats 1985b). In governance's spirit, it recommended '. . . mak[ing] a political virtue of the necessity to increase economic efficiency' and '. . . mix[ing] good development policy [with] good politics . . .' by folding transnational development aid within national strategies drawn in collaboration with representative coalitions of local NGOs and social elites (Poats 1985b, 35). Translated in operational terms, the 1985 'Review' brought the OECDs beyond harsh conditionality (dismissed later by DAC Chairman James H. Michel as a set 'of conditions imposed by donors to coerce poor countries to do things they don't want to do in order to obtain resources they need' (Michel 1995, 7). Over the next five years, DAC working groups defined new operational procedures endorsed later by high-level meetings: 'Guiding Principles for Aid-Co-ordination with Developing Countries' (adopted in 1986); 'Principles for Project Appraisal' (1988); 'Principles for New Orientations in Technical Co-operation' (1991); 'Principles for Programme Assistance' (1991); 'Principles for Aid Evaluation' (1991); and 'Good Practices for Environmental Impact Assessment of Development Projects' (1991). All emphasized inclusivity and participatory development as necessary to 'project survival and viability' (OECD (Development Assistance Committee) 1992, 9). On the field, OECD operatives were encouraged to form 'Consultative Groups and Round Tables', often in collaboration with The World Bank (one of the principal recommendations of the 1986 'Guiding Principles' was to increase collaboration with the Bank in structuring local participation (OECD (Development Assistance Committee) 1992, 27).

In 1994, the OECD established an *ad hoc* 'Working Group on Participatory Development and Good Governance' that led to a key policy statement on 'Development Partnership in the New Global Context' which 'consecrated the unity of 'people-centered development, local ownership, global integration and international partnership' (Michel 1996, 3). This statement was endorsed by a high-level meeting of the DAC in May 1995, and again a year later, when the DAC confirmed that 'investment of development resources in democratic governance will contribute to more accountable, transparent and participatory societies conducive to development progress'.[24]

Beyond global summitry and great civic gatherings, then, the move to governance in the world economy has also brought global regulatory agencies (and even organizations that are part of the inner sanctum of globalizing *élites*) in closer contact with NGOs of all sorts.[25] To solve global problems, restore authority and ensure efficiency, NGOs, CONGOs, DONGOs and other representatives of global civil society have received increased financing, and they have been 'upstreamed' and 'mainstreamed' into transnational policy processes.

Already, this has had a considerable impact on the structuring of the 'NGO phenomenon'. Indeed, an NGO *nébuleuse* is beginning to take shape (or a 'galaxy' in Antonio Donini's term, or 'a swarm' for the Rand Corporation).[26] At its centre are what might be termed 'executant' or 'contractor' NGOs, useful for their cost-effectiveness, low overheads, flexibility and closeness to the terrain (Poats 1985a; The World Bank 1988). They are recruited by regulatory agencies for their efficiency in 'deliver[ing] benefits ... at a low administrative cost', for their effectiveness in crisis situations and for their capacity to build enduring networks (OECD 1990). A good example of low-cost 'contractor NGOs' (Salmen and Eaves 1991) is the Women's World Banking (WWB), a gentler World Bank founded in 1980 as a micro-credit provider and loan guarantor (OECD 1988). Among important relief organ-izations are families or federations of international NGOs that have, quite literally, cornered the official aid market: World Vision International, Oxfam (whose workers have become 'as expert in the minutia of debt reduction procedures as the bureaucrats at the IMF and World Bank'[27]), *Médecins sans frontières*, Save the Children Federation, *Coopération Internationale pour le Développement et la Solidarité*, the Association of Protestant Development Organizations in Europe, Eurostep (the main coalition of secular European NGOs), and so on. To underline their place in the development aid market, Antonio Donini wrote of 'the increasing oligopolization of the NGO market' (Donini 1995). Also among worthy contractors are innumerable local NGOs and coalitions. By way of example, Leon Gordenker and Thomas G. Weiss wrote of the 'Khartoum-based Emergency Relief Desk [which] was backed by a number of European NGOs and then reorganized and adapted to help crossborder operations into Eritrea and Tigray' (Gordenker and Weiss 1996, 27). In the same vein, Ernesto D. Garilao gave two examples of contractor NGOs: (1) 'The Bangladesh Rural Advancement Committee', established in 1971 to respond to the tremendous refugee problem brought about by the war and to organize programmes of oral rehydration therapy for the millions of children in the country; (2) the 'Philippine Business for Social Progress', founded by businessmen in 1969, in the midst of growing unrest and societal tensions, 'to participate in implementing solutions to ... national problems' (Garilao 1987).

To work out sustainable and efficient solutions to particular problems, 'production-related' NGOs ('e.g. water user' societies, pastoral associations, consumer and credit co-operatives, farm equipment purchase and lease associations, tree-grower associations) and 'business-council NGOs' (The International Executive Service Corps, Volunteers in International Technical Assistance, Senior Expert Service, Canadian Executive Service Overseas, British Executive Services Overseas, Management Consultancy Programmes, the International Chamber of Commerce) have also been brought into gov-ernance's fold by regulatory agencies (OECD 1990). Sometimes they have been expressly created, as was the Global Alliance for Transnational Edu-cation, set up by the WTO 'to catalogue what could be challenged as trade restrictive practices in higher education' (Gould 1999).

Also central to the emerging NGO *nébuleuse* are 'participation-oriented' NGOs recruited to serve as 'effective intermediaries in ... projects that depend on participation and capacity-building at the community level' and, in the words of OMS 5.30, to facilitate the 'social dimensions of adjustment' (Cernea 1988, 44; The World Bank 1996b, 243). Adept at 'drawing the whole population into the active life of their countries', they act as 'a source of information, a broker of resources, a negotiator of deals' (Gordenker and Weiss 1996, 27). Beyond this, they also serve as guarantors of the sustainability and reproducibility of adjustment measures: 'ideally . . . development activities are not only continued, but become self-supportive' (Salmen and Eaves 1991, 108). Representative examples of 'bridging' NGOs include: FADVO (the *Forum des Organisations Volontaires Africaines de Développement*), the Asian NGO Coalition for Agrarian Reform and Rural Development (ANGOC Asia), the Society for Participatory Research in Asia (PRIA), and the Savings Development Movement (SDM, Zimbabwe).

Also occupying an important place in the emerging *nébuleuse* are 'policy-minded' NGOs that are concerned principally with establishing policy dialogue with regulatory agencies, or interested in reforming them. For the most part, these are located in New York or in other places where gather regulatory agencies. Relevant examples include: Human Rights Watch, Friends of the Earth International, the Environmental Defense Fund, the United Planetary Federation's plans for United Peoples Advocates and Global Virtual Assembly, the Global Policy Forum, the International Network for a Second Assembly (later incorporated into the 'Campaign for a More Democratic United Nations', a 'not-for-profit international network for generating ideas and organizing meetings on building a peaceful world order through a more democratic United Nations' launched in 1989 at the annual 'World Citizens' Assembly' in New York City).[28]

Excluded from the emerging NGO *nébuleuse* are what Ken Conca called 'political NGOs', which raise political questions and gather social forces for extraneous, non-governance purposes (Conca 1995). Relevant examples include groups and organizations mentioned in Chapter 3. As the reason for their exclusion from governance's fold we can cite the International Chamber of Commerce (which co-ordinated the participation of 450 heads of multi-national corporations in the MIA negotiations), writing as an NGO to others:

> ICC recognizes how societies are changing, with citizens speaking up and expressing their deep-felt concerns. However, in some respects, the emergence of activist pressure groups risks weakening the effectiveness of public rules, legitimate institutions and democratic process. These institutions should place emphasis on legitimizing themselves, improving their internal democracy, transparency and accountability. They should assume full responsibility for the consequences of their activity. Where this does not take place, rules establishing their rights and responsibilities should be considered. . . . What we question is the proliferation of activist groups that do not accept . . . self-disciplinary criteria.[29]

Regional governance

Certainly, regional processes are a less synthetic lot than global-level ones. Regions of the world economy face particular circumstances, have varying degrees of autonomy *vis-à-vis* regulatory agencies of the world economy, and distinct casts of social forces assemble which move different regions at different rhythms. Still, there are unmistakeable echoes of governance's civic calls in what Anthony Giddens called 'regional zoning' in the world economy (a broad term that encompasses all manners of schemes, programmes and blueprints to combine distinct countries into broader spaces, be they continents, hemispheres, regions or zones (Giddens 1985b, 272). Everywhere, regional zoning has been framed in terms of civic partnership, good governance and sustainable development.

To a degree, 'regional zoning' is built into the civic reform of transnational regulatory agencies. The World Bank's 'Participation and NGO Group', for instance, began gathering regional networks of NGOs in the early 1990s, and, in 1994, the 'NGO–World Bank Committee' started emphasizing regional-level discussions (to the point where, starting in 1995, it divided its annual spring meeting into regional meetings).[30] In addition, the GEF works from 'Regional NGO Focal Points': 'voluntary network of NGOs . . . that have offered to organize outreach to the NGO community . . . [and] serve to gather NGO input on the GEF and its Council Meetings, and to disseminate related information on Council Meetings and GEF-NGO consultations.' For the most part however, regional-level governance is best understood from a region-specific perspective.

In the Americas, the drive for hemispheric integration initiated by the 'Enterprise for the Americas Initiative' (EAI, June 1990) has been accompanied by talk of social covenants and good governance in the hemisphere, and it has interpellated some social forces as civic partners of capital, or fellow drawers of 'a development model which is sustainable in political, economic, social, cultural and environmental terms' (Drainville 1997). In true governance fashion, there have been great civic gatherings. The first notable moments were IDB conferences on 'Strengthening Civil Society' and 'Civic Participation and Socioeconomic Participation' in 1994 (IDB 1994). Still in 1994, the IDB held a hemispheric forum on 'Women in the Americas: Participation and Development'. At the March 1998 IDB Annual Meeting in Cartageana, Executive Vice-President Nancy Birdsall and Edmundo Jarquin of the newly created 'State and Civil Society Division' both addressed participants at the 'Social Programs, Poverty and Citizen Involvement' seminar, telling them of the inevitability of citizens' involvement in sustainable development. The two-day seminar concluded on an indisputable governance note:

> Citizen participation, properly channeled, generates savings, mobilized additional financial and human resources, promotes equity and makes a

decisive contribution to the strengthening of society, and the democratic system.

(IDB 1998)

In January 1999, the IDB co-sponsored a 'Global Meeting of Generations', in Washington, DC, along with the 'International Association of Students in Economics and Management', 'Youth for Development and Cooperation', the UNDP and the 'International Development Conference'. There 'one hundred young social entrepreneurs from around the world' sat with 'global, national and grassroots development organizations', to 'discuss key issues and opportunities facing humanity in the 21st century', and to draw civic blueprints.[31]

Beyond discourses and grand gatherings, regional zoning in the Americas has also brought about concrete efforts to select civic-minded interlocutors and structure their participation in regional affairs. Tellingly, these efforts have been led by the Bank for Inter-American Development, a regional affiliate of The World Bank and a central agency of governance in the hemisphere (Carrillo 1996).

Before governance, only the 'Small Project Program' (1979) provided a structured, sustained link between NGOs and the IDB, and would-be representatives of civil society were involved with the IDB only in exceptional circumstances – and then only in a service-delivery capacity (Fox 1996; IDB 1997a). In the past decade and a half, however, the IDB has conducted what Executive Vice-President Nancy Birdsall called a 'diagnostic survey of the present status of civil society in the region' (Hamilton 1994, 7), and set up a variety of outreach and consultation programmes for NGOs. In addition, new funding windows and 'social investment funds' have been opened that encourage and structure NGO participation. In 1987, a 'Social Investment Fund' was established that was explicitly demand-driven and aimed at fostering the active involvement of community organizations and NGOs in all stages of the project cycle. In 1991, the Indigenous Peoples Fund (IPF) was set up to 'promote the long-term, sustainable development of the native peoples of Latin America and the Caribbean'. The IPF encouraged structured consultations of all sorts (from information sharing to decision-making, in project identification and in project design) between native leadership and the IDB. Significantly, it is governed by a tripartite body that 'allocates equal representation to indigenous peoples, regional governments and international donors in its decision making bodies' (Schwartz and Deruyttere 1996). In the same spirit, the Multilateral Investment Fund (MIF) (1992) has concerned itself with building partnerships between NGOs and private voluntary organizations, particularly those representing people who are usually left out of the economic mainstream. The three investment 'windows' of the MIF – the 'Technical Cooperation Facility', the 'Human Resources Facility' and the 'Small Enterprise Development Facility' – all provide services to build knowledge, encourage economic empowerment, and involve women and youth in the 'enterprise economy'.

Beyond opening up new funding windows, the IDB has also opened new agencies and has created new policy guidelines to mainstream and upstream NGOs and other would-be representatives of civil society in the Americas, and to further participatory development, 'defined in broad terms as the process through which people with a legitimate interest (stakeholders) influence and share control over development initiatives, and the decisions and resources which affect them' (IDB 1997a). In the spirit of governance's reformism, the IDB seeks efficiency, both political and economic.

> Participation improves project design by reducing the cost of obtaining accurate and site-specific data on environmental, social and cultural factors as well as stakeholders' felt needs and priorities. Also, project managers can get input from all groups, including people often marginalized in the development process.
>
> (IDB 1997a)

In the early 1990s the IDB set up a 'State and Civil Society Division' and a 'Social Programs and Sustainable Development Department'. As well, a Women in Development (WID) unit was founded in 1994 that begat a 'Fund for Women's Leadership and Representation' which aspires to create a generation of women leaders for the new century, by directing funds to organizations that promote women's active participation and leadership at national, regional and local levels, in economic, political and social spheres (Editors 1993; IDB 1994; 1996 1997b;).

By 1995, the IDB was able to publish a 'Resource Book on Participation' where significant examples of participatory practice in the IDB project cycle could be listed:

> The National System for Sustainable Development (SINADES, Costa Rica 1994) brings all sectors of society together, through a number of institutions and mechanisms, to work towards the formulation of a national strategy for sustainable development. The National Sustainable Development Council, comprised of representatives from public agencies, NGOs, community organizations, universities, private businesses and producer cooperatives, serves as a forum for civil society's participation in the development and strengthening of SINADES.

> . . .

> The environmental investment sub-program of the National Environmental Program (Colombia 1993) provides financing for environmental projects and initiatives of regional and local origin as well as incentives

for direct community participation. As part of the criteria for granting funds, the Ministry of Environment requires that the local and regional public entities submitting project proposals present evidence of direct community participation in the preparation and execution of that project (PR-1935).

. . .

National Rural Development Program (PNDR, Nicaragua 1994). Projects are identified either through requests by national or regional public agencies, specialized institutions or NGOs as well as through processes by which the communities and beneficiary organizations identify their problems and propose solutions. After undergoing a program of institutional strengthening, municipalities, producers' organizations or NGOs participate actively in project preparation as well as in the execution and management of the projects.

. . .

Municipal Development Program, (Mexico 1994). This program provides funds (US$779.4 million) in support of the government's Solidarity Municipal Funds Program (FMS), which supports small-scale projects identified, designed and executed by communities. New FMS norms and procedures have been drawn up under the program that encourages localities to form project committees at an earlier stage of the cycle and enable them to hire technical experts for project preparation and supervision.

Until very recently, the Organization of American States had played a minor role in gathering hemispheric civil society (though sometimes it did act as a secretariat for hemispheric integration – as it did in Lima in June 1997, when OAS ministers of foreign relations set the agenda for the Santiago Summit of the Americas).[32] After the 1998 meeting of heads of states of the Americas, a 'Unit for the Promotion of Democracy' was created that has worked, modestly, through state institutions, 'to consolidate both civic practices and mechanisms of participation in the political process'.[33] In June 1999, a 'Committee on Civil Society Participation' was created 'to establish clear, transparent, modern procedures for interaction between civil society and the political organs of the OAS'.[34] These procedures allowed the Committee to consult with more than 900 organizations, and to assemble a store of policy proposals. At the 'Hemispheric Meeting' (Miami, 18–20 January 2001), these proposals were synthesized into the 'Final Document: Recommendations by Civil Society Organizations' that were part of what was discussed in Québec city.[35]

As well as the IDB and the OAS, other governing agencies in the

Americas have also worked to define efficient and sustainable terms of hemispheric social relations by hosting meetings with designated representatives of civil society. At their fourth meeting in San José (Costa Rica) in March 1998, trade ministers established the 'Committee of Government Representatives on the Participation of Civil Society'. In November, the Committee issued an 'Open Invitation to Civil Society', which detailed both its desire to work with civil society representatives and the terms of collaboration. The Committee met twice in the summer of 1999. On 4 November 1999, during the fifth meeting of the trade ministers of the Americas in Toronto, the Committee's report was made public.[36] In the spring of 2000, a second 'Open Invitation to Civil Society' was extended, in preparation for Québec's Summit of the Americas, arguably the most important gathering of the hemispheric growth machine, both quantitatively and in terms of policy readiness: never did so many gather with such defined purpose, with, in the background, such a decorous, 'colourful tapestry of cultures, values and traditions'.[37]

Central to the structuring of social relations in the Americas is the integration of opposition into people's summits, the second of which met in Québec city during the Summit of the Americas.

For a decade between the mid-1980s and mid-1990s social forces opposed to neoliberal integration in the Americas organized summits, gatherings and *encuentros*. In North America, the FTA and NAFTA negotiations occasioned a veritable explosion of trans-border summits between the Action Canada Network (ACN), the American Fair Trade Campaign (FTC) and the *Red Mexicana de Acción Frente Libre Comercio* (Kidder and McGinn 1995). Among notable summits were: the ANC–RMLAC *Encuentro* (Mexico, October 1990), the ACN–RMLAC-FTC Summit (Mexico, April 1991), the San Ygnacio *encuentro* of environmental groups (April 1991), the Zacatenas meeting (October 1991), the Trinational Working Women's Conference (*Valle de Bravo*, February 1992) and the tri-national cross-border meeting between representatives of the ACN, the RMLAC, the CTC and the American Alliance for Responsible Trade (Niagara Falls, October 1993). This was the last tri-national summit before the NAFTA came into effect in January 1994. After NAFTA, two *Encuentro por la Humanidad y contra el Neoliberalismo* were organized in Mexico by the *Ejército Zapatista de Liberación National*: the first took place in Chiapas in July to August 1996, the second in *Belem do Para*, from 6–11 December 1999.

In the same period, transborder summits were also being organized nearer Brazil, another pole of transnational integration. The São Paulo Forum was founded in 1990, by Brazil's *Partido Dos Trabalhadores* and representatives from Left organizations and movements, including the Sandinista National Liberation Front of Nicaragua, the Farabundo Marti National Liberation Front of EL Salvador, the Broad Front of Uruguay, Bolivia's Free Bolivar Movement, Peru's United Left and the Cuban Communist Party.[38] The second meeting of the São Paulo Forum was held in Mexico City, in June 1991;

the third in Managua in July 1992, the fourth in Havana in July 1993 and the last in 1995 in Montevideo. A gathering of more than 200 Left movements, parties and organizations, it was heralded by Libya's Mu'ammar al-Qadhafi as the embryo of a 'Popular World Front'.[39]

But fronts born of popular summitry did not hold up. Less than four years after Niagara Falls and two after Montevideo, popular summits were already being folded into the process of hemispheric governance. In 1997, the *Nossa América* popular forum was held in Belo Horizonte, besides the 'Third Summit Meeting of Ministers for Commerce' and the 'Third Business Forum of the Americas'. In true governance fashion, it both gave birth to a new transnational subject (the 'Hemispheric Social Alliance' (HSA)) and, on its behalf, produced a syncretic, reformist agenda accepting of what Michel Chossudovsky called the 'dominant counter-discourse' (which presses for the inclusion of environmental, labour and human rights clauses within trade agreements, and pushes for poverty alleviation schemes and institutional reforms).[40]

In April 1998, the First People's Summit, convened by the Hemispheric Social Alliance, was held in Santiago, alongside the second Summit of the Americas (Feinberg and Rosenberg 1999). 'Two thousand delegates met in twelve sectoral forums, workshopping ideas for an alternative social and economic model in the hemisphere.' The first 'People's Hemispheric Agreement' (PHA) was drafted, entitled 'Alternatives for the Americas'. Key to this was the people's acceptance of free trade and foreign investments as privileged 'instruments for achieving just and sustainable development'.[41] The HSA's campaign continued in March 1999 in Costa Rica, where a Coordinating Group was chosen – that included Common Frontiers and the RQIC – to pilot the PHA's push for inclusion and reform. A further draft of the PHA was prepared at a 'civil society meeting' in Rio in June 1999 (held in parallel with the meeting of heads of states from the European Union of Latin Americas and the Caribbean). And during the 'citizens' forum' held prior to the fourth Summit of Trade Ministers of the Hemisphere (Toronto, November 1999) the PHA draft was discussed and updated during the Second People's Summit in Québec city.

In Asia, the move to governance has been more recent, more modest and less celebrated than in the Americas. By way of an example, the 1999 'Social Forum' in Manila was the first conference of note to bring together NGOs and local regulatory agencies in a significant, policy-minded way, and the Asian Development Bank (ADB) – a sister institution to the IDB and a regional affiliate of The World Bank – has yet to operationalize strategies to involve NGOs and other would-be representatives of Asian civil society in the policy process.

Still, region-building in Asia is becoming a governance process. Since the late 1980s, the ADB has been moving towards social adjustment and participatory development. In governance spirit, this move was motivated by reasons of efficiency:

[The ADB] recognizes that the direct involvement of affected people in programs and projects can help avoid implementation problems. At the same time, shrinking aid resources has forced governments to look toward communities sharing the costs of new facilities and services being provided. Cost recovery, whether partial or full, is difficult unless projects are designed in cooperation with beneficiaries, to meet their priority needs in the most efficient and effective ways possible. . . . One way of ensuring closer beneficiary involvement is to work with and through non governmental organizations.

(ADB n.d.)

In 1987, the ADB approved a policy paper to facilitate co-operation with NGOs, especially in poverty relief and environmental protection (Kappagoda 1995; Korten 1991; Salmen and Eaves 1991). In 1989, the Bank initiated studies in several countries to examine co-operation with NGOs in agricultural and rural development, and it organized a first 'ADB–NGO Consultative Meeting on Environment and Natural Resource Management'. Consultations led to working arrangements in several member countries. In 1992, the ADB created a 'Social Dimensions Unit' that became the focal point of contact for NGOs and the institutional centre of soft conditionality (Kappagoda 1995, 160). In 1993, a 'Task Force on Improving Project Quality' was set up that recommended 'mainstreaming' and 'upstreaming' NGO participation and initiated programmes to further broaden and structure the relationship between the ADB and NGOs. In 1994, the Bank approved regional technical assistance to strengthen the capacities of women's NGOs across the region. Close to 200 NGOs received ADB assistance 'in developing systems for planning, monitoring and evaluating projects', to increase efficiency and sustainability of programmes (ADB n.d.).

At the epicentre of the global debt crisis, sub-Saharan Africa belongs less to itself than it does to the world economy as a whole. Not surprisingly, global regulatory agencies – and The World Bank in particular – have played a leading role in initiating the turn to governance, whether by fighting corruption, inefficiency and other practices of bad governance, or by significantly increasing funding for NGOs and would-be representatives of civil society.

Throughout the 1990s The World Bank carefully monitored the effectiveness of sectoral activities in countries where it was most involved, in marked contrast with slack monitoring in the first phase of the debt crisis, that relied principally on the work of individual state agencies. In 1994, The World Bank conducted a broad comparative review of 'Social Funds' and 'Public Works and Employment' projects. Especially at issue were the first two phases of the 'Special Program of Assistance for Africa' (SPA-1, SPA-2, 1988–1993), a partnership programme between donors and creditors created, in governance spirit, with two objectives in mind:

To ensure that adequate balance of payments finance is available for reform programs; and . . . to provide a forum for improving the effectiveness and efficiency of donor assistance for these programs.

(The World Bank 1994a)

In 1996, The World Bank conducted reviews of 'National Environmental Action Plans' in West Central Africa (The World Bank 1996a), and in 1997, it reviewed the restructuring of the banking sector in seven Sub-Saharan countries at the heart of the debt crisis: *Bénin, Côte d'Ivoire*, Ghana, Kenya, Tanzania, Uganda and Mozambique (Deschamps and Bonnardeaux 1997). Unerringly, lessons learned from these reviews emphasized the hazards of banking on states as sole transmission belts for adjustment measures; the fallibility, inefficiency and passivity of state agencies. Importantly, the reviews also emphasized the need to bolster adjustment measures by building capacity and connections amongst stakeholders, to mainstream social issues and increase stakeholders' ownership in both political and economic senses of the term (The World Bank 1996a). Looking towards SPA-3 (1994–1996), The World Bank emphasized the need for 'more realistic conditionalities', including measures to increase 'country ownership and political commitment to reform programs'; 'expand the role of private investment, on which countries will have to rely heavily if growth rates are to be raised'; strengthen 'local management and institutional capacity', and improve monitoring efforts and prospects for sustainability of adjustment measures, all features that were picked up again most recently by the New Partnership for African Development (NEPAD) endorsed by the G8 meeting in Kananaskis, Canada, from 26 to 27 June 2002. In governance fashion, key to these measures is the role of NGOs and representatives of African civil society, particularly women (The World Bank 1994a).

Once removed from The World Bank, and possessing relatively little autonomy, is the African Development Bank. Here as well, institutional changes and new operational procedures have underlined the move to participatory development. In 1985, the African Development Bank (ADB) created a WID policy unit that launched several modest projects to increase women's leadership and participation (English and Mule 1996). In 1987, the ADB set up a 'Socio-Environmental Division' (later renamed the 'Environmental and Social Policy Division') and it initiated the 'Social Dimension of Adjustment Program' (SDAP 1987–1992), perhaps the most explicit expression of participatory development. As part of the SDAP, the ADB helped launch the 'Network for Environmental and Sustainable Development in Africa' (NESDA) (1991) and it created an 'Environment and Sustainable Development Unit' (OESU), which now serves as the institutional focal point for addressing questions of environment, population, gender, poverty reduction and so on. It is also the principal point of contact with the NGO community. At the operational level, the ADB adopted a new 'Poverty Alleviation Strategy and Action Programme' (PASAP) (1992), that spoke of erecting an efficient and sustainable policy framework on the bedrock of restored institutions and of building a strong consensus between state agencies, donors, NGOs, grass-roots groups ('women in particular') and all other would-be representatives of African civil society (English and Mule 1996). In governance fashion, PASAP wants to mainstream and upstream NGOs, and it invites:

> the poor and other vulnerable groups to fully participate in the conceptualization, design, execution and management of poverty reduction projects and/or programs.[42]

In 1997, OESU established the Environmental Resource Center (ERC) as part of the Bank's institutional strengthening programme for environmental management.[43] Initially given an information gathering and disseminating mandate ('to create a locus for all of the most current data and research on environmental issues of relevance to Africa . . . to provide Bank Group staff with state of the art environmental techniques, concepts and designs for use in project/program formulation and development . . . to facilitate access to printed materials, computer data linkages, computer-aided design tools, other resource centers and libraries around the world for the utilization by the Bank Group's technical staff as well as other users'), the ERC has grown into a meeting place for African NGOs.[44]

In Europe, governance has worked in continuity with well-established practices dating from the Rome Treaty of 1957 (when the Economic and Social Council was mandated to involve economic and social interest groups in the establishment of the Common Market, and to provide institutional machinery for briefing the European Commission and the Council of Ministers on European Union issues). The first general assembly of NGOs of the European Union took place in 1967. In 1976, an NGO/EC Liaison Committee was created, and, in 1982, a budget opened to finance European NGO action in developing countries (Commission européenne 1997).

In the 1980s and 1990s, efforts to develop a 'European Social Model' moved NGOs to the forefront of regulatory initiatives, especially during the Delors presidency, when

> social and economic cohesion was needed to promote economic convergence and prevent disruptive social dumping. At the same time, it embodie[d] new commitments to inter-state regional solidarity to serve as a precedent for breaking with earlier EC member-state egoism. Economically, the social dimension was a way of regulating the consequences of the Single Market, to prevent the emergence of unfair trade in the labour market. It was also an avenue to greater dialogue and negotiation between employers and workers on European level, a way to counteract market based tendencies undercutting industrial relation systems on national levels.
>
> (Ross 1995)

The Single European Act (1986), the Maastricht Treaty (1992) and the Amsterdam Treaty (1997) all increased the amplitude of civic gatherings in Europe. However, the European social dialogue was well contained within established institutions, and there were few grand civic gatherings (the March (1998) 'Citizen's Europe' conference in Luxembourg was a notable exception).

At the end of the 1990s, governance's inclusive ways have caught up with corporatist participation in the European region, and the ESC has begun looking for ways to further NGO involvement. At its plenary session of January 1999, the 'Economic and Social Committee' (ESC) drew up an 'own-initiative opinion':

> The concept of civil society is thus very important as the third compon-
> ent of the state system. Whereas the 'statist society' model sees the citizen
> first and foremost as a citizen of the state, the 'market society' model sees
> the citizen as a market player. The citizen as a member of civil society
> (*homo civicus*) mediates between the two, by embodying all three aspects
> (*homo politicus, homo economicus and homo civicus*).[45]

To 'give more people the opportunity to participate' and 'make more use of contributions from experts', the ESC declared its intention to set up a new civil society institution, as yet unnamed. In October 1999, the European ESC convened the 'First Convention on Civil Society Organized at European Level' in Brussels. Workshop 3 on 'The Contribution of Civil Society to Growth and Competitiveness' concluded that:

> Improved competitiveness and faster growth are important for wealth
> creation, employment generation and welfare distribution. . . . Organized
> civil society has a major role to play in improving competitiveness and
> growth because . . . it helps to reconcile the conflicts between multiple
> objectives . . . to reconcile the views of the different stakeholders . . . it
> helps society to adapt to pressures for constant change [and] it helps to
> fill the gaps in welfare delivery mechanisms that governments cannot
> satisfy.

As if to better clarify the intent of governance's civic gathering, Workshop 3 further concluded that:

> Organized civil society can contribute directly and indirectly to improv-
> ing competitiveness and increasing growth. The direct contributions
> include: assistance with the delivery of public services such as education,
> health and social services; assistance with local economic development;
> the regeneration of depressed areas and the integration of socially and
> economically excluded individuals and groups.[46]

City-level governance

Real-concrete cities are where attempts to set the terms of global civility have taken what is perhaps their most explicit form. Before governance, situating urban questions in a global context was a relatively marginal activity, at least in terms of transnational politics. Although calls issued for global standards and practices sometimes had a considerable impact on the quotidian practice of architects and urbanists, they had little influence on transnational policy-making, and urban affairs remained very much internal – that is to say national – affairs. In 1978, for instance, the OECD fashioned 'Urban Environmental Indicators' that did not go beyond putting national data side by side. Tellingly, these were 'descriptive' and not 'performance' indicators that took note of the result of national and intra-national policies, but did not look at, or attempt to synthesize, policies (OECD 1997).

In the 1980s, the Brandt, Palme, Brundltand and Nyerere commissions began situating urban questions within a global whole, and such groups as the 'International Academy of Architecture' (1987) and the World Health Organization operationalized new ideas on 'sustainable cities' (UNCHS 1993, 8). In 1987, the General Assembly of the United Nations adopted the 'Global Strategy for Shelter to the Year 2000' (UNCHS 1988). Like the OECD, the GSS relied strictly on national indicators and nationally bound political commitments (UNCHS 1990a; 1990b; 1991a; 1991b). Urban affairs were still internal affairs.

As civic reformism replaced coercive transnationalism as a dominant mode of regulation in the world economy, global regulatory agencies quite literally discovered cities. As Siefried Brenke of the OECD's Urban Affairs Division put it urban affairs were no longer 'internal affairs' (Brenke 1992).

About the birth of civic reformism in the nineteenth century, Christine Boyer wrote of a 'set sequence' of events:

> First came recognition by a body of prominent citizens that an economic and social pathology existed and was infecting society. Second, improvers sought to amass data concerning the problem. Third was the publication of a plan, communications in popular journals, . . . and the molding of public opinion. And fourth was the expectation of voluntary cooperative conformance to planned remedies, freed from governmental enforcement but strengthened by the assumptions of an enlightened opinion.
>
> (Boyer 1994)

In similar fashion, global governance began by cataloguing what we may economically describe as the evils of twentieth-century cities in an urbanized world:

> the slums and ghettos, the homeless, the paralyzing traffic, the poisoning of our urban air and water, drugs, crime, the alienation of our youth, the

resurgence of old diseases such as tuberculosis, and the spread of new ones such as AIDS. Every city knows the signs; every city must fight them.

(UNCHS 1996)

youth unemployment in African cities; chronic water shortages in Dakar; water pollution and waste management in Rio de Janeiro, Dar es Salaam and Ismailia; squatting in Rio, Nairobi and Dhaka; homelessness, violence and urban anarchy everywhere.

(Camargo 1995; UNCHS 1996; UNDP 1996)

Second, global civic improvers have amassed data concerning global problems. In 1990, the UNCHS and The World Bank established a joint 'Housing Indicators Programme' with the intent of creating 'a more solid analytical, empirical and institutional base for the conduct of housing policy' (UNCHS 1996). Twenty-five key indicators were regrouped under five headings that emphasized the explicitly political intent of governance's civicism: political commitment to shelter, definition of national shelter objectives, reorganization of the shelter sector, mobilization and allocation of financial resources, shelter production and improvement. Fifty-two cities were compared and contrasted (UNCHS 1990a; 1996).

In contrast to the OECD's retiring look at the result of national policies, UNCHS/World Bank indicators put national political processes themselves under global gaze. A year after their inception, UNCHS/World Bank indicators were combined into an 'Enabling Index' used to conduct an extensive survey and rank cities on a global scale. Again, the focus was explicitly put on political adjustment, and on measuring 'the degree to which the policy and institutional context is judged to facilitate the activities of actors in the housing sector' (OECD 1997, 37). In March 1994, the UNCHS launched the 'Habitat Indicators programme' to 'measur[e] the performance of a city . . . and . . . test, collect and analyze . . . indicators around the world' (OECD 1997, 38). In tune, the OECD began working 'to implement permanent data collection in order to establish a database that permits the regular monitoring of conditions in cities and of the effects of specific policies in different sectors' (OECD 1997, 38–39). In 1995, the UNCHS introduced a 'Global Urban Indicators Database', fed by collaborators from 237 cities in 110 countries.

To enlighten global public opinion, the 'Global Urban Indicators Database' was put on the Web and made searchable, with a set of fifty key data entries in a spreadsheet form (in Excel and Lotus), together with definitions and methods for compilation. In addition, all manner of global plans, standardized and profitable practices have detailed what Le Cobusier would have called *la bonne solution* (the unique, economical solution fitting into a grand scheme (Le Corbusier 1994 [1925]). In preparation for Habitat II, 'Best Practices' were invented to identify political arrangements susceptible to be 'replicated in other cities and countries that face similar . . . problems'

(Kreimer *et al.* 1995, xi). In 1995, the International Conference on 'Best Practices in Improving Living Environments' (Dubai, November 1995), endorsed twenty-five 'new and innovative ways to solve . . . urban problems' (UNDP 1996). Among criteria used to select sanctionable behaviour were: sustainability and the formation of lasting partnerships between governments, community organizations, the private sector and international agencies (UNDP 1996). After Istanbul, ways to reduce favelization (growth of squatters' barrios) in Rio de Janeiro became ways to solve squatting in 'megacities' everywhere, and local ways of doing sustainable things in Chattanooga (Tennessee) or Curitiba (Brazil) became global models of civic behaviour (Kreimer *et al.* 1995). Rio de Janeiro (a case much studied under governance) provided cities of the world economy that wished to turn natural beauty into commercial assets, and 'mainstream' their squatters into responsible stakeholders with a useful exemplar (Camargo 1995; IDB 1997c; UNCHS 1988; The World Bank 1996b). About squatters, the UNCHS's 'enabling approach' (UNCHS 1991a) has worked to bring them 'into the mainstream of the housing process' through interim land-tenure programmes that try to regularize their position and 'put them on an equal footing with other participants' (UNCHS 1991b). Mainstreaming slum-dwellers was also behind the UNCHS sponsoring of SPARC (Brazil's National Slum-Dwellers Federation). Through SPARC-recruited squatters, the UNCHS created community events ('a huge celebration, which might be a concert, drama, or a welcome for visiting dignitaries or representatives from other low-income communities'), and later occasioned informal exchanges with the community. These, as the UNCHS put it, are 'both an outstanding method of mobilization and an exceptionally accurate way of identifying issues that people in the community regard as relevant' (UNCHS 1996, 327). 'The way a squatter responds to the inquiries of a fellow squatter is very relevant from, and more relevant than, the way the same squatter responds to the social scientist or researcher' (UNCHS 1996, 327).

In April 1998, The World Bank sponsored an installation by the 'Adventist Development Relief Agency' (ADRA) that was displayed on the Mall in Washington, DC. It is perhaps the most striking single artefact of global governance. Gathered together 'for the benefit of schoolchildren' were ten generic 'Global Village Habitats'. Introduced as a 'life-sized re-creation of 10 habitats portraying how people live in different parts of the world', the collection contained such archetypal habitats as the 'Stilt House', the 'Choza', the 'Refugee Camp', the 'Favela', the 'Kraal' and the 'Homeless Environment' ("Homeless people will make their home anywhere – in their cars, in cardboard boxes tucked in an alley or in recesses underneath highway overpasses").[47]

A 'tenement' was also on display ('In poor areas of large cities, including North America, people live in apartment buildings or tenements. Often located in crime-ridden neighbourhoods, these buildings are usually crowded and in need of repair.'). Seen beside such telling fragments as *la maison insalubre* of the 1889 Universal Exhibition in Paris, ADRA's tenement is an eloquent reminder of the link between nineteenth-century civic reformism and global governance at the close of the twentieth century.

To encourage and frame voluntary conformance, the General Assembly of the United Nations called on the UNCHS (resolution 51/177, December 1996) to 'involve in its work the representatives of local authorities or international association of local authorities . . . and the relevant actors of civil society' (N'Dow 1997). Following a UNCHS meeting at the *Maison de l'Habitat* in Geneva, The World Bank and the UNCHS set up the Global Urban Observatory (GUO) programme in December 1997, to 'mobilize people into organized structures' (Cernea 1988).

To borrow Patrick Geddes' term, the GUO is a worldwide network of 'Outlook Towers' (Geddes 1908, xi) that works to produce and exchange information related to housing and urban indicators, to encourage the exchange of best practices and to increase compliance with global standards (Garau 1997). Together with associated Local Urban Observatories (LUOs), 'a . . . unit where a team of people come together to develop effective and relevant tools . . . to address common issues', and Urban Ateliers, 'a university faculty, a strong municipal agency, a local branch of a national or provincial ministry, an urban NGO, a private firm or some other entity', GUO institutions work, in effect, as surveillance and policy dissemination facilities (Auclair 1997; UNCHS 1997a, 10). In Foucauldian terminology, there are institutional supports to the capillary function of power.

At The World Bank, encouraging inclusivity in city-level governance has meant organizing 'town meetings' in Benin, gathering 'slum-dwellers' in Brazil, Bedouins in Egypt, influential women and other community leaders in Gujarat and Tamil Nadu (India), and so on (The World Bank 1996b). In Rio's favelas, 'the most famous slums in the world', The World Bank's first step was:

> to be present in the community when the people themselves were present . . . This initial phase served to identify who were the key stakeholders and in particular who were the community leaders. They came from all walks of life and places, but mainly were associated with religious, sports, or other types of clubs that exist in communities everywhere. . . . It was the women's clubs, however, that proved the most effective instruments for working with the community.
>
> (The World Bank 1996b)

In the process, World Bank associates helped community leaders and other stakeholders 'learned together what was possible and not possible, what they really wanted, and how they had to behave to get what they wanted' (Maija 1996, 32).

In Mumbai (India), a UNCHS/World Bank sponsored project 'offered tenants of over 50,000 inner-city tenements the option to purchase houses on the condition that the tenants form a cooperative to manage repair and installation of services'. In *Concepción* (Chile), the Sustainable Cities Programme (UNCHS/UNEP)

> initiated a project involving several partners to improve the quality of water in the seven urban lakes in the municipality. Neighborhood organizations, corporations, NGOs, sanitary services, health services, the tourism board, municipal and government bodies, universities and businesses were all invited.
>
> (Warah 1997)

Many enabling programmes and instances of city-level participative arrangements could be cited, but no more are needed to show real concrete cities in the process of becoming ancillary sites of global governance.

Conclusion

Global governance is structural reformism for the world economy. Until the mid-1980s, reformism was a peripheral movement, rooted in marginal sites of transnational politics (e.g. the UNESCO, UNCTAD, and UNCLOS III global conferences in Stockholm, Bucharest or Vancouver). Working against both state power and the unilateral transnationalism of central regulatory agencies, reformism did have a measure of influence over policy-making, and it did secure piecemeal reforms and treaties, but it did not bring about a wholesale reinvention of modes of authority in the world economy.

When troubles stemming from the crisis of the Bretton Woods system (the threatening collapse of debtor economies, the instability of currencies, the political and economic costs of adjustment, monetary overhangs) could not be solved by means of inter-state negotiations, neoliberal concepts of control (from monetarism to the 'new constitutionalism') were invented to discipline accumulation in the world economy. Beyond state-centred regulation, they sought to impress a particular strategy out of the crisis on to all countries of the world economy, creditors and debtors alike. In the former, monetarist policies tried to discipline monetary aggregates, with remarkably little concern for the difficulties of monetary targeting, and remarkable indifference to politics (Drainville 1995a). In debtor countries, harsh conditionality was applied, with no more concern for the politics of adjustment. When neoliberal concepts of control proved unable to solve global problems – what World Bank Managing Director James D. Wolfensohn called 'timebomb' issues – and to ensure a swift, efficient, return to business as usual in the world economy, reformism moved from the periphery to the centre of transnational power (Wolfensohn 1997, 6). Then, moral reformism gave way to the structural reformism of global governance.

Working to 'bring more orderly and reliable responses to social and political issues' (Gordenker and Weiss 1996,17) and to 'improv[e] the enabling environment for private sector development' (OECD 1990; OECD

(Development Assistance Committee) 1992), governance wants to contain politics and establish sustainable foundations for global order.

In reformist manner, global governance begins with circumscribed problems giving cause for gatherings and setting boundaries for action:

> in the global neighborhood, citizens have to co-operate for many purposes: to maintain peace and order, expand economic activity, tackle pollution, halt or minimize climate change, combat pandemic diseases, curb the spread of weapons, prevent desertification, preserve genetic and species diversities, deter terrorism, ward off famine, defeat economic recession, share scare resources, arrest drug traffickers, and so on.
>
> (Commission on Global Governance 1995)

These problems correspond to governance's store of workable solutions, plans, programmes, searchable databases and best, most portable, practices. Companions to other standards of global performance (from 'global benchmarking' practices prevalent in multinational corporations to the 'Global Performance Index' discussed at last year's World Economic Forum) they aim to establish unvarying standards of acceptable engagement (Pénicaut 2001).[48]

Beyond policy issues, global governance is also a radical political programme intent on putting in place the social and political infrastructure of a sustainable global order free of irritants and resistance. It is, to borrow from Le Corbusier, a 'revolution by solutions' (*On ne révolutionne pas en révolutionnant. On révolutionne en solutionnant.*).[49]

To reduce political costs and increase the efficiency of its solutions, governance works to assemble what structural reformists at the beginning of the nineteenth century would have called a 'growth machine', that is to say a broad coalition of social forces that share an apolitical, ostensibly 'value-free' understanding of economic growth (Molotch 1976), and that have moved 'beyond opposition to proposition' to define a consensual path for growth. This is what Henri Lefebvre called 'integrative participation' (*la participation integration*), that works to secure the pre-emptive acquiescence of interested and concerned people (Lefebvre 1968, 105). Driving this global growth machine is a new global subject. William Allen White (who wrote *The Old Order Changeth*, as triumphalist a pamphlet as there ever was of American reformism) would have called this subject a 'New Citizen'.[50] More critically, Antonio Gramsci would have written of 'a new type of man', created to match 'a new type of work and productive process' (Hoare and Smith 1998).

In marked contrast to the subject being born of transnational campaigning, new citizens of the world economy are made by severance and decontextualization. As severance between the means and the social relations of production defined the 'capitalist mode of production' for Marx, and as separation between quotidian life and its spectacular representation defined 'spectacular modernity' for Guy Debord, severance from place can be said to define governance's mode of relation to the world economy. Addressing local examples of global problems, looking for portable solutions, global citizens are rooted not in contexts but in managerial issues. Looking down unto compartimentalized places, they see problems that need to be solved and they work on finding the most efficient solutions.

Already, places exist where this new type of citizen may be visited and observed. The curious will want to attend global conferences, certainly the most spectacular sites born of governance. Similar to savages brought to universal expositions to show the ways and means of colonialism – and to accompany colonial plunder – these model citizens are part of the governance's spectacle. They are Global Civil Society incarnate, a living panorama constructed to contextualize and justify global governance. Without it, global social contracts would seem empty affairs.

Unlike Samoans in San Francisco, governance's citizenry participates actively in all phases of the spectacle (thus reaching what Guy Debord called *le spectaculaire intégré*).[51] In preparation for global conferences, would-be citizens of the world gather in places where they are accredited, sponsored, vetted, and where they circumscribe problems and prepare policy positions detailing relevant, efficient solutions. Moving from local places to the global space, would-be global citizens shed context and meet other designated representatives of global civil society in allotted sites on the margins of inter-state

Figure 4.1 Colonial spectacle of humanity: Samoan natives at the California Midwinter International Exposition, San Francisco, 1894
Source: from I.W. Taber, *Album of Photographs of California Midwinter International Exposition*, San Francisco Room, San Francisco Public Library

gatherings. From places to space, the movement of global citizens is directed efficiently, purposefully, with minimum leakage and vagrancy, by various and sundry leadership programmes and participation grants. It ends in a political *non-lieu*, a point in space outside context. Already in Rio, Copenhagen or Vienna, new global citizens gather into a parliament of experts working to synthesize solutions into portable, workable plans. Sanctified, captured and cornered, they work with assigned purpose, negotiating and drafting agendas. Sometimes, they are rewarded for their initiative by visits from an appointed authority.

In the last scene of the spectacle of global civic unity, programmes of action, global contracts, charters, declarations and agendas drawn up by gatherings of global citizens are merged with those negotiated 'upstairs', and signed on everyone's behalf. Spectacular icons of humanity's will, they will be hung in a corner and celebrated at designated times (see Table 0.1, p. 2).

Governance's spectacular gatherings, of course, are only the most visible, and most spectacular, moments of a broader division of labour, themselves indicative of a new mode of relation to the world economy. Also worth visiting are other, more permanent sites where global citizens gather to work out enduring solutions and foster apolitical comity. The curious will want to visit nodal points in the 'upstreaming' and 'mainstreaming' (the NGO–World Bank Committee, for instance), attend World Bank-sponsored town meetings in *Concepción*, Gujarat or Tamil Nadu, or work alongside 'executant' or

Figure 4.2 Neoliberal spectacle of humanity: signing the Earth Pledge, the United Nations Conference on Environment and Development, Rio de Janeiro, June 1992
Source: Photo by Charles V. Barber, World Resources Institute

'contractor' NGOs and neighbourhood corporations where global managers, local stakeholders and community leaders are assembled in policy-minded communities, to gather information, broker resources, build local capabilities and assemble pre-emptive coalitions of local *élites* that know – or learn – what is possible and not possible, what they really want and how they have to behave to get it.

In contrast to conjunctural places of transnational struggles, governance sites are not made by social forces answering tactical solicitations. Rather, they answer to the ordering spirit of civic reformism. They are apolitical locations, set aside for purposes of political and economic efficiency, where citizens, community leaders, stakeholders, shareholders and other partners assist in the delivery of services and facilitate social adjustment. Rather than places pregnant with possibilities, they are anchoring points of order in the world economy.

5   Integrated world creation
Outlines of a radical articulation

Revolution is not showing life to people; it is making them live.

(Guy Debord)[1]

Seen from the vantage point of 'modes of relations to the world economy', contemporary global politics seems a Manichaean struggle between (1) transnational historical subjects moved by the exigencies of their many campaigns, who hop and skip across the terrain of the world economy, carrying bundles of contextualized issues and, along with these, what Ralph Miliband would have called 'the actual structures of work and life', preparing the ground for a successful, self-supportive and self-governing global neighbourhood *à la* Jane Jacobs, and (2) abstract subjects gathered by globalizing *élites* in civic coalitions and global goo-goo (good government) clubs, who look to the world economy as a levelled space and labour to create a settled and perfectly efficient place to be administered on purely business principles.[2]

In this fable, global governance is another moment of alienation: a further breaking down of social ensembles on behalf of a more abstract 'species-being', endowed with a still more 'unreal universality' than that Marx wrote of in 'On the Jewish Question' (Marx 1975). By the same token, the transnational campaigns we documented in Chapter 3 can only be thought of as struggles against alienation, and, as such, linked to all other struggles to further real liberation against illusive sovereignty. Staying with this fable a while longer – to learn from it as much as we can before submitting our findings to the blind and blinding light of *realpolitics* assessment – we can begin moving towards a more synthetical and political understanding of the present juncture.

What we have done so far to think about the world economy as a field of concrete and situated practices lets us move beyond generalities to address political questions in a more conjunctural manner. The question, then, is not one of politics in general, (of the kind that necessarily invites perfectly condescending and alienating grand plans for the reordering of the world), but of historically and conjuncturally situated concepts of struggle.

Again, thinking urban thoughts allows us to concretize and radicalize our thinking. Specifically, concepts of *situation, dérive* and *détournement* will move us towards what Ernesto Laclau and Chantal Mouffe called the moment of 'hegemonic articulation' (Laclau and Mouffe 2001). Weapons in the struggle against modern urbanism – the most concrete and definite expression of capitalist ordering – these concepts are at the heart of *l'urbanisme unitaire* ('integrated city creation'), arguably the most concrete and radical of all avant-garde practices.

In a crucial moment when assembling a compliant global subject is becoming integral to the making of world order, and when – for the first time in the history of capitalism organized on a world scale – social forces are installing themselves on the terrain of the world economy, it is both urgent and propitious to think of hegemonical and counter-hegemonical practices beyond national social formations, on the terrain of the world economy.

Elements of hegemonical articulation

Works of international political economy often mine Gramsci's writing to present us with absolutely irreconcilable, ideal-typical scenarios: either we are in the West, civil society has gelled into a relatively autonomous whole, bourgeois hegemony can be rooted in social consensus and we must begin engaging in the patient politics of position-building (scenario I: A war of position); or we are in the East, civil society has not gelled, there is domination rather than hegemony and active sorties against the state can be envisioned (scenario II: A war of movement).

Less concerned with categorical righteousness than with practical exigencies related to the construction of situations, situationist concepts rather encourage us to think about a more conjunctural and purposeful articulation between matters of position and of movement.

Positions

The furthest point on the horizon of Situationist thinking, in relation to which *Situationnistes* themselves defined their practice, was the small, incisive space of everyday life. There, human beings could regain a sense of the significance of their existence and recapture the capacity to re-create themselves as whole, unalienated, beings.

> The punctual space of quotidian life steals an external parcel of time by which gets created a small space-time. This is the space-time of lived moments. Of creativity, of pleasure, of orgasm. The site of such alchemy is tiny but, within it, life is lived with such intensity that it has unequal fascination to most people.
>
> (Vaneigem 1967, 235)

In modern cities, Situationists argued, such places had been almost gridded out of existence by functionalist urbanism. To unearth them was a fundamental task *Situs* set for themselves. The first place they wrote about, that remained their reference for unalienated life in the city, was *Les Halles*, Paris' central marketplace since the middle ages (Sadler 1998, 63). A polysemic place (of commercial exchange, social relations and deterioration, acculturation, drinking, prostitution, inhabited and traversed by a mixed population), it offered the most remarkable example of unitary ambience in all of Paris (Khatib 1958).[3]

To reproduce and generalize this ambience were objectives to which Situationists subsumed all questions of tactics and strategy. Thus, the *dérives* they engage in were both unalienated experiences unto themselves and means to discover unalienated places (Debord 1958). On the *dérive* model, the *Internationale Situationniste* later defined 'the model revolutionary organization' as both an organization in the most processual (and political) sense of the term, and as a position unto itself.

> The ultimate criterion of [a revolutionary organization] is its totalness. Such an organization is ultimately a critique of politics. It must explicitely aim to dissolve itself as a separate organization at the moment of its victory.[4]

For a decade, Situationists stayed in the realm of experimental politics, working on unitary ambiences, contenting themselves with principled variations on the theme of the necessary unity of organization and position. Debord's own contribution, for instance (a take on more expressly political *problématiques* developed by the *Socialisme ou barbarie* group) was his affirmation that the proletariat could only be whole – thus both object and subject – in workers' councils:

> Within councils . . . the proletarian movement is its own product, and, in turn, that product itself becomes a producer. It is, in of itself, its own product.
>
> (Debord 1992)

The radical turn taken by the student movement in Paris in the spring of 1968 (the first global anti-systemic movement that Situationists' thinking helped inspired, with Debord's own *Société du spectacle* and Raoul Vaneigem's *Traité de savoir-vivre*, both published in 1967) forced the movement to engage itself more seriously in concrete matters of organization (Bourseiller 2001; Labelle-Rojoux 2001).[5] The Nanterre *Enragés*, who ignited the spark that launched the *mouvement du 22 mars* that provoked the student uprising in Paris, were *Situationnistes*. So were the principals of the *Conseil pour le maintien des occupations* (CMDO), formed on 16 May, three days after the Sorbonne was first occupied, as the occupation movement began to reach beyond the *quartier des barricades* on the Left Bank to the most important manufacturing concerns in France (Renault-Billancourt, the largest factory in the country, was occupied from 16 May) and beyond (there were occupations in Antwerp, London, Berkeley, Germany, Stockholm, Bruxelles, Tokyo, Istanbul).

Moving from the reflexive micro-politics of a few avant-garde artists 'passing through a rather brief moment in time' (the title of Debord's 1959 film) to the real world of social forces in movement in the world economy (a move Situationists themselves would have scorned for its crass instrumentalism) what can we make of the universe of institutions born in the past twenty years (from the transnational institutes, think-tanks, TSMOs and information clearing-houses presented in Chapter 3, to the sundry organizations presented in Chapter 4)?

This move, of course, is not an easy one. Raoul Vaneigem himself failed to make much of it in his later work. Published in 1996, *Nous qui désirons sans fin* (a globalized version of the *Traité*) put forth a simplistic and undiscriminating enjoinder to occupy factories of the world economy, to retool them to local use:

> To occupy factories ruined by shareholders, to control their production without regard for bureaucratic rules of competition, to transform them if needed in order to produce quality goods that are useful to the region where they are installed, to look to local interests for a reason that an international consciousness can solidify everywhere.
>
> (Vaneigem 1996, 103)

In 1999, Vaneigem wrote an important book, *Pour une international du genre humain*, which showed great insight into the historical uniqueness of the present moment, but said nothing about how a new, grounded and situated international had come to constitute itself; what did, or could, sustain it, how situations could be constructed from it, or how to restore *le mode d'être de la vie humaine* (Vaneigem 1999, 30). In 2001, Vaneigem drew up a grandiloquent *Déclaration universelle des droits de l'être humain* that, for all its grounding in *l'espace-temps du vécu*, was as abstracting as any cosmopolitan grand plan (Vaneigem 2001).

Better informed about the ways in which social forces are installing themselves on the terrain of the world economy, as well as about neoliberal attempts to create an efficient, settled and perfectly apolitical world economy, can we move beyond this unknowing stance?

In Chapter 3, we got a sense that 'transnational institutions' born of transnational campaigns (listed in Tables 3.1 and 3.2) could be both organizations in the instrumental and strategic senses of the term as well as positions unto themselves. Born of, and tied to, actually existing struggles, and creative of resistance communities (both near as their point of origin – think BS/FS 'Camp Justice' and GAP pickets – as well as far from it – think PGA-inspired events in Hyderabad, Seville or Montréal), transnational institutions are the very heart of a dialectics of presence in the world economy. Traversed by the multiple, unresolved and contingent issues of everyday life, as polysemic as *Les Halles* themselves, they offer the most remarkable examples of global unitary ambience. *In situ*, humanity can be both an articulating subject and an historically contingent, situated object.

A contrario, the many bureaux, agencies and learning and working groups set up by global regulatory agencies in their attempt to 'mainstream' and 'upstream' civil society participation only have reasons as instrumental, dedicated, organization. Rather than birthing places of a new transnational subject, they are the ground-zero of decontextualization, where experience begins to be impoverished beyond politics.

To radicalize and generalize practices of liberation and to move towards a more integrated practice, what is called for is (1) the continued occupation, and development, of the significant positions that have already emerged since the beginning of the crisis of the Bretton Woods world order, and (2) the opening up of critical sites of decontextualization. This, of course, goes well beyond the occupation and retooling of factories that Vaneigem called for, to take into account the breadth of ordering mechanisms put in place by neoliberal governance.

By the tools of analysis most often used in the analysis of social and political relationships in the world economy, significant positions and sites of decontextualization are all but indistinguishable from one another. Both contain people who labour to devise strategies to find responses to issues that go beyond the capacities of states to address individually, both contain actors who use new communication technologies and make themselves into network subjects, are transnationally aware and contribute to the opening of a global public sphere; everywhere the human capacity to create alternatives is on display, and everywhere are movements that could be linked up to counter-hegemonic strategies. Only by thinking with reference to ways of entering the world economy and of organizing the occupation of the new terrain can we make political sense of the present juncture. Just as we have to set Tammany Hall's clambakes, wigwams and goo-goo clubs in relation to the broader rise of a more abstact and commodified relationship to the city in order to make political sense of them, and just as we have to enquire into the construction of hemispheric subjects in the Americas to understand DFAIT events and carnivalesque happenings at the *Ilôt Fleuri* or in the *Faubourg Saint-Jean Baptiste*, we need to situate 'transnational institutions' and governance's bureaux in the broader making of 'modes of relation to the world economy' to see that they belong to radically different political ensembles.

To move beyond these very slack pronouncements, we need to be able to say something much more pointed about specific contexts of struggles. To do this, we need to bring general concepts developed here to bear on specific experiences. What are 'actually existing', radically unresolved issues of everyday life (specific, close to daily occuring disputes, effective and real), as opposed to 'abstract' and pre-bound problems, is a matter of empirical enquiry, as is, in the end, what is a significant position and what is a site of ctritical decontextualization. We know (because we have read Henri Lefebvre and have lived in the world) that housing is a more concrete issue, related to everyday life in the city, and that 'habitat' is a more abstract category, intimately linked since the mid-nineteenth century, to a commodified, speculative view of the city (Lefebvre 1968). Thus we think that the GUOs and LUOs born of governance, that are trying to 'mobilize people into organized structures' (Cernea 1988) address themselves not to contingent and situated communities but to humans as a 'species-being' in the sense that Marx understood it. We believe that they create, by design, a global absentee subject inattentive to the creative possibilities of everyday life. We also know that struggles against sexual tourism, *karoshi* or patriarchy in export zones, or for living wages for garment workers and for BS/FS or New Otani workers matter more than do issues of population control; that Ken Saro-Wiwa was a real human being (multiple, irreducible until death), and not an abstract bearer of rights, and that the fate of Mumia Abu-Jamal and the sons of the mothers of the *Plaza de mayo*, or workplace safety say more about democracy and human rights than do global conferences, or projects to reform the United Nations. Thus we think that institutions which are carrying these issues are more open, and more charged with unalienated life than those created by The World Bank *et al.* to draw 'the whole population into the active life of their countries'. The closer we get to the heart of the NGO *nébuleuse*, and the more we reach the centre of global problem-solving of the governance kind, the more we are severed from the manifold warp of global circumstances, and from the possibility of unalienated life. Organizational imperatives assume greater autonomy and the radical possibilities of daily life evaporate. That much seems established. Work we did in Chapter 3 and Chapter 4 does allow us to begin to have an intuitive sense of which is which, but this is far too general to be useful. However, only by conducting empirical enquiries that do not rise above practice but are guided by it can we move with more intelligence beyond the general lists I have assembled and unearth significant positions.

In operational, terms, we need to identify, among institutions listed in Tables 3.1 and 3.3 and others like them, which are at once positions and organizations, and which are places where everyday life gets shrunk beyond all politics. This work, of course, needs to be ongoing, for significant positions only stay so for a while, in a given context. Sometimes, they disappear entirely: *Les Halles* were destroyed in 1971, to make way for an RER station underground, and above it, for the *Centre Pompidou*, which hosted the first retrospective exhibition on the Situationist Internationals in 1989 (Sadler 1998, 66). Identifying significant positions and sites of decontextualization, then, is work that needs constant updating. This is a crucial step in the development of a political articulation.

Movement

Until his resignation in the summer of 1960, Constant (Constant Nieuwen-huys) worked within the *Internationale Situationniste* on plans for a 'New Babylon', building maquettes of elevated and covered cities made up of a 'great number of different traversable spaces' (Constant 1997, 110). Although they took for granted exactly the kind of revolutionary upheaval I want to problematize, and though they stood high on *pilotis*, as severed from everyday life in the modern city as any Corbusean grand plan, Constant's maquettes do offer the most striking model of the IS's visions of the city as a 'ceaselessly changing, endlessly dramatic' ideally unalienating, radically free, place (Wollen 1989a).

From Constant's maquettes, can we learn something about the real world of social forces in movement in the world economy? A first thought concerns ways to break with the emerging neoliberal framework for action.

The will to break with alienating contexts and continuities, of course, was at the heart of the *International Situationniste*. For Debord, Vaneigem and others, all that had been revolutionary about the modern ability to picture – and thus to seize – the world had already settled into a regime to govern daily life by emptying it of radical possibilities (Wollen 1989b, 70). The constitutive principle of this modern regime was the willed and active separation between atomized individuals reduced to passive consumers of images, and shallow moments of false unity. Severed from experience, modern society was 'without community', only whole in passive moments when it consumed alienating spectacles (Debord 1987).

To break with the modern spectacle, Situationists hurled insults and wrote injurious manifestos. To them, Gallimard was shit (*raclure de bidet*) and art critics incoherent imbeciles (Debord *et al.* 1969; IS 1958a). Against revolutionary vanguards that share in 'the ineffectiveness and mystification of political specialization as a means of transforming the world' (Bernstein 1964), Situationists put themselves at the centre of their own world:

> I speak today, and no one, in the name of Alabama or South Africa, or in the name of spectacular exploitation, can make me forget that I stand at the epicentre of such troubles, alongside every other humiliated being. I will not abandon my rightful share of violence.
>
> (Vaneigem 1967)

Against sacred history and capitalism's *chantage à l'utilité* (*'le capitalisme moderne fait renoncer à toute critique par le simple argument qu'il faut un toit . . .*), Situationists dared called social housing concentration camps: 'si les nazis avaient connu les, urbanistes contemporains, ils auraient tranformé les camps de concentration en H.L.M.' (Vaneigem 1961).

Against the alienating spectacle of the cold war and what E.P. Thompson termed 'exterminism' they vowed 'never . . . under any circumstances, [to] set foot in an atomic shelter' (Nash 1964).[6]

To break with the established patterns of urbanists, Constant imagined endlessly traversable cities that were sites of continuous – and continuously creative – drifts. In practice, of course, Guy Debord *et al.* did participate in *dérives*. Wilfully abandoning their usual reasons for moving about the city, rather following scattered hints and 'solicitation' from ambient architecture, as well as chance encounters, they moved about in a manner that was in tune with the creative unity of the city (Debord and Fillion 1954; Debord 1958; Home 1996; IS 1958b; Ivain 1958).

What Constant sought to provoke, and what Debord *et al.* wanted to experience, was the conjunctural unity between subjective knowledge of drifters and objective knowledge of the city as a terrain of experience. This unitary knowledge is what Situationists grandiloquently dubbed 'psychogeography', the scientific framework that underpinned *l'urbanisme unitaire*. In the archives of avant-garde thinking about politics (admittedly a peculiar collection) it is the most tactical of knowledge (Debord sometimes spoke of becoming 'street-wise'; Tuan, cited at the beginning of Chapter 3, on developing 'the feel of a place'). To borrow another, more usual, reference, it is a concrete, reflexive and situated expression of Antonio Gramsci's 'social instinct' (born of 'daily experiences illuminated by common sense').[7]

> The power of psychogeography, it seems, lay precisely in its intoxicating combination of subjective and objective . . . approaches to urban exploration. Psychogeography was merely a preparation, a reconnaissance for the day when the city would be seized for real.
>
> (Sadler 1998, 81)

Of course, social forces involved in transnational campaigns actually move about the world economy via *dérives*. Abandoning for a while their usual trajectories through the world economy, avoiding the grand avenues opened by neoliberal governance, moved by the tactical necessities of polysemic struggles, transnational campaigners eschew internationalist and cosmopolitan high roads to follow more direct routes. Out of obligation and opportunism, they prey on corporate structures, lobby politicians, travel in solidarity, meet Swiss and Dutch bankers, lean on the notoriety and influence of a Nobel laureate, and work to mobilize Czechoslovakian and Brazilian workers. Gathering contrapuntal energies, they fight regional integration in the Americas, sexual tourism in Asia, the putting-out system, the MIA or the ways of Nike, PVH, GAP, the IMF or the World Trade Organization. Dynamized by placed struggles in factories, export zones, prisons and homes, in Manila, Montréal, Osaka, New York or San Francisco, they fight to stop Saipan sweatshops, to save Mumia or Timerman's life, for better pay and in defence of work and safety issues, for abortion rights, to ensure the human rights of trafficked women, and to celebrate International Workers' Day.

Fused for a while by the exigencies of their struggles, transnational campaigners drift about the world economy, exploring it, circumstantially and purposefully, one step at a time, looking for like-minded groups to exchange with and draw from, and for protective societal relationships to build.[8] Hitherto barren, the world economy becomes the context for a while, and fragmented struggles gain amplitude, resonance and social significance. Thus, against the depoliticizing efforts of The World Bank *et al.*, is politics brought to the world economy, not by organizational fiat, but by social forces elbowing for a place in the world economy, 'grop[ing] their way uncertainly into a dimly perceived world, discovering and creating the rules as they go along' (Morris-Suzuki 2000).

This, in words that are more germane to actual practice on the terrain of the contemporary world economy, is what Fredric Jameson (who situated his enquiry in a transcending 'postmodern hyperspace') called 'cognitive mapping', 'a code word for ... class consciousness of a new and hitherto undreamed of kind' (Jameson 1991, 418). A key to the rise of a broader and more political sense of place in the world economy, it offers a foothold into thinking about the kind of counter-hegemonic articulation that works of 'transnational historical materialism' have, too exclusively, been looking for at the level of national social formations.

It is the process of *dérive* that matters most in the development of this new, global, class-consciousness, and not the network form so celebrated by the sociology of globalization (and in such popular books as Naomi Klein's *No Logo*).[9] Reasoning by metonymy, these works imagine a transnational subject that is as free and unattached as flows themselves. But about how subjects are actually constituted, and about their relationship to, and relative autonomy from, other subjects in other moments and contexts, they say little. Drawn from practice, the concept of *dérive* allows us to theorize what is a form of critical engagement with the world, and it lets us build dialectically on practice rather than wait for it to invest, as if by magic, pre-theorized forms and flows. *Dérives* are not things unto themselves, but critical movements agains the gridding process (the authority behind the flow), that are constitutive of an articulating subject.

A second thought concerns matters of organization. Places unto themselves (and as such 'gap[s] in the Parisian spectacle'), sites of unitary ambiance unearthed by Situationist *dérives* and psychogeographic investigations (*Les Halles* in the example cited above) also served as *plaque tournantes*, or 'hubs', much in the same manner that, for E.P. Thompson, the London Corresponding Society was a 'junction point' for working men of London. The very contingency and the polysemism that made them privileged sites of unitary ambience (their 'totalness' and their embeddness in the moving structures of work and life), also allowed them to serve as unitary connecting points between hitherto distinct or unconnected moments. (A good, clear example of how connections can be made in *plaque tournantes* is the broadening of dockworkers' struggles to stevedores on 17 August 1889.)

Again, we got a sense from Chapter 3 that some of the transnational institutions listed in Tables 3.1 and 3.2 do now serve as *plaque tournantes*, and could thus be crucial links in the 'chains of equivalance' that Ernesto Laclau and Chantal Mouffe argued were core to radical democratic politics (Laclau and Mouffe 1985). Perhaps more importantly (because still closer to everyday life in the contemporary world economy), we got a sense that the many places occupied by resistance communities (whether Nike Towns during 'Nike Days of Action', Bangkok brothels being picketed by GAATW activists, Maquilladora communities linked by *Mujer Obrera*, or the Coalition for Justice in the Maquilladora, cities that are sites of anti-summit protests or high schools, universities or places of worship animated by anti-sweatshop campaigns) could be junction points in *dérives*.

A contrario, we got a sense in Chapter 4 that bureaux and agencies born of governance are not *plaque tournantes* at all, but points where the best practices and global benchmarks are developed and enforced that are the gridding principles at the core of global governance, linking together the 'worldwide grid of strategic places' identified by Saskia Sassen (Sassen 1998).

Again, this is a crucial political difference which the existing literature does not allow us to make. Of course, works that discuss specific sites of global politics often insist on the 'glocal' character of happenings. This is important, but too descriptive. Certainly, GUOs and LUOs are 'glocal' institutions, and IMF and World Bank 'town meetings' in Benin and Tamil Nadu are 'glocal' events, as are everyday acts of resistance in export factories and anti-summit protests in Seattle, Québec city, Prague or Genoa. But to say this is to leave unproblematized what is most crucial about how the limits and possibilities of political action in the world economy are being defined at the present moment: the manner in which both the passage of social forces to the terrain of the world and their relationship to it is being structured. All that is 'glocal' does not share the same political significance.

Again, we need much more specific empirical work to proceed beyond these general pronouncements. It is a matter of empirical enquiry as to what are the movements that are actually animated by direct, strategic solicitations and not disciplined by cosmopolitan designs (either those of The World Bank and so on or those of academics and political drawers of grand plans for the re-invention of the world). We cannot see into *positions* by reasoning above conjunctural struggles. We do know that docks served as *plaques tournantes* during the dockworkers' strikes of 1889; we could make an argument that the whole East End was animated by a unitary ambience in this period, and that, had the whole city been so animated, London might have known such a festive moment as the Paris Commune (but we also know that, by the 1890s, suburban and colonial developments had already made this unitary ambience difficult to construct). We know that the processions of dockworkers were *dérives* and that, moved as they were by the exigencies of their struggle to go beyond their usual places, dockworkers and their supporters linked the 'two Englands' just as they were most divided, and thus challenged the functional cadastering of the city. We also know that sites of Tammany Hall politics were not positions at all but fiefdoms invested by established power. Thus, there was no unitary ambience in places of Tammany power, nor were significant *dérives* likely. During Québec city's Summit of the Americas, the difference between creative drifting and depoliticizing obedience for the grid was as evident as could be. When union marshalls steered their members away from those who organized the *carnaval anti-capitaliste*, they were enforcing the depoliticizing grid.

Clear in specific instances, gridding principles and *dérives* become more difficult to see in general. Again, there is a need for more empirical work. What is a *plaque tournante* and what is a point in the grid is a conjunctural matter; prospectively, what *plaques tournantes* can serve which struggles, which are traversed by more significant struggles, what gridding point can be charged with quotidian meaning and made into a *plaque tournante*, are all matters of conjunctural intelligence.

In this respect there are no more urgent tasks for engaged intellectuals than to work on a strategic guide to the world economy (which could perhaps be called a *Guide transnational l'économie mondiale*, to evoke Guy Debord and Asger Jorn's *Guide psychogeographique de Paris*). An aid to necessary drifts, this *Guide* is needed preparation for the day when the world economy can be seized for real. If *positions* and *plaque tournantes* do indeed exist in the contemporary world economy, we need to unearth them. They are crucial elements of what may be a global social revolution that can challenge governance's attempt at a political revolution.

Détournement

Actually existing politics, it bears emphasizing, is not the fable we theorized. Although they can be separated from one another in theory (evidently at the price of some semantic and theoretical convolutions) actors considered here have not in reality constituted themselves into distinct political subjects (what Michel de Certeau calls *sujets de vouloir et de pouvoir*).[10] Transnational drifts do not yet have, and may never acquire, an expressly 'political' character (in the sense of 'a type of action whose objective is the transformation of a social relation which constructs a subject in a relationship of subordination' (Laclau and Mouffe 1985). By the same token, governance-led attempts to create a new social order of capital have not installed themselves as a hegemonic strategy. Indeed, what Susan George called 'ultraliberalism' – the politically insouciant 'concepts of control' we associated with the incipient phase of global neoliberalism – still rules the day in such core regulatory agencies as the Trilateral Commission, the World Trade Organization and the Bank for International Settlements, and in private regulatory institutions such as debt securities and bond-rating agencies.

In the absence of structuring struggles, it would be vain and foolish to jump from these few thoughts about position and movement to programmatic thinking. In the present context, updating Lenine's twenty-one conditions would be as useless as drawing yet another grand plan to hurl at the world, calling for transnational dialogue between ghostly interlocutors (Beck 1999), or inventing still another universal that 'we currently embrace as meaningful ideals upon which to let our imagination roam' (Harvey 2000). As I hope to have shown, the planetary 'us' implicit in these calls is, in itself, problematic, and the question of its making need be addressed before all else. Although it would certainly be satisfying from the points of view of typological neatness and strategic rectitude to declare this group or that gathering irrevocably bound to this or that mode of relationship to the global city, to distinguish the reds and the greens from the yellows, or to praise radicals and condemn reformists (or vice versa), forcing political issues would serve no purpose, either intellectually or politically.

Programmatic thinking is not what is needed, but letting our imagination roam is not sufficient. We live in a crucial moment when a regime to discipline access to the terrain of the world economy and movement accross it is taking shape. A mode of relation to the world economy is being constructed and another one risks disappearing just as it is being born. What is being fixed now will, for a while at least, determine the conditions of global practice.

Rather than plans or programmes, what is needed to give a measure of coherence to the unearthing and defending of positions, to necessary *dérives* and to the articulation between the two, is a more general concept of struggle. To be useful, this concept has to tie together existing practices of both order and change, and it has to bring us further towards a political understanding of the present moment. I believe *détournement* to be just such a concept.

Defined either operationally ('putting artistic elements to new uses in different contexts' (IS 1959b), or by its impact ('a violent excision of elements . . . from their original contexts, and a consequent destabilization and recontextualization'), *détournement* was a key practice of the *Internationale Situationniste*.

The best example of *détournement* is the eponymous journal of the *Internationale Situationniste*, 'a rich collection of montage/collage work on pieces of commodity culture, including . . . recaptioned or reworked advertisements, comic strips, newspaper photographs, problematic description of scantily clad women, illustrations from industrial manuals, graphs, and so forth' (Levin 1989, 74). Animating the journal were trafficked cartoons in which quotidian thoughts burst through the plastic surface of the spectacle (in one instance, dialogue in three panels showing a couple kissing amorously was restored to its ostensibly truer meaning: *Regardez la Commune de Paris . . . C'était la dictature . . . du prolétariat* (IS 1969).

Guy Debord's *Société du spectacle* – a key document of the *IS* – was also a defining example of *détournement* (Debord 1987). Opening with a play on the first sentence of *Capital* ('the whole life of societies where reign modern conditions of production appear as an immense accumulation of spectacles'), *La société du spectacle* followed with a late-modern variation on the first sentence of the *Manifesto's* most lyrical passage ('All that was lived has become a representation'), that is used again throughout the book to réformes : en janvier 1968 un « programme d'action » est adopté, consacrant la montée de l'équipe Dubcek et l'éloignement de Novotny. Outre le plan économique de Ota Sik, définitivement adopté, ce programme nouveau programme, un certain nombre de mesures d'ordre politique étaient fièrement affirmées, par la nouvelle direction. Parmi toutes les « libertés » formelles que voudraient garantir, ces qui constitue une orientation tout à fait originale pour les régimes bureaucratiques. C'est dire l'importance de l'enjeu et la gravité de la situation. Les éléments radicaux, profitant de ces concessions bureaucratiques, vont leur donner leur véritable valeur : à savoir les mesures *nécessaires* pour la sauvegarde de la domination bureaucratique. Le plus libéral parmi les membres nouvellement promus, Sunkovsky, explicite lui-même la vérité du libéralisme bureaucratique : Sachant que, même dans une société socialiste, l'évolution a lieu par une lutte constante d'intérêts dans les domaines économique, social et politique, nous cherchons à établir un système de *direction politique* qui permet le règlement de tous les conflits sociaux et exclut la nécessité d'interventions administratives extraordinaires. Cependant, la nouvelle bureaucratie, en renonçant à ces « interventions extraordinaires », qui constituent, en réalité, sa seule façon de gouverner, ne saurait pas qu'elle livrait son régime à l'emploi de la critique radicale. La liberté d'expression culturelle et politique, et d'association, fut une véritable orgie de la vérité critique. L'idée que le Parti doit « enclicher, intégrer au niveau des organisations de base, fondée sur la capacité des fonctionnaires communistes à travailler et à agir partout battue en brèche, et la nouvelles exigences d'organisation autonome des travailleurs commencent à s'affirmer. La fin du printemps 1968, la bureaucratie dubcekiste donnait la ridicule impression de vouloir à la fois « manger son gâteau et le garder ». Elle réaffirmait son intention de maintenir son monopole politique. Si la résolution du Comité Central de juin 1968, en-

l'expriment dit « d'attaquer à ce fait historique du droit du Parti à commander », le Parti mobilisera toutes les forces du peuple et de l'État socialiste pour repousser et réduire à néant cette tentative aventuriste ». Mais, la réforme bureaucratique remettant tout à la décision de la majorité du Parti, comment les grandes majorités, en dehors du Parti ne voudraient-elles pas décider elles aussi ? Quand on le s'empare de l'État et de l'économie, là où l'intérêt général de l'État devient un intérêt réel, par suite, au sommet le bureaucratie commence à lutter contre le prolétariat comme toute conséquence pratique de ses présuppositions.

« regardez la Commune de Paris »

À partir de la les tendances révolutionnaires vont orienter leur critique vers la démocratisation du libéralisme radical. Jusqu'ici la démocratie a été, en quelque sorte, « imposée » aux masses de la même manière que la dictature leur était imposée ; c'est-à-dire en excluant leur participation réelle. Tout le monde sait que Novotny est arrivé au pouvoir comme partisan de la libéralisation et que, des lors, une « régression » du type communiste » n'étant le danger n'est le mouvement de Dubcek. On ne transforme pas une société en changeant d'appareil, mais en la bouleversant de fond en comble. De là, l'on en vient à critiquer la conception bolchevik du parti dirigeant de la classe ouvrière, et à exiger une organisation autonome du prolétariat ; ce qui signifiait pour la bureaucratie une mort prochaine. C'est que, pour elle, le prolétariat ne peut exister

que comme une puissance *imaginaire* ; elle le ravale, ou prétend que l'travailleur n'est jusqu'ici ne plus être qu'une apparence, mais elle veut que cette apparence existe et croit à sa propre existence. Fondant son pouvoir sur le formalisme de l'idéologie, la bureaucratie au fait de ses buts *formels* en conflit avec ses buts *réels*, et ainsi elle entre partout en conflit avec les buts réels.

« c'est la dictature »

même pour le contre-projet, manifestement rédigé par des syndicalistes, présenté le 29 juin 1968 par l'usine mécanique Wilhelm Pieck. La critique du léninisme, présenté par « certains philosophes », comme étant « déjà une déformation du marxisme puisqu'il contient dans sa logique le stalinisme » a été, non comme le pensent les ânes de *Rouge* « une idée saugrenue parce qu'à terme elle nie le rôle dirigeant du prolétariat » (!), mais le plus haut point de la critique théorique atteint dans un pays bureaucratique. Dubcek lui-même, a été ridiculisé par les étudiants révolutionnaires tchèques, et son « anarcho-maoïsme » rejeté avec mépris comme « absurde, comique et ne méritant pas l'attention d'enfants de quinze ans ». Toute cette critique qui, naturellement, ne pouvait aboutir qu'à la mise en question pratique du *pouvoir de classe de la bureaucratie*, était encore, colée, et même parfois encouragée, par le dubcekisme tant qu'il pouvait la *récupérer* comme une légitime défense contre des « erreurs stalinonovotnystes », dénonce ses propres crimes, mais toujours comme étant commis par *d'autres*, il lui suffit de détacher une partie d'elle-même, de l'ériger en entité autonome, de la condamner au sacrifice est, depuis les temps les plus reculés, la pratique préférée de la bureaucratie, pour perpétuer son pouvoir. Pologne et en Hongrie, le nationalisme a été, en

Mais le mouvement de contestation — consécutif à la réforme bureaucratique — n'a fait que dans le chemin. Il n'a pas trouvé le temps de s'affirmer dans ses conséquences pratiques. La dénonciation théorique et sans concessions de la « dictature bureaucratique » et du totalitarisme stalinien a été à peine reprise à son propre compte par la grande majorité de la population, que la néo-bureaucratie russe, déjà brandissant la menace russe, déjà présente à la fin du mois de mai. On peut dire que la brutalité du mouvement tchécoslovaque a été quelquefois pas intervenue comme une force autonome et décisive : Les thèmes de « l'autogestion », les conseils ouvriers », contenus dans la réforme technocratique d'Ota Sik, n'ont pas dépassé les perspectives bureaucratique-à-la-yougoslave ; ceci

« du prolétariat »

Figure 5.1 Détournement
Source: Internationale Situationniste, vol. 12, September 1969

punctuate the analysis. In like spirit were Asger Jorn's *peintures détournées*, and Debord's own interrupted and all but invisible films (broken up and withdrawn from circulation by Debord himself).

Of course, Constant's maquettes for a New Babylon, that used urbanist techniques not to control circulation but to create traversable cities were graphic examples of *détournements* (Andersen 1989). Key here is the re-appropriation of existing elements. Specifically, *détournements* were about taking hold ('hijacking' is a possible translation of the term, 'embezzlement' another) of the most advanced, and abstracted, commodity forms, where the modern spectacle was most ubiquitous, but also most extended and thus most fragile.[11]

> Western capitalism [the IS] realized, was taking a risk by dangling the spectacle under people's noses. What if spectators transgressed the rules of consumerism by stealing and redistributing its product and images, for themselves, making good its vacuous promises of a better world?
>
> (Sadler 1998, 19)

In this scheme, the Watts riots of 1966 were, for Situationists, more pregnant with revolutionary meaning than civil rights marches:

> The riots in Los Angeles represent a revolt against merchandise, against the world of merchandise, where workers-consumers are reduced to the measure of merchandise. Blacks in Los Angeles ... are taking at face value the propaganda of modern capitalism, its publicity of abundance. They want, right now, all the things that are shown by capitalism but are only available in the abstract, because they want to make use of it now.
>
> (IS 1966)

More specifically relating to the city, Situationists suggested diverting the most empty and functionally reduced scenes of contemporary urbanism, to invest them with radical, unitary behaviour:

> Open the Metro at night after the trains stop running. Keep the corridors and tunnels poorly lit by means of weak, intermittently functioning lights. With a careful rearrangement of fire escapes, and the creation of walkways where needed, open the roofs of Paris for strolling. Leave the public garden at night. Keep them dark.
>
> (Sadler 1998, 109)[12]

In similar spirit, Debord wrote in his *Mémoires* of a 'project for a realist urbanism':

> replace the stairways in Piranesi with lifts – transform the tombs and buildings – align sewers with the planting of trees – recast dustbins in

ivory – stack up the shantytowns and build all these cities in the form of a museum.

(Sadler 1998, 108)

As we saw in Chapter 3, the spirit of *détournement* is very evident during transnational campaigns. Black-flagging Bridgestone/Firestone at Indy Car races is a *détournement*, as is charging basketball and golf tournaments with political meaning, or occupying streets in the financial district. The spirit of *détournement*, of course, is also alive and well in Adbusters' highjacking of brand marks, the most ubiquitous and fragile artefact of contemporay capitalism.

Détournement practices are also highly visible during anti-summit protests. Reappropriating (and 'Reclaiming', to make explicit reference to the English group whose practices have influenced anti-summit protests) the very spaces reserved by globalizing *élites* for levelling activities and dutiful problem-solving, anti-summit protesters directly question governance's strategy for the ordering of the world. To governance's severance, they oppose essential moments of creative wholeness, comparable to other moments when artistic desires to create and political desires to change the world have been conjuncturally linked: 'De Sade liberated form the Bastille in 1789, Beaudelaire on the barricades in 1848, Courbet tearing down the Vendôme Column in 1870' (Wollen 1989a). Of global situations there can be no better examples. This unitary ambience is what made protests in Seattle, Prague and elsewhere so resonant and important (it is indeed crucially important that, in less time than it took the First International to ratify its provisional rules, anti-summit protests have created their own, relatively coherent, aesthetics).

Beyond giving us reason to understand the importance and resonance of *Adbusters* campaigns and anti-summit protests, the concept of *détournements* also gives us ways to begin thinking of a more deliberate, political practice (less taken with what are perhaps modish ways and more concerned with constructing a less alienating style of relation to the world economy).

As we saw in Chapter 4, 'global governance' is an extension of neoliberal ordering. In the past twenty years, global regulatory agencies have involved themselves as never before in the structuring of everyday life in the world economy. 'Upstreaming' and 'mainstreaming', creating NGOs as they go, gathering local leaders, stakeholders and users, assembling stores of best practices and global benchmarks, The World Bank and others have brought global decontextualization closer to the ground level of social life. Severance is the structuring principle behind funding, it informs the creation of new institutions (from the 'Center for Women's Global Leadership' to local urban observatories) and it is the ordering principle of the NGO *nébuleuse* that is being born of governance. Civic cosmopolitanism, then, is not just a discourse, but the official ideology of the global, neoliberal regulation of daily life.

Governance practices have made members of the global growth machine (neoliberalism's 'New Citizen') as ubiquitous as Tammany's 'braves' and 'sagamores' in New York's Lower East Side at the end of the nineteenth century. This presence, of course, is most obvious in debtor countries, or in countries in transition from state-planned economies, where global regulatory agencies have greater room to manoeuvre and where governance often bypasses state mechanisms, to install more efficient mechanisms of financial surveillance.

Ubiquitous, governance's people also occupy the most fragile sites of neoliberal regulation. Until global governance has in fact succeeded in fixing hegemonical terms of presence in the world economy (until the earthworks of hegemony have been dug and solidified, in Gramscian parlance), global capitalism is taking a risk by dangling global civility under people's noses. In a crucial moment of transition, governance is, at once, trying to define new terms of global order and to invent a society to sustain it. This represents a formidable extension over previous mechanisms of world order, that relied on a mix of transnational coercion and nationally constituted, or enforced, consensus (Drainville 1995c). This extension leaves global neoliberalism greatly exposed. Were decontextualizing sites to be diverted now, that governance could actually end up creating *plaque tournantes* where it wanted to make sites of decontextualization, and furthering *dérives* where it wanted to grid. Thus governance could be diverted to make exactly the opposite of the depoliticized humanity which global neoliberalism wishes to create. Not in a wholesale manner, of course, but site by site.

To divert sites of global governance is to rupture their links with decontextualizing machineries and to reset them in the continuum of experience. This seems a very abstract (and very academic) strategy, but it is actually very close to transnational practices, both past and present. *Détournement* is exactly what French and English workers who met at the Great Exhibition in London in 1851 did (with significant results). It is also what women who brought up issues of excision, sexual tourism or abortion rights at the World Conference on Human Rights in Vienna did, and what housing-right activists did at Habitat II in Istanbul. Although The World Bank and others would like them to have learned what is possible and how they had to behave to get what they want, they also loaded the moment with multiple, irreducible issues.

Again, global conferences clarify what are diffused and endemic processes and choices. All social forces present on the terrain of the world economy, whether constituted as NGOs, local unions or social movements, are necessarily involved in both modes of relation to the world economy. At the present time, these are not exclusive ensembles. There is a part of both in any practice, as well as in all institutions (few of the transnational institutions listed in Tables 3.1 and 3.2 could not find a place in the NGO *nébuleuse* discussed in Chapter 4; by the same token, few sites of governance are not traversed by multiple issues, some of which are as quotidian and irreducible as they come). Breaking with governance and resetting in the continuum of experience are but ends of a situation where actually-existing social forces have to navigate, mindful of compromises that are the lot of all practice. Thinking with reference to modes of relations to the world economy is not a means to substitute automatisms for what are necessarily conjunctural decisions, but a way to introduce concepts of struggle to strengthen the coherence of unalienating practices.

Again, more specific intelligence is required to move beyond these general pronouncements. Which instance of governance can be diverted, at what moment at what cost and for which profit can governance's problem-solving enterprise be made matters of political contention, what are ways to reset transnational struggles in experience and to further presence, what is *détournement* and what is petty opportunism, what can be hijacked and what is unredeemable, are all matters too specific to be discussed here. Again, concepts introduced here are not meant as substitutes for empirical work and tactical evaluations, but to inform the broad process of cognitive mapping that is already ongoing and, in the end, to move to a more political articulation between individual experiences.

Conclusion

Here, then, are a few *banalités de base* about politics in the world economy. Animated by the urgency of thinking beyond cosmopolitan accommodation before global neoliberalism has succeeded in establishing stronger footholds, I have exploited as much as possible the uncompromising, poetic vernacular of the *Internationale Situationnistes*, without the exegete's concern for the lineages of their thinking, or the care that a historian of ideas would have taken to situate them in relation to theories and strategies born of other moments of struggle (from council communism to Guevara's *foco in foco*, to more recent thoughts on transgression, resistance and 'affinity groups'). To rescue transnational subjects from the immense condescension of cosmopolitan ideology and problematize their making, I have written an account that allows us to see as clearly as possible what is currently at stake.

To move further ahead in the political articulation, more careful, and situated, empirical work needs to be done. In the Introduction to this book, I suggested that ten thousand E.P. Thompsons working with as many Walter Benjamins and a million area specialists would be needed to rescue experience from the oblivion of cosmopolitan generalities. Such is the strength of practice these days that these resources are available in social forces in action.

Conclusion

[I]n the era of globalization . . . we must live by consensus or die. . . . If we do not accept such a submission to a world authority we shall not get peace.

(Shridath Ramphal)[1]

C'est un beau moment que celui où se met en mouvement un assaut contre l'ordre du monde.

(Debord 1999)

In the 1880s and 1890s, two cities at the core of the world economy became loci of political struggles. The outcome of these struggles, of course, was determined by circumstantial happenings. The dockworkers' strike was won because stevedores and sailors organized successful pickets that kept black-legs out; because over extended and under-capitalized dock companies stuck to an archaic work regime that made them fight the City as well as dockers and their supporters; because Ben Tillet disciplined the *residuum* into respectability; because, in spite of its failure, the 'no-work' manifesto did underline the threat of a general social strike in London; because the City supported an orderly end to the strike; because Australian trade unions contributed massively to the strike fund; and because the casualization of work in the East End increased the resonance of the dockers' case. In New York, the 1894 mayoralty race was lost by Tammany Hall because moral and structural reformists rallied together for a while; because Reverend Parkhurst successfully turned the public's growing taste for the sordid (in the 1880s the Five Points district was one of New York's principal tourist sites) into fear of Tammany's boozy mob; because the Ninth Avenue 'El' opened up the Upper West Side for expansion; because Tammany Hall undermined the power of the popular press and because of the publicity given to the Lexow hearings.

After dockers got their tanner, the sense of place in the East End dissipated as quickly as it had taken hold, a more efficient work regime was put in place and dockworking became, as Sydney Buxton put it, an 'organized and regular industry' (Buxton 1890). Dockers became regular employees, all enrolled in the 'Dock, Wharf, Riverside and General Labourers' Union', financed by fixed contributions from members, and as hostile as any union to 'the riff-raff: the wretched wastrels that have disgraced the docks', determinately not in the spirit of the 'new unionism' (Thompson 1967, 51). For their part, 'casuals' on whose behalf stevedores and others had come out 'for entirely unselfish motives' – and who were central to placing the dockers' strike in the East End – found their position more precarious than ever. By the winter of 1890 to 1891, the new employment regime had effectively excluded them from dock employment (Stedman Jones 1971, 318–319). In 1900, the strike of dockworkers was met with strong police measures, blacklegs were hired by the thousand, stevedores and other skilled workers refused to join in and, in the East End, processions were 'tiny and pathetic' when compared with patriotic marches for imperialist expansion (Schneer 1994). Rather than becoming a challenge to industrial capitalism, or creating socialism in England, the dockworkers' strike signalled the end of a fifty-year period of mobilization (starting with the 'Open Space movement' in the mid-1850s) and the beginning of the deradicalization of London's working class.[2] 'Proud citizens of the first city in the world', as Ben Tillet presented dockers to Lord Mayor Whitehead at the conclusion of the 1889 strike, workers settled for the spectacle of parliamentary socialism, 'a system to contain pressure from below' (Miliband 1982, 1). New places were charged with new, apolitical meaning:

> the most prominent developments in working-class life in late-Victorian and Edwardian London were the decay of artisan radicalism, the marginal impact of socialism, the largely passive acceptance of imperialism and the throne, and the growing usurpation of political and educational interests by a way of life centered round the pub, the race course and the music hall. In sum, its impermeability to the classes above it were no longer threatening or subversive, but conservative and defensive.
>
> (Stedman Jones 1974, 484)

The conjunctural sense of place that socialized and radicalized the dockworkers' struggle, then, did not automatically translate into structural transformation. By the same token, the victory of civic reformism in New York did not by itself empty places in the Lower East Side of politics, nor did it, in the short term, displace Tammany Hall (that endured, under the new dynamics of 'city comptroller governance', until well after the Second World War). Gridding politics out of place is not so easily done, as another, less ambiguous episode could have taught us. Only a few years after Georges Eugène Haussmann undertook the strategic beautification of Paris, with the intent of pacifying and disciplining the turbulent working class, the Commune created what David Harvey called 'the greatest class-based communal uprising in capitalist history' (Harvey 1985, 154).

In the 1980s and 1990s, the world economy, that had been the almost exclusive preserve of globalizing *élites*, became a loci of political struggles, arguably for the first time in the history of capitalist accumulation on a world scale. In Chapter 3, I gave short accounts of some representative struggles. The uncertain score sheet presented in the conclusion (victories for Ravenswood and BS/FS workers, defeat for partisans of Ken Saro-Wiwa and opponents of NAFTA, no end in sight to campaigns for the rights of Saipan, Nike and Reebok workers, for abortion rights, wages for housework, against excision, sexual tourism, and gender exploitation), hints at the relative indeterminacy of further struggles on the terrain of the world economy, and gives us cause to think in broader, more political, terms.

What will come of further struggles on the terrain of the world economy – what structural transformation they will bring about, what possibilities will open up for broader struggles and which will disappear, what will be settled and what will remain open for questions and movements – will depend entirely on matters of *realpolitik* about which very little has been said in this book. To problematize what cosmopolitan ideology takes for granted and see into how social forces are moving themselves to the terrain of the world economy, or are being taken to it, I have worked from relatively abstract *thought-images* and *real-abstract concepts* to create a heuristic device that operates more sensibly than do fashionable political categories. This has allowed me to posit that there may be radically distinct 'modes of relationship to the world economy' being born in the present moment, but it may also have had the perverse effect of encouraging me to treat minor episodes as matters of world-historical importance. In conclusion, I want to distance myself from tiny details and say something about the broad political prospects and the relevance of my analysis to actually-existing politics.

In the academic and popular presses as well as in debates among militants, political analyses of actually-existing processes of order and counter-order in the world economy most often limit themselves to the most spectacular events, from UN global conferences to Zapatistas' *Encuentros*, to G-8, The World Bank, IMF and WTO summits and counter-meetings, to gatherings in Porto Alegre's protest pit. Trapped in the spectacle of purposeful and circumscribed events, many take 'civil society', the fellowship of Davos, and kins of the rogue people of Seattle to be actually-existing subjects. Cosmopolitan ideology and what Cameron McCarthy and Greg Dimitriades called the conversationalizing discourse of the media culture encourage this fabulation, from which political positions are established that structure false debates: the reasonable ones among us, perhaps social democrats, invariably wish for a discussion to take place (Kellner 2000); radicals, anarchists, libertarians, autonomists and sundry other revolutionaries speak in favour of a diversity of tactics, many arguing that another world is indeed possible; cautious radicals worry that Porto Alegre II was 'perhaps too happy, too celebratory and not conflictual enough' (Hardt and Negri 2000). Little, if anything, is said about what should give us political reason for celebration, happiness, conflict or discussion, and about what is possible and what can be done to help make another world, that is not over-determined by cosmopolitan ideology.

Beyond cautious platitudes and some folksy sense that there is more truth in batik than in fine wool and more justice and equality in what seems to come from below (or from the would-be people's big tent) than in what seems to come from above (or from convention centres where Davos' people meet), what can help us get a political sense of whether we should celebrate or criticize happenings in Davos and Porto Alegre, or World Bank overtures to civil society, or victories and defeats in given transnational campaigns? Beyond principled and ideological stances, what, to put it as operationally as possible, should help us think through our political choices? What politics, then, are we to navigate by and what is indeed possible (two questions that are intimately related for everyone except ascetics, puritans and academics who put blind faith in ghosts of the sort presented in Chapter 1)?

To answer these questions, we need to question the unreal universality of cosmopolitan ideology and look into contemporary happenings as material events. This is what I tried to do in Chapter 2, when I looked into the making of transnational subjects in preparation for Québec city's Summit of the Americas. Building my heuristic machine and putting it to the test of a real occasion, I concluded that we could see not one but two radically distinct modes of relation to the world economy at work: the 'civic-consensual mode', that operated in preparation for the People's Summit and the heads-of-state summit, and the 'unitary mode' at work in the making of events in the *faubourg Saint-Jean Baptiste*, at the *Ilôt Fleuri* and elsewhere.

Were the distinction between modes of relation to the world economy to be observable only during spectacular events, then its importance would be wholly theoretical, in the most pejorative sense of the term. 'Modes', then, would be but ways of partaking in spectacles. However, as I hope to have argued successfully in Chapter 3, when I looked into some transnational campaigns, and in Chapter 4, when I looked into global, regional, national and city-level governance, two 'modes of relation to the world economy' can also be seen at work in more ordinary, and thus significant, happenings. They are part and parcel of the practice of all social forces that are taking themselves to the world economy, or that are being taken to it. As such, they already have a history that is far from inconsequential. Born of the meeting of social forces in particular circumstances, they structure, inform, shape or over-determine considerable movements of social forces, whose relative strength has yet to be assessed, but must be investigated.

To give more *realpolitik* intelligence to our reading of the current moment, and to inform strategic and tactical choices, I propose, then, to distinguish between what goes in the direction of civic governance and what goes in the direction of unitary globalism, and to get a sense of the real forces on each side. From Chapters 3 and 4, the implications of this distinction are, I hope, as clear as possible: civic governance should be understood as another moment of alienation, unitary globalism as a promise of being whole in creating a new world.

This is not to say, of course, that modes have already gelled into something that can over-determine the movement of social forces, that they have been reflexively integrated into strategies of power and counter-power, or that they can be directly transposed into practices. Modes exist in theory, which is not to say that they do not exist at all in politics, but that they do so in a manner that is relatively autonomous from conjunctural happenings; they can be read into practices but they do not (yet?) define struggles. Social forces have not fallen into camps, nor should they be made to fall into them. Nothing could be further from the purpose of this book than to encourage those who wish to rush to programmatic coherence, or to draw up exclusive lists of who are the good people and who the bad, true revolutionary and social fascists (to evoke the righteous position of the Third International during the rise of fascism, arguably the most tragic mistake of the Left).

Nor can we argue for transnational strategies unrelated to struggles going on in other national social formations. In a text published a little under a decade ago (Drainville 1995c), I concluded from a brief, spatially informed analysis of efforts by transnational regulatory agencies to manage transition in Eastern Europe, and to solve the debt and migration crises,

> that political transformation in the world economy is not only incomplete, but it relies both on the confinement of political and social relationships to the space of national social formations, and on the capacity of states to structure political participation.

In arguing here that global regulatory agencies have also been furthering a specific mode of relation to the world economy, and that a radically distinct style can be seen operating in transnational campaigns, I certainly do not wish to imply that we need no longer to think about the relation between distinct moments of struggle.

Rather than exclusive categories, what we need are articulating principles that give political intelligence to tactical and strategic choices, and allow us to strengthen and radicalize existing links between separate movements at different moments. This, I hope, is what specific modes provide.

By the same token, we also need political categories to guide the mapping of efforts by global regulatory agencies to socialize global neoliberalism. This, of course, is only part of what may be understood as the neoliberal hegemonic project. As surely as the rise of gated communities in Los Angeles is linked to the militarization of the Southern Californian landscape (Davis 1998, [1946] 361), the making of a 'civic' growth machine is related to coercive politics, to what Perry Anderson labelled 'the reconstruction of the world in the American image' (Anderson 2002), and to practices of consensus and coercion in national social formations. One sets the context, and the limits, of the other. Thinking only about national social formations, for instance, it is very possible that globalization and the internationalization of states will beget a new kind of political division of labour: to global regulatory agencies and associate members of the 'global growth machine' might go legitimation functions and the spoils of the new order, to states 'market-driven politics' (that is to say no politics at all), and the containment of uncivil societies. It is easy to imagine a world of unpolitical freedom cadastered into productive places, and nation-states as prisons. Again, thinking in terms of 'modes of relation to the world economy' can inform strategic choices. In the present context, it is not enough to speak for a 'war of position' beginning with 'the long, laborious effort to build new historic blocs within national boundaries' (Cox 1983, 174). As I argued in Chapter 5, global capitalism is taking a considerable risk by dangling global civility under people's noses. In a crucial moment of transition, when governance is, all at once, trying to define new terms of global order and to invent a society to sustain it, more than a patient war of position is possible, and necessary. In some sites, more varied and engaged forms of struggle can be imagined that can both bring victories now and help establish new positions (or diverse positions opened but not held by agencies of governance). To map which sites are worth taking at what cost, what positions should be established, where movement is appropriate and where new positions should be defined, it is key to think with reference to 'modes of relation to the world economy'.

For politics to be done, it has to be seen. Immodestly, this is what this book has been about. Relying on the eloquence of historical vignettes and the strength of Situationist vernacular, work done here allows us to raise an incredible, yet eminently realist, hypothesis: Perhaps not one, but two quite distinct humanities are now beginning to rise. One is an abstract creation, severed from inherited ways of life and struggle, never wholly outside of ordering processes, a mechanical part of a mechanical system (to paraphrase from Luckas). The other is a radically indeterminate and situated subject. Perhaps we are living at the beginning of a global social revolution that will challenge governance's attempt at a political revolution.

A little more than a year after Québec's Summit of the Americas, we can see what comes of different 'modes of relationship to the world economy'. Born of severance and apolitical recomposition, the People's Summit was commemorated by a sad parade, a wake really, that dragged the People's corpse away from where the fence had been, to a cul-de-sac. In remarkable contrast, people engaged in the occupation movement in the *faubourg Saint-Jean Baptiste* and at the *Ilôt Fleuri* continued their action in a way that could not have highlighted better the creative dialectic we saw operating in the Bridgestone/Firestone and Ravenswood strikes – and could have observed with the Landless movement in Brazil after 1984, in the Chiapas, or in Paris during the strike movement of December 1995, described by *Le Monde* as 'the first revolt against globalization'.[3] On 17 May, 300 people marched in support of a new squat being inaugurated in an empty two-storey apartment building at *920 de La Chevrotière*, in the *Ilôt Berthelot*, a stone's throw away from where the Summit of the Americas' fence had stood (and fell). In the three months of its existence, the Québec city squat (part of a provincial-wide movement co-ordinated in large part by the *Front populaire en réaménagement urbain*) had received widespread support: neighbourhood merchants are putting signs of support in their windows, a majority of the twenty-seven co-ops in *Saint-Jean Baptiste* neighbourhood declared their support for the occupation, as did the *Conseil de quartier* and many of the organizations that had been active in the staging of protests in Québec city: les *AmiEs de la Terre, Droit de Parole*, Coalition OQP-2001, la CLAC, ATTAC, the CADEUL and the *Association des étudiantes et étudiants en sciences sociales de l'université Laval* (Comité populaire Saint-Jean Baptiste 2002a, 2002b; Phébus 2002; Porter and Gouin 2002).

Thus, the sense of place that radicalized and socialized anti-FTAA protests in Québec city seems to have endured long enough to radicalize and socialize another struggle. This, of course, will not automatically translate into structural transformation, but it is part of the dialectics of presence in the world economy.

Notes

Introduction

1 See Cassani (1995) About the Tobin tax and related proposals; (1995); Tobin (1978). About a second UN assembly and related reforms, see Archibugi, (1993); Archibugi and Held (1995); Goldblatt (1997); Held (1991, 1995); Kreml and Kegley (1996). About a global social contract (an idea more often discussed in the French literature), see Groupe de Lisbonne (1995); Petrella (1994, 1997).

2 On thought-images in Benjamin, see Benjamin (1998); and Gilloch (1996, 2–3, 37–38).

3 Henri Lefebvre cited in Harvey (1985, 16).

4 René Descartes cited in Braudel (1979, 20).

5 Henry James cited in Lewis Mumford, *The City in History* (London: Penguin Books, 1961).

6 In *Le temps du monde*, Braudel used the image of the *nébuleuse* (nebulae), to convey the relatively loose unity of merchants of the Hanseatic League. Robert Cox applied the image to transnational organizations managing the world economy in Cox (1992). In contemporary international political economy, the term is now widely used in Cox's fashion and usually written in French.

7 On 'Haussmanization' (strategic demolition and beautification) see 'Haussmanisation, combats de barricades', in Benjamin (1993). In *The housing question*, Engels had already also generalized 'Haussman' as a practice. On this see Deutche (1996).

8 Frank Lloyd Wright 'On Creativity' in Patrick J. Meehan (ed.), *The Master Architect: Conversation with Frank Lloyd Wright* (New York: John Wiley & Sons 1984), p. 67.

9 About semantization of usage, see Pierre Bourdieu, *Propos sur le champ politique* (Lyon: Presses Universitaires de Lyons, 2000); Barthes (1964).

10 Marshall Berman, *All That is Solid Melts into Air: The Experience of Modernity* (New York: Penguin, 1988), cited in Harvey (1985, 29).

11 About the spatial fix, 'capitalism turning "to geographical reorganization . . . as a partial solution to its crises and impasses"', see Harvey (2000).

12 See Tuan (1977).

13 Christine Boyer commenting on Michel Foucault's critique of modern urbanism in Boyer (1994, 33).

14 Walter Benjamin, 'Paris, Capitale du XIX siècle' (May 1935), in Benjamin (1993).

1 More than ghosts: subjects in places in the world economy

1 Mattelart (1999).

2 Quotes are from R.B.J. Walker 'Security, Sovereignty, and the Challenge of World Politics', *Alternatives* 15 (1) (winter, 1990): 11.

3 Haas (1992), cited in Della Porta and Kriesi (1999, 19).

4 In World Bank vernacular CBOs are Community-Based Organizations. GONGOs are Government Organized Non-Governmental Organizations (that belonged principally to the cold war period); NGOs, of course, are Non-Governmental Organizations; QUANGOs are Quasi-Non-Governmental Organizations (e.g. the International Committee of the Red Cross); GOINGOs are Government Induced Non-Governmental Organizations; CONGOs are Co-ordinating Bodies of Non-Governmental Organizations (e.g. the UN's ECOSOC); INGOs are International Non-Governmental Organizations.

5 On this, the most synthetical position, see Morin and Naïr (1997). In the same spirit, see Morin (1993).

6 See Mattelart (1999, 205). On the tendency 'within early French sociological trad-ition to equate that which is most basically social (or societal) with the notion of humanity', see Robertson (1992, 23).

7 An excellent presentation of McLuhan's ideas and their influence may be found in Waters (1995). The quote from Wallerstein is from Wallerstein (1987), cited in Robertson (1992, 49).

8 Mitchell (1995); see also Stephen G. Jones. 'From Where to Who Knows?', in *Cybersociety*, edited by S. Jones (London: Sage, 1995). On this, see also J. Carey, *Communication as Culture*. (Boston, MA: Unwin-Hyman, 1989).

9 Lyotard (1993), quoted in Linklater (2001, 28). On the idea of a global public sphere, see also Habermas (1996, 122); and Gupta and Ferguson (1992). On Habermas' idealization of the public space, see Deutche (1996).

10 MUDs (Multiple-User Dungeons – later Multiple-User Domains) are collective role-playing sites. According to William J. Mitchell, the first one, based on the fantasy game 'Dungeons and Dragon', was written at the University of Sussex by Roy Trubshaw and Richard Bartle. A decade after their inception, MUDs begat MUAs (Multi-User Adventures), MUSEs (Multiple-User Social Environments), MUSHes (Multiple-User Social Hosts) and MOOs (Muds-Object Oriented). Moving from texts to more evocative graphic-based formats, the MU world took on civic attributes and names. Lucasfilm's *Habitat*, for instance, was a city of 20,000 'Avatars', created for the Commodore 64, that was equipped with the usual panoply of all American cities (from ATM machines to garbage cans, traffic jams, weapons and drugs), and with new features announcing the complete commodifi-cation of human life (e.g. 'Change-o-Matic' sex-change machines). When it was acquired by Fujitsu, *Habitat* was renamed *Populopolis* and moved to a main frame. At last count, it was home to 1.5 million citizens. In the same vein are *Cyberion city* (a learning community) and *Islandia* (arguably the most commodi-fied civic place); see Mitchell (1995); see also Morningstar, Chip and Farmer (1991); Rheingold (1993a). For a more experimental enquiry into the process of invention and alternative personae, see Stone (1995).

11 Marshall McLuhan and Q. Fiore, *The Medium is the Massage* (London: Allen Lane, 1967), cited in Waters (1995).

12 Stone (1995).

13 See also Frederick (1993).

14 Examples of transportation and communication technologies are taken from Lash and Urry (1994).

15 Immanuel Wallerstein *The Capitalist World Economy* (Cambridge: Cambridge University Press, 1980) p. 230. In the same spirit, see Giovanni Arrighi *Geometry of Imperialism* (London: NLB, 1978), p. 113.

16 Giovanni Arrighi, Terence K. Hopkins and Immanuel Wallerstein *Antisystemic Movements* (London: Verso, 1989), p. 51.

17 Bourdieu and Passeron (1977), cited in Shields (1991).

18 Fernand Braudel *La Dynamique du capitalisme* (Paris: Flammarion Champs,

1985) pp. 12–13. On the emergence of the 'mercantile art' in Venice and Treviso, see Frank J. Swetz, *Capitalism and Arithmetic: the New Math of the 15th Century* (La Salle: Open Court 1987).

19 Wilson and Wimal (1996); Vertovec (1999); Vertovec and Cohen (1999); Werbner (1999). On 'global ethnoscapes', see Arjun Appadurai 'Global Ethnoscapes: Notes and Queries for a Transnational Anthropology', in *Recapturing Anthropology: Working in the Present*, edited by Richard Fox (Santa Fe: School of American Research Press, 1991); Arjun Apparduai 'Disjuncture and Difference in the Global Cultural Economy', in *Global Culture, Nationalism, Globalization and Modernity*, edited by M. Featherstone (London: Sage, 1990).

Beyond these specific texts, references to 'transnational imaginary' and diasporic cultures are nods to a small but significant literature that has taken as its point of departure a critique of disembedded conceptualizations of the world economy as an abstract 'third space' located 'in between' significant locations. Desirous 'to introduce intellectual order and accountability into this newly dynamic space of gushingly unrestrained sentiments, pieties, and urgencies for which no adequately discriminating lexicon has had time to develop', this literature has sought to document and theorize transnational social structures 'sustained by social networks in migration and their attendant modes of social organization – home town associations, economic remittances, social clubs, celebrations and other bi-national social processes as well as by more indirect technological means of transportation and communication now available to facilitate the reproduction of transnational social fields such as jet airplanes, satellite dishes, telephone, faxes and e-mail.' For good accounts, see: Smith and Guarnizo (1998b); Robbins (1998, 9); and Smith and Guarnizo (1998a).

20 Ricardo Petrella, 'Le Retour des conquérants', *Monde Diplomatique*, cited in Georges Thill D'une dépendance globale à une solidarité planétaire responsable. *La Revue Nouvelle* 10 (October 1995), pp. 52–64; 55. On the same theme see Petrella (1994, 1996).

21 Anthony D. King documented the growing interest in 'globally-oriented urban research' in the second chapter of his *Global Cities* (1990). 'Global cities' are defined by Jan G. Lambooy as cities 'with functions that have a worldwide importance'. See *Global Cities and the World-Wide Economic System: Rivalry and Decision-Making*, Research Memorandum No. 8803, Department of Economics, University of Amsterdam (1987); Davis (1992); Anthony D. King *Urbanism, Colonialism and the World Economy: Cultural and Spatial Foundations of the World Urban System* (London: Routledge, 1990), p. 2; Saskia Sassen *The Global City: New-York, London, Tokyo* (Princeton: Princeton University Press 1993). On this, see also Magnusson (1996, 355, note 3).

22 A good early review of the literature can be found in Dear and Scott (1981). Patrick Geddes is usually credited with having popularized the term 'world cities', borrowed from the German *Weltstadt*, that came into common usage in the nineteenth century: see Geddes (1908). The founding text of the modern literature on 'world cities' is Friedmann and Wolff (1982). Friedman himself credits Manuel Castells and David Harvey for having linked 'city-forming processes to the larger historical movement of industrial capitalism' in Friedmann (1986). On this subject see also Clark (1996); Johnston (1994); King (1990); Knox (1995). On world cities as 'technopoles', see Castells and Hall (1994). On 'world cities' as nodal points, see Sassen (2000).

23 Vaneigem, cited in Sadler (1998, 16).

2 Three episodes from cities in the world economy

1 The citation is from Smith and Nash (1984 [1890], 24).

2 In the same spirit, see also Eric Hobsbawm on May Day processions in London, in Hobsbawm (1984).

3 For a succinct survey of social movements that gathered under the '50 years is enough' umbrella, see *New Internationalist*, No. 257, 'Squeezing the South', July 1994.

4 'The plus-system may be defined as a system of piece-work combined with time-work. Upon a ship's coming into dock, the dock superintendent takes her tonnage and calculates what it ought to cost to discharge her in a given time with a given number of men. The calculation is made on a basis of rates specifying so much money to the ton, and so many tons to the hours. ... The amount having been fixed, one of the dock company's officials engages the requisite number of men at a *minimum* wage of 5d an hour, it being understood that, if the work is done in a shorter time than calculated by the dock company, the unexhausted balance of the money, called *plus*, will be divided among the permanent workmen, the "Royals" as they are called, of whom there are a certain proportion to each gang'. 'The Dock Labourers Strike', *Illustrated London News*, 7 September 1889, p. 295. See also Lovell (1969, 94).

5 'The Strike of Dock Labourers', *The Times* (London), 23 August 1889, p. 6.

6 'The Great Strike Still Extending', *Pall Mall Gazette*, 27 August 1889. p. 1.

7 'The Dock Labourers' Strike', *The Times* (London), 21 August 1889, p. 9.

8 'According to Burns, "there were at the height of the stoppage as many as 3000 pickets in operation, some of them operating from boats on the river" (Lovell 1969, 107).

9 'The Strikes', *The Times* (London), 10 September 1889, pp. 3–4.

10 On the importance of strike-breakers in dock strikes in the 1850s and 1860s see Pattison (1966).

11 'Bombarding the dock gates meant that the leaders of the strikers, going off with different parties, went round in the early morning with bands and yelled in the hope, which was sometimes realized, of inducing those who were within to come out' (Ballhatchet 1991). On intimidation and violence on the pickets, see 'The Strikes at the East-End', *The Times* (London), 27 August 1889, p. 6.

12 'The Dock Labourers' Strike', *The Times* (London), 21 August 1889, p. 5.

13 'The Strikes at the East-End', *The Times* (London), 24 August 1889, p. 10.

14 'The Dock Labourers Strike', *Illustrated London News*, 7 September 1889, p. 295.

15 'The Great Strike', *Pall Mall Gazette*, 28 August 1889, p. 1.

16 On processions see also Robert (1996).

17 On this, see also Ballhatchet (1991).

18 'The Strikes', *The Times* (London), 4 September 1889, p. 7; Smith and Nash (1984 [1890]).

19 On the growing sense of community in the East End at the time of the dockworkers' strike, see Garside (1984); Ross (1983); and Savage and Miles (1994).

20 'The Strikes at the East-End', *The Times* (London) 24 August 1889, p. 10.

21 'The Strikes at the East-End' *The Times* (London), 26 August 1889, pp. 3–4.

22 'The Strikes', *The Times* (London), 6 September 1889, p. 4.

23 Oram, R.B. (1964, 538). A shorter version of this banner was reprinted in 'The Strikes', *The Times* (London), 10 September 1889, p. 3.

24 W.J. Fisherman, *East End 1888: Life in a London Borough among the Laboring Poor*, cited in Walkowitz (1992).

25 A good contemporary account of the riot is provided in Headly (1970 [1873]). See also Cook (1974).

26 Tammany retained native-style names for offices, titles and ceremonies until almost the end of the nineteenth century. Thus were masters of ceremonies called 'sagamores', doorkeepers 'wiskinskys', ordinary members 'braves' and members of the executive 'sachems', each responsible for a 'tribe' named for an American

mammal. Their leader was the 'Grand Sachem'. Until 1871 the President of the United States was known as the 'Kitchi Okemaw', or 'Great Grand Sachem'. In Tammany vernacular, states were animals (New York an eagle, Massachusetts a panther and so on), months were moons and seasons were of blossom, fruits, hunting and snow. Tammany's first 'Wigwam' was in the House of Talmadge Hall, then in various taverns: Barden's on Broadway, the City Tavern on Broad Street, Martling's at the Corner of Nassau: see Peel (1968 [1935]). In 1812 the Wigwam moved into its first dedicated building, at the corner of Nassau and Frankfort Street. In 1867 it moved uptown on fourteenth street, to a building it occupied until 1929: see Allen (1993b); Myers (1968 [1917]); Peel (1968 [1935]).

27 James Bryce's *The American Commonwealth*, cited in Hammack (1982).
28 Peel (1968 [1935]).
29 On anti-Semitism among New York's social *élites*, see Hammack (1982).
30 Callow (1976a).
31 DeForest and Veiller (1903), cited in Kenneth T. Jackson. The Capital of Capitalism: The New York Metropolitan Region, 1890–1940. In *Metropolis 1890–1940*, edited by A. Sutcliffe (Chicago, IL: The University of Chicago Press, 1984), p. 350.
32 For the complete text of the EAI announcement, see *Public Papers of the Presidents of the United States, George Bush: January 1 to June 30, 1990* (Washington: United States Government Printing Office, 1991), pp. 873–877.
33 Members of OQP included one neighbourhood committee (the *Comité populaire Saint-Jean Baptiste*), several student associations (the *Comité de mobilisation de l'Association étudiante du CEGEP de F-X Garneau*, the *Comité de mobilisation de l'Association étudiante du CEGEP de Saint-Foy*, the *Coalition de l'Université Laval sur le libre-échange dans les Amériques,*), Left parties and NGOs (the *Parti pour la Démocratie Socialiste, ATTAC*, the *Rassemblement pour une Alternative Populaire*, the *Parti Communiste du Québec, Alternatives*), locally based unions (the *Syndicat des Employés de la Fonction Publique*, the *Syndicats des professeurs du CEGEP de Sainte-Foy*) as well as solidarity NGOs (*Carrefour Tiers-Monde, Casa latino Americaine de Québec, Plan Nagua*).
34 n.d. (2001).
35 The defence of the security perimeter was, the police admitted, 'the largest police operation in Canadian history' (CIEPAC 1999); Samson (2000a, 2000b).
36 By itself the *Sureté du Québec* – only one of three police corps handling security at the Summit – fired more than 300 plastic bullets at individuals and 1,700 smoke bombs into the crowd (François Cardinal 'Pleins Gaz à Québec!', *Le Devoir* (26 April 2001), p. A2). At the time of writing, reports from other police corps had not yet been presented.
37 At the June 2000 camp, *formateurs* and *formatrices* were given a *Cahier de formation* as well as several thematic kits (on 'éducation et mondialisation', 'écologie et mondialisation', 'programmes sociaux', 'droits de la personne', 'femmes et mondialisation', 'droits du travail' and so on).
38 OQP 2001, 'Communiqué de Presse' (Opération Québec Printemps 2001).
39 It is a measure of the shortness of this history that Québec's bid to host the April 2001 Summit of the Americas was presented to the federal government in April 1999, six months before the Seattle WTO summit see Robert Fleury 'L'Allier nuance ses propos', *Le Soleil*, (27 March 2001), p. A3.
40 Citations are, in order, from Cockburn, St Clair and Sekula (2000), and Adam Sternbergh 'The Dirty Kids who Show up for the Gathering,' *This Magazine*, November/December 1998, pp. 28–31.
41 http://www.agp.org/agp/en/PGAInfos/bulletin2/bulletin2b.html.
42 NEFAC (2001); Philippis and Losson (2000).
43 Teamster leader James Hoffa Jr, cited in Cockburn *et al.* (2000). On 'the myth of Seattle', see: n.d. (2001); *Le Maquis*, (n.d., 3–4).

44 SalAMI (2000).

45 The *Manifeste contre le Sommet des Amériques et la Zone de libre-échange des Amériques* was made public on 20 March, a month before the summit. See Jean-Simon Gagné 'Sommet des Amériques: Un manifeste percutant contre la ZLÉA', *Le Soleil* (21 March 2001), p. A12.

46 Before Seattle, *The Economist* called for a 'fight for globalization' after it took to accusing protestors of having fomented it. See 'Countdown to Ruckus', *The Economist*, 4 December 1999, p. 26; 'The Battle in Seattle', *The Economist*, 27 November 1999, pp. 21–23.

47 A dozen protesters were kept in jail in the week that followed. Most notable was the CLAC's Jaggi Singh, who was, for seventeen days, Québec's Mumia Abu-Jamal. To support him and others, OQP and the CASA (now the *Comité d'adieu au Sommet des Amériques*) organized demonstrations at the Orsainville penitentiary in Charlesbourg and at the *Palais de Justice* in Lower Town, a short walk from the now-empty site of the People's Summit. On 1 May the CASA organized a support march for political prisoners that started at the Parc de l'Amérique française near the security perimeter and ended at the *Palais de Justice*.

48 Created in January 1889, the London and India Docks Joint Committee represented only two of five principal dock companies on the river, but it was the most important interlocutor of dockers: 'it cannot be said that up to the present time, the other dock companies have shown any noticeable inclination to follow any course other than that to which the Joint Committee have persistently, some say obstinately, adhered.' 'The Strikes', *The Times* (London), 5 September 1889, p. 3.

49 Since the beginning of the century, wharehousing fees had been the principal source of revenue for dock companies; see Pattison (1966); Lovell (1969).

50 'The Trade of the Dock', *The Times* (London), 2 September 1889, pp. 6, 9; 'The Dock Labourers' Strike', *The Times* (London), 21 August 1889, p. 9: 'The Dock Labourers' Strike', *The Times* (London), 22 August 1889, p. 4.

51 See also Lovell (1969, 43ff.).

52 Robson (1939), cited in Hall (1998, 700).

53 See also Garside (1984).

54 Charles Booth, cited in Stedman Jones (1971, 160). Lord Rosenbery, cited in Garside (1984).

55 By no means did the creation of the London County Council in 1888 simply pave the way to more instrumental governance of the city. In 1892 already, the Metropolitan Management Acts Amendment Bill reconstituted vestries as municipal councils (with mayors but no aldermen), thus restoring a measure of decentralization in London, and detracting from the importance and efficiency of the LCC as a political body. See Young and Garside (1982).

56 The 'No-Work Manifesto' is reprinted in the Annex of Henry Hyde Champion, *The Great Dock Strike, Social Science Series* (London: Swan Sonnenschein & Co, 1890), and in Appendix C of Smith and Nash (1984 [1890]).

57 'The Strikes', *The Times* (London), 2 September 1889, pp. 4–5.

58 *The Times* (London), 24 August 1889, p. 10.

59 Ballhatchet, Joan. (1991, 60).

60 'The Strikes', *The Times* (London), 31 August 1889, pp. 5–6.

61 'The Strikes', *The Times* (London), 31 August 1889, pp. 5–6.

62 'The Strikes', *The Times* (London), 3 September 1889, p. 4.

63 'The Strikes', *The Times* (London), 6 September 1889, p. 3.

64 'The Strikes', *The Times* (London), 6 September 1889, p. 4.

65 'The Strikes', *The Times* (London), 6 September 1889, p. 4.

66 'The Strikes', *The Times* (London), 7 September 1889, p. 6.

67 Champion (1890); see also 'The Strikes', *The Times* (London), 3 September 1889, p. 3; 'The Strikes', *The Times* (London), 7 September 1889, p. 6; 'The Strikes', *The*

Times (London), 10 September 1889, p. 4: 'The Strikes', *The Times* (London), 12 September 1889, p. 4.

68 'The Strikes', *The Times* (London), 4 September 1889, p. 4.

69 'The Strikes', *The Times* (London), 7 September 1889, p. 6.

70 'The Dock Labourers', *Illustrated London News*, No. 2629, Vol. xcv, 28 September 1889, p. 394.

71 The expression 'Friendly visitor' takes its name from M. Richmond's *Friendly Visiting Among the Poor* (1863), a Charity Organization Society manual that encouraged visitors to visit poor neighbourhoods, 'simply to establish a human tie across the barriers of class, religion, and nationality'. Cited in Boyer (1994). On later political travails of the Charity Organization movement, see Lui (1995).

72 The Women's Municipal League, for instance, which was formed in 1894 at the inception of Reverend Parkhurst, deliberately stayed away from 'the old "dirty" business'. 'The new "clean" arena of non-partisan work on city problems was, [the League] asserted, women's territory as well as that of progressive-minded men.' (Monoson 1990, 101).

73 Jacob Riis 'The Battle with the Slums', *Atlantic Monthly* (May 1899), cited in Boyer (1994).

74 The first elevated railroad opened in the 1870s, but the consolidation of the public transport system in New York did not begin in earnest until the Sixth Avenue 'El' opened in 1877. The Third Avenue 'El' opened a year later, and the Second and Ninth Avenue 'El's' in 1880; see Brooks (1997); Lockwood (1976).

75 Parkhurst (1970 [1895]). On the distinction between moral/social reform and structural reform see Holli, (1976).

76 Schlesinger (1983). See also Schlesinger, *The Rise of the City*, cited in Stern *et al.* (1983, 17).

77 John DeWitt Warner *et al.*, 'Matters that Suggest Themselves', *Municipal Affairs*, 2 March 1898, cited in Stern, *et al.* (1983, 27).

78 'The Seventy Ready for Work', *New York Times*, 20 September 1894, p. 9.

79 Parkhurst, cited in Todd (1993).

80 'See a Charm in Seventy', *New York Times*, 7 September 1894, p. 1.

81 'The Conferences have Begun: Good Government Clubs Delegates meet the Seventy men', *New York Times*, 22 September 1894, p. 9.

82 'Strong', *New York Times*, 7 November 1894, p. 1.

83 Stern *et al.* (1983).

84 At the time of writing, details of DFAIT events could still be found at http://www.holaquebec.ca. In the spirit of inter-agency collaboration the *Institut* also served as a DFAIT temp agency, recruiting *agents et agentes de liaison* and other support staff for the Summit of the Americas, and it was host to several Summit officials, including (three times) Marc Lortie, the Prime Minister's sherpa. A press release detailing the conclusions of the colloquium may be found at the Institut's website: http://www.ulaval.ca/scom/Communiques.de.presse/2001/avril/IQHEIzlea.

85 Founded in 1994, the RQIC is under the hegemonic guidance of Québec's main union confederations (the *Confédération des Syndicat Nationaux*, the *Centrale des enseignants du Québec* and the *Fédération des travailleurs et travailleuses du Québec*). Its membership also includes another, much smaller, union confederation (the *Centrale des syndicats du Québec*,), union-made or union-funded NGOs (most notably the *Centre international de solidarité ouvrière* and *Solidarité populaire Québec*), a professional appendage of the union movement (the *Association canadienne des avocats du mouvement syndical*), two state-funded NGOs (the *Association québécoise des organismes de coopération internationale* and the *Fédération des femmes du Québec*) and two research centres based in Montréal

universities that are also close to unions (McGill's *Centre d'études sur les régions en développement* and UQUAM's RQIC).

86 About 'protest pits' and anti-summit movements, see Cockburn *et al.* (2000, 19).
87 Matthew Arnold, cited in Stedman Jones (1971, 241).
88 Shawn Desmond, *London Nights of Long Ago* (London, 1927), cited in Stedman Jones (1974).

3 Occupying places in the world economy

1 Van Hoolthon and van der Linden, 'Introduction' (1988, vii). On the beginning of 'anti-systemic social movements', see Immanuel Wallerstein, 'Antisystemic Movements: History and Dilemmas', in Samir Amin, Giovanni Arrighi, Andre Gunder Frank and Immanuel Wallerstein, *Transforming the Revolution: Social Movements and the World-System.* (New York: Monthly Review Press, 1990).
2 Marx's instructions to delegates at the Geneva Congress of the First International in 1866, cited in van Hoolthon and van der Linden. (1988, 124).
3 See also Harvey (1985).
4 *Third Annual Report of the IWMA*, cited in D.E. DeVreese (1988, 286). Marx, cited in the 'Provisional Rules of the Association', in K. Marx and F. Engels, *Collected Works*, Vol. 20 (New York: International Publishers, 1975).
5 Wilhelm Eichhoff, 'The International Working Men's Association; Its Establishment, Organisation, Political and Social Activity, and Growth', Reprinted in Marx and Engels (1975, Vol. 21, 322–380).
6 Karl Marx 'Letter to Abraham Lincoln, President of the United States of America', 22–29 November 1864, *MEW* (New York: International Publishers, 1975), Vol. 20, 19–21.
7 Cited from a letter by Isabella M.S. Todd to Susan B. Anthony (an ICW founding member), 17 February 1884, in Regine Deutsch, *The International Woman Suffrage Alliance: its History from 1904 to 1929* (London: no publisher, 1929), International Informatiecentrum en archief voor de Vrouwenbeweging, Amsterdam, p.21. Louise C.A. van Eeghen. 1938. *The Spirit and Work of the I.C.W.* Aberdeen: International Council of Women, p. 4.
8 Ministère du Commerce, de l'Industrie des Postes et des Télégraphes, *Congrès international de la condition et des droits des femmes tenu à Paris du 5 au 8 Septembre 1900* (Paris: Imprimerie Nationale, 1901).
9 Bureau International du Travail, *La règlementation du travail féminin* (Genève, série 'Études et Documents', 1931, No. 2).
10 Emma Goldman, draft for 'The Tragic Plight of the Political Exile', IISH archives, Amsterdam 2012–2103, II/6.
11 The anti-slavery campaign is discussed in Chapter 2 of Keck and Sikkink (1998), along with three other case studies of 'historical precursors to modern Transnational Advocacy Networks': 'the efforts of the international suffrage movement to secure the vote for women between 1888 and 1928, the campaign from 1874 to 1911 by Western missionaries and Chinese reformers to eradicate footbinding in China, and efforts by Western missionaries and British Colonial authorities to end the practice of female circumcision among the Kikuyu of Kenya in 1920–1931.'
12 Baldemar Velasquez, President of the U.S. Farm Labour Organizing Committee, speaking of labour's response to NAFTA. Quoted in Alexander and Gilmore (1994).
13 ICEM Update 13 December 1996: http://www.icem.org/update/upd1996/upd-96–76.html.
14 Details are given in the USWA's report 'One Day Longer. The Road to Victory at Bridgestone/Firestone' at: http://www.uswa.org/news/bridgestone.html.

15 ICEM Update 10 October 1996: http://www.icem.org/update/upd1996/upd-96–57.html.

16 '[P]attern bargaining means that companies in the sector have similar wage and benefits packages and compete on the basis of product quality and productivity rather than solely on the basis of labour costs. Bridgestone was the last of several tyre multinationals to try to break this system' (ICEM Update, 7 November 7 1996): http://www.icem.org/update/upd1996/upd96–70.html.

17 *Karoshi* was discussed, for instance, at a Japan–Korea joint seminar on occupation safety and health, sponsored by Japan's Occupational Safety and Health Resource Center, and the Korea Worker's Safety Research Association held 22–23 July 1995 at Akira, Suziki in 1995. Japan and Korea Joint Seminar on Labor and Health: *APWSL/Japan (Newsletter From Japan Committee of Asian Pacific Worker's Solidarity Links)*, November, p. 5.

18 On the *Lunafil* campaign, see also 'Solidarity Success Stories', in *Horizon* (Nanaimo: Global Village, September 1992), Vol. 8, No. 7, p. 5.

19 For details of the *Camisas* campaign, see: http://www.uaw.org/breaktime/news_to_you/Guatemala.html.

20 An excellent starting point to document brand name campaigns is the Campaign for Labor Rights' online 'Documents Library': http://www.summersault.com/~agj/clr/doc_lib.html.

21 Details of campaigns against GAP, Guess, Nike and Reebok may be found on the CLR's website (http://www.summersault.com/~agj/clr/alerts/). A significant player in the GAP campaign was the Global Survival Network (www.globalsurvival.net). The anti-GE campaign (1991–1993) was motivated by the company's involvement in nuclear weaponry and organized by the Methodist Federation for Social Action. For details, see Methodist Federation for Social Action (1993). The Mitsubishi campaign was led by Rainforest Action Network (http://www.ran.org/ran). On the Suzuki campaign, see Yoko (1998).

22 Cockburn *et al.* (2000, 73).

23 The only offshore export zone in the USA, Saipan does not have to abide by federal labour standards. Producers installed there pay no US import tariffs, face no quota restrictions and benefit from lax immigration laws. Over 90 per cent of garment industry jobs in the Marianas are held by 'guest workers', mostly from China, the Philippines, Bangladesh and Thailand; see Ellison (1998). See also Campaign for Labor Rights Action Alerts, 29 July 1999: http://www.summersault.com/~agj/clr/alerts/gapcampaignupdate.html#5

24 ICEM Update 6 February 1996: http://www.icem.org/update/upd1996/upd-96–1.html.

25 Of interest here is the work of the International Network Against Female Sexual Slavery and Traffic in Women (INFSSTW) and of The Global Alliance Against Traffic in Women (GAATW). On the campaign to protect the rights of workers in the sex trade see: http://www.monde-diplomatique.fr/1997/03/LOUIS/8027.html.

26 'Big-Honkin' Radical Anti-Assimilationist Terrorist Super-Queer' (BRATS) cited in Tim Davis, The Diversity of Queer Politics and the Redefinition of Sexual Identity and Community in Urban Spaces. In *Mapping Desire*, edited by David Bell and Gill Valentine (New York: Routledge, 1995).

27 Marx's letter to Lafargue, 19 April 1870, quoted in Labande (1976). My translation.

28 TSMOs are Transnational Social Movement Organizations, especially concerned to 'facilitate and routinize communication, consultation, coordination and cooperation among its members' (Pagnucco and Atwood 1994).

29 In 1991 and 1992, for instance, the ICCSASW organized solidarity campaigns in the Philippines, Nicaragua, the Dominican Republic, Brazil, Haiti, Canada and Thailand (ICCSASW 1991, 1992). In 1993, the ICCSASW campaigned on behalf

of Nicaraguan sugar workers against the privatization of sugar refineries and defended the rights of Dominican and Haitian cane-cutters to organize unions. See *Sugar World: A Newsletter on Issues of Concern to Sugar Workers*, Vol. 16, nos 2, 3 (March and May 1993).

30 'Proposal for action: US–Mexico–Canada Labor Solidarity Network Submitted by United Electrical Workers (UE) of US and the *Frente Auténtico del Trabajo* of Mexico', quoted in Barry Carr, Labor Internationalism in the Era of NAFTA: Past and Present. In *Labor, Free Trade and Economic Integration in the Americas: National Labor Union Responses to a Transnational World*, edited by John D. French and Russell E. Smith (Durham, NC: Duke University Press, 1994) Paper presented at the 'Labor, Free Trade and Economic Integration in the Americas' conference', 25–27 August, at Duke University. See also Moody (1995).

31 http://www.igc.org/unitedelect/#About Alliance.

32 On this subject, see Allen (1993); also Jeroen Peijnenberg, 'Workers in Trans-national Corporations: Meeting the Corporate Challenge' (pp. 108–120) and Werner Olle and Wolfgang Schoeller, 'World Market Competition and Restrictions Upon International Trade Union Policies', (pp. 39–58), both in Peter Waterman, *For A New Labour Internationalism: A Set of Reprints and Working Papers* (Birmingham: Third World Publications, with the International Labour Education, Research and Information Foundation, 1984).

33 The first WCCs were created in 1966 by the United Automobile, Aerospace and Agricultural Implement Workers of America (UAW), in co-operation with the International Metalworkers' Federation (IMF) and the ICFTU: the General Motor WCC, the Ford WCC and the Chrysler WCC. All three were based in Detroit. In 1967, the International Harvester WCC (Geneva) became the first non-American WCC, followed by the Philips WCC (Brussels). See Herod (1995b).

34 Quoted from 'Global Exchange Reality Tours', at: http://www.globalexchange.-org/tours/.

35 http://www.igc.org/unitedelect/#About Alliance.

36 http://www.inet.co.th/org/gaatw/activity.htm.

37 See also: http://www.icem.org/networks/bridge/july12.html.

38 http://www.summersault.com/~agj/clr/index.html.

39 http://www.icem.org/networks/bridge/july12us.html.

40 http://www.icem.org/networks/bridge/justice.html.

41 http://www.icem.org/networks/bridge/july10.html.

42 http://www.icem.org/networks/bridge/july15.html.

43 http://www.summersault.com/~agj/clr/index.html.

44 http://www.summersault.com/~agj/clr/alerts/pvhleafletingplans.html.

45 http://www.summersault.com/~agj/clr/alerts/gapcampaignupdate.html.

46 E-mail from juliette@globalexchange.org.

47 http://www.igc.org/igc/ln/hl/99061028056/hl5.html;http://www.igc.org/igc/wn/aa/99050315981/aa2.html.

48 http://www.summersault.com/~agj/clr/alerts/nike_campus_activism.html.

49 For a good factual presentation of the birth of PP21, see 'Will the future be ours? We Propose a People's Plan for the 21st century', *AMPO: Japan-Asia Quarterly Review* 20, (1 and 2): 3–13.

50 Sampled from accounts of actions posted on the PGA site at: http://www.agp.org/agp/en/PGAInfos/bulletin2/bulletin2b.html.

51 http://www.alternatives.ca/salami/.

52 See also Maquila Solidarity Network (n.d.).

4 The civic ordering of global social relations

1 *La production de l'espace* (1974), cited in Harvey (1985).

2 On the IMF's call for a more 'pluralist' policy outlook, see e.g. *IMF Survey*, 2 February 1982. In like spirit, the Joint Statement issued at the end of the June 1982 meeting of the G7 in Versailles called for a renewed convergence of national economic policies, not on the basis of monetary targeting but for 'renewed growth' and 'the cooperative stimulation of employment'. See *IMF Survey*, 21 June 1982, pp. 177–189. On renewed calls for pluralism and discretion in monetary policy, see also BIS, *Fifty-Third Annual Report*, June 1983.

3 *Shaping the 21st century: The Contribution of Development-Co-operation*, report adopted at the DAC High Level Meeting of 6–7-May 1996 and endorsed by the OECD Council, May 1996.

4 Michel Camdessus, 'Opening Adddress', in *Central and Eastern Europe: Roads to Growth* (Washington: International Monetary Fund and the Austrian National Bank, 1992, p. 16). With this address, Camdessus opened a seminar on 'Central and Eastern Europe: Roads to Growth' organized jointly by the Austrian National Bank and the IMF. The seminar was held at Baden, Austria in April 1991.

5 On monads as 'fragment[s] within which the totality . . . may be discerned', see Gilloch (1996).

6 In the apolitical language of contemporary cosmopolitanism, the 'third sector' is a residual category of sorts, where are tossed all non-profit or non-governmental organizations ('neither prince nor merchant'), regardless of political orientation, class origin, project, resources, influence, affiliation, position in the world economy and so on. For a good example of a recent text celebrating the emergence of such an undifferentiated and underconceptualized whole, see Oliveira and Tandon (1994).

7 Cited in Interim Committee to Consultative Non-Governmental Organizations (1948 [1978]).

8 Quoted from Article 71 of the UN Charter (on 'Arrangements for Consultation with Non-Governmental Organizations'), by Gordenker and Weiss (1996).

9 A well-known exception was the International Labour Organization, which placed non-governmental representatives of employers and employees on an equal footing with governmental representatives. Interim Committee to Consultative Non-Governmental Organizations (1948 [1978]), 15.

10 The International Labour Assistance (ILA, 1951) has distant historical roots in the 'International Fund to Help the Labour Movement in Countries without Democracy', created in 1926 and nicknamed 'the Matteotti' in honour of Italian Socialist Giacomo Matteotti. More directly, the ILA was born of the 'Refugee Subcommittee' created in 1946 by the COMISCO (Committee of the International Socialist Conference) to support families of imprisoned and displaced socialist refugees. In 1950, the 'Refugee Subcommittee' was renamed the International Socialist Assistance (ISA). The ISA had a broader mandate than the Refugee Subcommittee and worked both to help displaced socialist workers (especially Spanish workers exiled by Franco) and to promote democratic socialism everywhere. In 1951, the ISA joined ECOSOC, UNICEF and UNESCO. It was then renamed the ILA, to reflect its mandate to help workers regardless of their political affiliation. See Julius Braunthal, The International Labour Assistance and the Socialist International. Bulletin Périodique (Entraide Ouvrière Internationale) (1952) 17: 3.

11 Translated from Lévy (1983); see also Malonew (1984).

12 So unimportant, in fact, were NGOs to the structuring of power in this period that when Robert Keohane and Joseph Nye published *Transnational Relations and World Politic*, a book concerned explicitly with emerging transnational relations beyond the realm of inter-state politics, transnational NGOs were relegated to a few marginal chapters, far from the more consequential 'Issues' chapters.

13 Donini (1995).

14 The official estimate was 6,000: http://www.idt.unit.no/~isfit/human.rights/fn.-konferanse.rapport.

15 As well as specific sources quoted, figures for NGO participation in UN global conferences were drawn from the following: Chase *et al.* (1994); Chen (1996). Conca (1995); Fisher (1993); Gordenker and Weiss (1996); UNCHS (1997a, 1997b).

16 For most intents and purposes, *chantiers* are 'building sites'. In the context of governance, however, *chantier* is a more appropriate term than its English near-equivalent, inasmuch as it evokes more readily not just the *on-site* social frame-work being erected – competently evoked by 'building site' – but also dynamics *outside* the building site itself. Famously, the Vichy regime used the term in this sense when it put together its mandatory work programme for youth in 1940: the *Chantiers de jeunesse*. See Alain Rey, *Dictionnaire historique de la langue française* (2 vols). Vol. I (Paris: Dictionnaires Le Robert, 1993).

17 Judith Randel, 'Aid, the Military and Humanitarian Assistance: An Attempt to Identify Recent Trends' in *Journal of International Development* (1994), 6 (3): 336, cited in Gordenker and Weiss (1996).

18 See also http://www.nsrc.org/AFRICA/KE/providers/elci.html.

19 On the crisis of the IMF, see Richard E. Feinberg and Catherine Gwin, 'Reform-ing the Fund'. In *The International Monetary Fund in a Multipolar World: Pulling Together*, edited by Catherine Gwin *et al.* (Washington, DC: Overseas Develop-ment Council, 1989). See also Richard E. Feinberg, *Between Two Worlds: The World Bank's Next Decade* (New York, Transaction Books 1986).

20 See Kenen (1989, 69). On the changing relationship between The World Bank and developing countries, and on the Social Dimensions of Adjustment programme, administered by The World Bank in co-operation with the United Nations Devel-opment Programme, see Banque Mondiale, *Obtenir des résultats: Ce que la Banque Mondiale veut faire pour mieux agir sur le développement* (Washington, DC: The World Bank, 1993). On SDA see also *Making Adjustment Work for the Poor* (Washington, DC: The World Bank, 1990).

21 The World Bank (1996b); see also The SDA Steering Committee, 'The Social Dimensions of Adjustment Program: A General Assessment' (Washington, DC: The World Bank. Human Resources and Poverty Division, Technical Department, Africa Region, 1993).

22 http://www.worldbank.org/html/gef/gef.htm.

23 See also Joan M. Nelson, 'The Politics of Pro-Poor Adjustment'. In *Fragile Coali-tions: The Politics of Economic Adjustment* (Washington, DC: Overseas Develop-ment Council, 1989).

24 http://www.oecd.org/dac/htm/pubs/p-pdggev.htm.

25 A year after the Rio Summit, the World Economic Forum decided to 'limit its activities to members and to their special guests only . . . in order to reinforce the club character of its network' (The World Economic Forum's *Timeline* http://www.weforum.org/the_foundation/history/). This decision was reversed at the beginning of the 1990s. In governance fashion, the latest forums have been both more closed to 'anti-globalization' activists, and more open to selected guests (as well as more conscious of global attention: to spruce up its image the Forum has hired Bennetton publicist Oliviero Toscani). In 2001, Lori Wallach, Director of Global Tradewatch and a key figure of Seattle protests, addressed WEF delegates at the personal invitation of the Forum's founder Klaus Schwab. See Hazan (2001); Pénicaut and Dutilleux (2001). After Seattle, an NGO ombudsman was created at the World Trade Organization: see Chossudovsky (2000).

26 Donini (1995); 'The Non-governmental Order', *The Economist*, 11 December 1999, pp. 20–21.

27 'The Non-governmental Order', *The Economist*, 11 December 1999, pp. 20–21.

28 http://www.globalpolicy.org/visitctr/about.htm. See also Jeffrey Segall (ed.), *United Nations and United Peoples Partnership for Peace* (London: CAMDUN, 1995).

29 Geneva Business declaration, cited in Freitag and Pineault (1999, 91).

30 Participation and NGO Group (1996).

31 At the moment of writing, the conference website was still active: www.idc.org/gmg.

32 About the OAS's turn to participatory development, see OAS, *Inter-American Strategy for Public Participation in Environment and Sustainable Development: Decision Making in the Americas* (Washington, DC: Organization of American States, 1996).

33 The Santiago Plan of Action designated the OAS as a privileged forum for 'the exchange of experience and information amongst civil society organizations'; see Organization of American States, *Work Plan of the Unit for the Promotion of Democracy*, cited in Guy Gosselin and Jean-Philippe Thérien, 'The Organization of American States and Hemispheric Regionalism'. In *The Americas in Transition: The Contours of Regionalism*, edited by Gordon Mace and Luyis Bélanger (Boulder, Co: Lynne Rienner, 1999), pp. 175–193.

34 See http://www.civil-society.oas.org.

35 The document is available at http://www.summit-americas.org/documents.

36 Comité de représentants gouvernementaux sur la participation de la société civile, 'Invitation ouverte à la société civile dans les pays de la ZLÉA' (http://www.ftaa-alca.org/spcomm/soc2_f.asp, 2000).

37 Translated from http://www.holaquebec.ca/bienvenue/intro_e.htlm.

38 Robinson (1992). On the São Paulo Forum, see also 'Left to Start Work on Alternative: Sao Pãulo Forum Offers Few Hints Regarding Content', *Latin America Weekly Report*, 15 June 1995, pp. 258–259; Raul Ronzoni, 'Latin America: The Left Meets to Discuss its Role and Integration', *Inter Press Service*, 25 May 1995.

39 BBC Summary of World Broadcasts, Wednesday, 31 May 1995.

40 Chossudovsky (2000). According to Julio Turra of the United Workers' Federation of Brazil, 'the whole idea of incorporating social clauses or social charters into these "free trade" pacts ... was really projected at the 1995 Social Summit in Copenhagen. The goal of integrating trade unions internationally into the whole apparatus of globalization was made explicit at that summit' ('Leader of the Brazilian United Workers' Federation (CUT) describes labour summit organized to respond to the extension of NAFTA throughout the Americas': http://www.igc.apc.org/workers/cut.html.

41 Alliance for Responsible Trade *et al.* (1998).

42 ADB Group, 'Poverty Alleviation Guidelines': http://www.afdb.org/about/oesu/povertyallev.html/.

43 ADB Group, 'Environment and Sustainable Development Unit Overview OESU's Mandate and Functions': http://www.afdb.org/about/oesu-overview.html.

44 ADB Group, 'Environment and Sustainable Development Unit, The Environmental Resource Center (ERC)': http://www.afdb.org/about/oesu-overview.html.

45 http://www.ces.eu.int/en/acs/forum/conclusions_123_EN.htm/;http://www.ces.eu.int/en/docs/docs_opinions/CES851–1999_AC_en.DOC/.

46 http://www.ces.eu.int/en/acs/forum/conclusions_123_EN.htm/.

47 Quotes from ADRA's Global Village Site, housed on The World Bank's server, at: http://www.worldbank.org/html/extdr/gvillage/default.htm.

48 Pénicaut (2001). About global benchmarking, 'a system of continuous improvements derived from systematic comparisons with world best practice'; see Sklair (2001).

49 'Revolutions are not made of revolution-making, but of problem-solving' (my translation) (Le Corbusier (1994 [1925], 284).

50 Cited in Hofstadter (1959).
51 Debord (1988).

5 Integrated world creation: outlines of a radical articulation

1 'Pour un jugement révolutionnaire de l'art', cited in Levin (1989, 101).
2 Ralph Miliband, *Marxism and Politics*, cited in Marston (1989, 256).
3 Sadler (1998), quoting Khatib (1958).
4 Document of the Seventh IS Conference 1966 'Minimum Definition of Revolutionary Organizations', cited in Bracken (1997, 124).
5 Wallerstein (1989 [1968]).
6 Thompson (1982). On IS's position, see also IS (1962).
7 Ralph Miliband, *Marxism and Politics*, cited in Marston, Sallie A. (1989, 256).
8 Sartre spoke of 'fused groups' as bundles of serialized individuals united by specific circumstances and particular struggles that form the raw material of class spontaneity. See Sartre (1970).
9 Klein (2000a, 2000b).
10 Michel de Certeau, *L'invention du quotidien: 1. arts de faire*. Vol. 146, *Folio/essais* (Paris: Gallimard, 1990).
11 Sadler (1998, 17).
12 The reference here is to the *Internationale Lettriste*, a precursor of the *Internationale Situationniste*.

Conclusion

1 Ramphal (1997).
2 On this subject, see the excellent study by Taylor (1995).
3 Cited in David McNally, *Another World is Possible: Globalization and Anticapitalism* (Winnipeg: Arbeiter Ring, 2002, p. 17).

Bibliography

Adam, Barry D. 1987. *The Rise of a Gay and Lesbian Movement*. Boston: Twayne Publishers.

ADB. n.d. *ADB and NGOs: Working Together*. Manila: Asian Development Bank.

Akira, Matsui. 1995a. Don't Buy Reebok: Support for Dismissed Filipino Workers. *APWSL/Japan (Newsletter From Japan Committee of Asian Pacific Workers' Solidarity Links)*, April: 2–4.

Akira, Suziki. 1995b. Japan and Korea Joint Seminar on Labor and Health Held. *APWSL/Japan (Newsletter From Japan Committee of Asian Pacific Workers' Solidarity Links)*, November: 5.

Alexander, Robin, and Peter Gilmore. 1994. The Emergence of Cross-Border Labor Solidarity. *NACLA Report on the Americas* 28 (1 (July–August)): 42–48.

Allen, Michael. 1993. Wordly Wisdom. *New Statesman and Society*, 21 May: xii–xiii.

Allen, Oliver E. 1993. *The Tiger: The Rise and Fall of Tammany Hall*. New York: Addison-Wesley.

Alliance for Responsible Trade *et al.* 1998. Alternatives for the Americas: Building a People's Hemispheric Agreement.

Amoore, L. *et al.* 1997. Overturning 'Globalisation': Resisting the Teleological, Reclaiming the Political. *New Political Economy* 2 (1).

Anderson, Perry. 2002. Internationalism: A Breviary. *New Left Review* (Second series) 14 (March–April): 5–25.

Andersen, Troels. 1989. Asger Jorn and the Situationist International. In *On the Passage of a Few People Through a Rather Brief Moment in Time: The Situationist International, 1957–1972*, edited by E. Sussman. Cambridge/Boston: The MIT Press/The Institute of Contemporary Art.

APSWL-Japan. 1994. Japanese Report: Migrant Workers and their Rights. *APSWL/Japan (Newsletter from Japan Committee of APWSL)*, September: 3–10.

Archibugi, Daniele. 1993. The Reform of the UN and Cosmopolitan Democracy: A Critical Review. *Journal of Peace Research* 30 (10): 301–315.

Archibugi, Daniele, and David Held (eds). 1995. *Cosmopolitan Democracy: An Agenda for a New World Order*. London: Polity Press.

Arroyo, Alberto P., and Mario B. Monroy. 1996. *Red Mexicana de Accion Frente al Libre Comercio: 5 anos de lucha (1991–1996)*. Mexico: RMALC.

Artaud, Antonin. 1979. Surréalisme et révolution. In *Messages révolutionnaires*, edited by A. Artaud. Paris: Gallimard.

Auclair, Christine. 1997. Local Urban Observatories: Tailoring Indicators to Local Needs. *UNCHS: Habitat Debate*, March, 1: 4–5.

Ballhatchet, Joan. 1991. The Police and the London Dock Strike of 1889. *History Workshop Journal* 32 (autumn 1991): 54–68.

Barlow, Maude. 1993. Message from the National Chair. *Canadian Perspectives, Ottawa, Council of Canadians* (autumn): 1.

Barthes, R. 1964. Éléments de sémiologie. *Communications* 4: 91–135.

Beck, Ulrich. 1999. *World Risk Society*. Cambridge: Polity Press.

Beck, Ulrich. 2000. *What is Globalization?* Cambridge: Polity Press.

Beckford, James. 2000. Religious Movements and Globalization. In *Global Social Movements*, edited by R. Cohen and S. M. Rai. London: The Athlone Press.

Beckmann, David. 1991. Recent Experiences and Emerging Trends. In *Nongovernmental Organizations and the World Bank: Cooperation for Development*, edited by S. Paul and A. Israel. Washington, DC: The World Bank.

Beigbeder, Yves. 1992. *Le rôle international des organisations non gouvernementales, Axes*. Paris: Librairie générale de droit et de jurisprudence.

Benjamin, Walter. 1973. Thesis on the Philosophy of History. In *Illuminations*, edited by H. Arendt. London: Fontana.

Benjamin, Walter. 1993. *Paris, capitale du XIXe siècle (Le livre des passages)*, translated by Jean Lacoste. Paris: Cerf.

Benjamin, Walter. 1998. *Images de pensées*, translated by Jean-François Poirier and Jean Lacoste, *Détroits*. Paris: Christian Bourgeois.

Berger, John. 1968. The Nature of Mass Demonstrations. *New Society*, 23 May: 754–755.

Bernstein, Michèle. 1964. The Situationist International. *Times Literary Supplement*, 3 September: 781.

Beyer, Paul. 1994. *Religion and Globalization*. London: Sage.

Boorman, John T. 1992. A View From the IMF. In *Policies for African Development*, edited by I. G. Patel. Washington, DC: IMF.

Bourdieu, Pierre, and J-C. Passeron. 1977. *Reproduction in Education, Society and Culture*. London: Sage.

Bourseiller, Christophe. 2001. Aux origines de Mai '68. *Magazine Littéraire*, June: 42–44.

Boutros-Ghali, Boutros. 1996. Foreword. In *NGOs, The UN, and Global Governance*, edited by T. G. Weiss and L. Gordenker. Boulder, Co: Lynne Rienner.

Boyer, M. Christine. 1994. *Dreaming the Rational City: The Myth of American City Planning*. Cambridge, MA: The MIT Press.

Boyer, M. Christine. 1996. *The City of Collective Memory: Its Historical Imagery and Architectural Entertainment*. Cambridge, MA: MIT Press.

Boyer, M. Christine. 1997. *Cybercities: Visual Perception in the Age of Electronic Communication*. New York: Princeton Architectural Press.

Boyer, Paul. 1978. *Urban Masses and Moral Order in America, 1820–1920*. Cambridge, MA: Harvard University Press.

Boyer, Robert. 1986. *La théorie de la régulation: une analyse critique*. Paris: Agalma/La Découverte.

Bracken, Len. 1997. *Guy Debord Revolutionary*. Venice, CA: Feral House.

Braudel, Fernand. 1979. *Civilisation matérielle, économie et capitalisme XVème–XVIIème siècle*, 3 vols. *Vol. III. Le temps du monde*. Paris: Armand Colin.

Braudel, Fernand. 1985. *Une leçon d'histoire de Fernand Braudel*. Paris: Arthaud-Flammarion.

Braunthal, Julius. 1967. *History of the International (1914–1943)*, translated by Henry Collins, and Kenneth Mitchell. Vol. 2. New York: Frederick A. Praeger.

Brecher, Jeremy, and Tim Costello. 1991a. Labor Goes Global II: A One World Strategy for Labor. *Z Magazine*, March: 90–97.

Brecher, Jeremy, and Tim Costello. 1991b. Labor Goes Global I: Global Village vs. Global Pillage. *Z Magazine*, January: 90–97.

Brenke, Siefried. 1992. The Role of Cities in Sustainable Development: A Call for New Partnership. In *Cities and New Technologies*, edited by OECD. Paris: OECD.

Breton, André. 1952. *Entretiens 1913–1952*. Paris: Gallimard.

Breyman, Steve. 1994. Movements Rising in the West. *Peace Review* 6 (4): 403–409.

Brock, Edwin A. 1955. *Representation of Non-Governmental Organizations at the United Nations, Public Administration Clearing House*. n.a.

Brooks, Michael W. 1997. *Subway City: Riding the Trains, Reading New York*. New Brunswick: Rutgers University Press.

Bunch, Charlotte. 1993. Organizing for Women's Human Rights Globally. In *Ours by Right: Women's Rights as Human Rights*, edited by J. Kerr. London: Zed Books.

Burgerman, Susan D. 1998. Mobilizing Principles: The Role of Transnational Activists in Promoting Human Rights Principles. *Human Rights Quarterly* 20 (4): 905–923.

Burnham, Peter. 1991. Neo-Gramscian Hegemony and International Order. *Capital and Class 45* (autumn): 73–93.

Burns, Elaine. 1991. Clothing the World. *Correspondencia* (autumn): 4–9.

Buxton, Sydney. 1890. Introduction. In *The Story of the Dockers' Strike Told by Two East Londoners*, edited by H. L. S. V. Nash. London: T. Fisher Unwin.

Callow, Alexander B. 1976a. Commentary. In *The City Boss in America*, edited by A. B. Callow. New York: Oxford University Press.

Callow, Alexander B. 1976b. The Crusade Against the Tweed Ring. In *The City Boss in America*, edited by A. B. Callow. New York: Oxford University Press.

Camargo, José Marcio. 1995. Rio de Janeiro: Natural Beauty as a Public Good. In *Towards A Sustainable Urban Environment: The Rio de Janiero Study*, edited by A. Kreimer, T. Lobo, B. Menezes, M. Munasinghe, R. Parker, and M. Preece. Washington, DC: The International Bank for Reconstruction and Development.

Canadian Center for Policy Alternatives. 1992a. *Which Way for the Americas: Analysis of NAFTA Proposals and the Impact on Canada*. Ottawa: CCPA.

Canadian Center for Policy Alternatives. 1992b. *Document 14(Selected Documents). Popular Sector Organizations and Trade: A Report to the Ministry of Industry. Trade and Technology, Government of Ontario*. Ottawa: CCPA.

Canel, Eduardo, 1992. New Social Movement Theory. In *Organizing Dissent: Contemporary Social Movements in Theory and in Practice*, edited by W. Carroll Toronto: Garamond.

Carr, Barry. 1994. Labor Internationalism in the Era of NAFTA: Past and Present. Paper read at Labor, Free Trade and Economic Integration in the Americas: National Labor Union Responses to a Transnational World, 25–27 August, at Duke University.

Carrillo, Fernando. 1996. Governance: The Region's Next Challenge. *The IDB (Inter-American Development Bank)*, November: 3.

Cassani, Robert. 1995. Financing Civil Society for a Global Responsibility. *Futures* 27 (March): 215–221.

Castells, Manuel. 1983. *The City and the Grassroots: A Cross-Cultural Theory of Urban Social Movements*. Berkeley, CA: Edward Arnold.

Castells, Manuel. 1996. *The Rise of the Network Society, The Information Age: Economy, Society and Culture*. Oxford: Blackwell.

Castells, Manuel, and Peter Hall. 1994. *Technopoles of the World: The Making of 21st Century Industrial Complexes*. London: Routledge.

Cernea, Michael M. 1988. *Nongovernmental Organizations and Local Development*. Washington, DC: The World Bank.

Céspedes, Roberto. 1994. El Movimiento Sindical Paraguayo Frente al Mercosur. Paper read at Labor, Free Trade and Economic Integration in the Americas: National Labor Union Responses to a Transnational World, 25–27 August, at Duke University.

Chalmers, Douglas A., Judy Gearhart, Andrea Hetling, Adam Jagelski, Kerianne Piester, and Caroline Tsilikounas. 1995. *Mexican Networks and Popular Participation*. North–South Center, University of Miami.

Champion, Henry Hyde. 1890. *The Great Dock Strike, Social Science Series*. London: Swan Sonnenschein & Co.

Chasek, Pamela, Anilla Cherian, Anne Charlotte de Fontaubert, and L. James Goree. 1994. Summary of the International Conference on Population and Development. *Earth Negotiations Bulletin*, 14 September.

Chen, Martha Alter. 1996. Engendering World Conferences: The International Women's Movement and the UN. In *NGOs, The UN, and Global Governance*, edited by T. G. Weiss and L. Gordenker. Boulder, Co: Lynne Rienner.

Chiang, Pei-Heng. 1981. *Non-Governmental Organizations at the United Nations: Identity, Role and Function*. New York: Praeger.

Chossudovsky, Michel. 2000. Seattle and Beyond: Disarming the New World Order. http://www.transnational.org/forum/meetéseattle.html: Transnational Foundation for Peace and Future Research.

Chua, Tian, and Wong Wai-Ling. 1993. Help! Is There a Way Out? *Asian Labour Update* (July): 1.

CIEPAC. 1999. *Seattle: The World Mobilization of the Century Against Globalization*. Chiapas: Centro de Investigaciones Economicas y politicas de Accion Comunitaria.

Clark, Anne-Marie. 1995. Non-Governmental Organizations and their Influence on International Society. *Journal of International Affairs* (winter): 507–525.

Clark, David. 1996. *Urban World/Global City*. London: Routledge.

Clark, T. J., and Donald Nicholson-Smith. 1997. Why Art Can't Kill the Situationist International. *October* 79 (winter): 15–31.

Cockburn, Alexander. 2000. So Who Did Win in Seattle? Liberals Rewrite History. http://www.antenna.nl/~waterman/cockburn.html: Global Solidarity Dialogue.

Cockburn, Alexander, Jeffrey St Clair, and Allan Sekula. 2000. *5 Days that Shook the World: Seattle and Beyond*. London: Verso.

Cockburn, Cynthia. 2000. The Women's Movement: Boundary-Crossing on Terrains of Conflict. In *Global Social Movements*, edited by R. Cohen and S. M. Rai. London and New Brunswick: Athlone Press.

Cohen, Robin, and Shirin M. Rai, eds. 2000a. *Global Social Movements*. London: Athlone Press.

Cohen, Robin, and Shirin M. Rai. 2000b. Global Social Movements; Towards a Cosmopolitan Politics. In *Global Social Movements*, edited by R. Cohen and S. M. Rai. London and New Brunswick: Athlone Press.

Colás, Alejandro. 2002. *International Civil Society*. London: Polity Press.

Comite populaire Saint-Jean Baptiste. 2002a. L'Ilot Berthelot: Point fort de la resistance urbaine 1.

Comite populaire Saint-Jean Baptiste. 2002b. Pour le droit au logement, reprenons nos quartiers! La lettre du compop 1.

Commission européenne. 1997. *Action 21: le bilan des cinq premières années*. Brussels: Office des publications officielles des Communautés européennes.

Commission on Global Governance. 1995. *Our Global Neighbourhood*. Oxford: Oxford University Press.

Conca, Ken. 1995. Greening the United Nations: Environmental Organizations and the UN System. *Third World Quarterly* 16 (summer): 441–457.

Constant. 1997. A Different City for a Different Life. *October* 79 (winter): 37–40.

Cook, Adrian. 1974. *The Armies of the Streets*. Lexington: The University Press of Kentucky.

Cook, Helena. 1996. Amnesty International at the UN. In *We the Peoples*, edited by P. Willetts. Washington, DC: Brookings Institution.

Cook, Maria Lorena. 1995. Mexican State–Labor Relations and the Political Implications of Free Trade. *Latin American perspectives* (winter): 77–94.

Correspondencia. 1994. Organizing Drives. *Correspondencia* 16 (May): 18.

Correspondencia. 1995. A Beleaguered Step on the Road to Beijing. *Correspondencia* 17 (May): 25.

Cottenier, Jo, and Kris Hertogen. 1991. *Le temps travaille pour nous: militant syndical dans les années 1990*. Brusseles: Editions EPO.

Cox, Robert W. 1986a. The Global Political Economy and Social Choice. In *The New Era in Global Competition: State Policy and Market Power*, edited by D. Drache, and M. S. Gertler. Montréal: McGill-Queen's University Press.

Cox, Robert W. 1986b. Social Forces, States and World Orders: Beyond International Relations Theory. In *Neorealism and Its Critics*, edited by R. O. Keohane. New York: Columbia University Press.

Cox, Robert W. 1987. *Production, Power and World Order: Social Forces in the Making of History*. New York: Columbia Univesity Press.

Cox, Robert W. 1992. Global Perestroika. In *The Socialist Register: New World Order*, edited by R. Miliband and L. Panitch. London: Merlin Press.

Cox, Robert W. 2001. The Way Ahead: Toward a New Ontology of World Order. In *Critical Theory and World Politics*, edited by R. W. Jones. Boulder, Co: Lynne Rienner.

Cox, W. 1983. Gramsci, Hegemony and International Relations: An Essay in Methods. *Millennium: Journal of International Studies* 12 (2)(summer): 162–175.

Cunningham, Frank. 1988. *Social Movements/Social Change: The Politics and Practice of Organizing, Socialist Studies*. Toronto: Between the Lines.

Czitrom, Daniel. 1991. Underworlds and Underdogs: Big Tim Sullivan and Metropolitan Politics in New York, 1889–1913. *Journal of American History* 78 (2) (September): 536–558.

Davis, Mike. 1992. *City of Quartz: Excavating the Future in Los Angeles*. New York: Random House.

de Bernis, Gérard Destanne. 1990. On a Marxist Theory of Regulation. *Monthly Review* 41 (8): 28–37.

de Certeau, Michel. 1990. *L'invention du quotidien: 1. arts de faire*. Vol. 146, *Folio/ essais*. Paris: Gallimard.

Dear, Michael, and Allen J. Scott (eds). 1981. *Urbanization and Urban Planning in Capitalist Society*. London: Methuen.

Debord, Guy-Ernest 1958. Théorie de la dérive. In *Internationale Situationniste*, edited by GE. Debord. Paris: IS.

Debord, Guy-Ernest. 1985. Rapport sur la construction des situation. In *Documents relatifs à la fondation de l'internationale situationniste (1948–1957)*, edited by G. Berreby. Paris: Allia.

Debord, Guy-Ernest 1987. *La société du spectacle (1971)*. Paris: Éditions Gérard Lebovici.

Debord, Guy-Ernest. 1988. *Commentaires sur la société du spectacle*. Vol. 2905, *Folio*. Paris: Gallimard.

Debord, Guy-Ernest. 1989. Two Accounts of the Dérive. In *On the Passage of a Few People Through a Rather Brief Moment in Time: The Situationist International, 1957–1972*, edited by E. Sussman. Cambridge/Boston: The MIT Press/The Institute of Contemporary Art.

Debord, Guy-Ernest *et al.* 1969. Correspondance avec un Éditeur. *Internationale Situationniste* (September): 115–116.

Debord, Guy-Ernest 1992. *La société du spectacle (1967)*. Paris: Gallimard.

Debord, Guy-Ernest 1999. *In girum imus nocte et consumimur igni, nrf.* Paris: Gallimard.

Debord, Guy-Ernest, and Jacques Fillion. 1954. Résumé 1954. *Potlatch*, 17–30 August: 63.

DeForest, Robert W., and Lawence Veiller. 1903. *The Tennement House Problem*, 2 vols. New York: Macmillan.

Della Porta, Donatella, and Hanspeter Kriesi. 1999. Introduction. In *Social Movements in a Globalizing World*, edited by D. Della Porta, H. Kriesi, and D. Rucht. London: Macmillan.

Deschamps, Jean-Jacques, and James Bonnardeaux. 1997. Bank Restructuring in Sub-Saharan Africa: Lessons from Selected Case Studies. *Findings (Africa Region, World Bank)*, June, http://www.worldbank.org/aftdr/findings/english/find89.htm.

Deutche, Rosalyn. 1996. *Evictions: Art and Spatial Politics*. Cambridge, MA: MIT Press.

Devetak, Richard, and Richard Higgott. 1999. Justice Unbound? Globalization, States and the Transformation of the Social Bond. *International Affairs* 75 (3): 483–498.

Domhoff, G. William. 1978. *Who Really Rules: New Heaven Community Power Re-Examined*. Santa Monica: Goodyear.

Donini, Antonio. 1995. The Bureaucracy and the Free Spirits: Stagnation and Innovation in the Relationship Between the UN and NGOs. *Third World Quarterly* 16 (summer): 421–439.

Donini, Antonio. 1996. The Bureaucracy and the Free Spirits: Stagnation and Innovation in the Relationship Between the UN and NGOs. In *NGOs, The UN, and Global Governance*, edited by T. G. Weiss, and L. Gordenker. Boulder, Co: Lynne Rienner.

Drainville, André C. 1995a. Left Internationalism and the Politics of Resistance in the New World Order. In *A New World Order: Global Transformations in the Late Twentieth Century*, edited by D. Smith, and J. Böröcz. Westport, Co: Praeger.

Drainville, André C. 1995b. Monetarism in Canada and the World Economy. *Studies in Political Economy* (46)(spring): 7–42.

Drainville, André C. 1995c. Of Social Spaces, Citizenship, and the Nature of Power in the World Economy. *Alternatives* 20 (spring): 51–79.

Drainville, André C. 1997. Continental Integration and Civil Society in the Americas. *Social Justice* (spring): 120–148.

Drainville, André C. 1999. Social Movements in the Americas: Regionalism from Below. In *The Americas in Transition: The Contours of Regionalism*, edited by G. Mace, and L. Bélanger. Boulder, Co: Lynne Rienner.

Drainville, André C. 2001. Cosmopolitan Ghosts and Resistance Communities: Québec City's Summit Of The Americas and the Making of Transnational Subjects. In *Socialist Register 2001*, edited by L. Panitch, and C. Leys.

Dunne, Tim, and Nicholas J. Wheeler (eds). 1999. *Human Rights in Global Politics*. Cambridge: Cambridge University Press.

Eco, Umberto. 1986. Travels in Hyperreality. In *Travels in Hyperreality: Essays*. San Diego: Harcourt Brace Jovanovich.

Ecumenical Coalition for Economic Justice. 1992. From the Double Day to the Endless Day. *Economic Justice Report* (December): 1, 8.

Editors. 1993. Citizens of the Rain Forest. *The IDB (Inter-American Development Bank)* (August): 3.

Ellison, Michael. 1998. Fashion Names Face Sweatshop Case. *Guardian Weekly*, 24 January: 7.

Encuentro Nacional de Organizaciones Ciudadanas. 1995. *Carte de los Derechos Ciudadanos*. Mexico: ENOC.

English, E. Philip, and Harris M. Mule. 1996. *The African Development Bank*. Vol. 1: *The Multilateral Development Banks*. Boulder, CA: Lynne Rienner/The North South Institute.

Enloe, Cynthia. 1989. *Bananas Beaches and Bases*. Berkeley: University of California Press.

Falk, Richard. 1993. The Making of Global Citizenship. In *Global Visions: Beyond the New World Order*, edited by J. Brecher, J.B. Childs and J. Cutler. Montréal: Black Rose Books.

Falk, Richard. 1995a. Liberalism at the Global Level: The Last of the Independent Commissions? *Millennium: Journal of International Studies* 24 (3): 563–576.

Falk, Richard. 1995b. *On Humane Governance: Towards a New Global Politics*. University Park: The Pennsylvania State University Press/World Order Models Project.

Feinberg, Richard, and Robin Rosenberg (eds). 1999. *Civil Society and the Summit of the Americas: The 1998 Santiago Summit*. Boulder, Co: Lynne Rienner.

Felix, David. 1995. The Tobin Tax Proposal: Background, Issues and Prospects. *Futures* 27 (2): 195–208.

Fisher, Julie. 1993. *The Road from Rio: Sustainable Development and the Nongovernmental Movement in the Third World*. Westport, Co: Praeger.

Fleming, J. Marcus. 1975. Floating Exchange Rates, Asymmetrical Interventions and the Management of International Liquidity. *IMF Staff Papers* 22 (2)(July): 276.

Flynn, Mike. 1997. New Otani Worker Solidarity Update: 6 Months of Actions in Japan to Support of L.A. Workers. *APWSL/Japan (Newsletter From Japan Committee of Asian Pacific Worker's Solidarity Links)* (April): 1–2.

Foucault, Michel. 1966. *Les mots et les choses*, translated by François Ewald, 4 vols, *Tel*. Paris: Gallimard.

Fougère, Henry. 1905. Les Délégations ouvrières aux expositions universelles sous le Second Empire. Thèse de Doctorat (Faculté de Droit), Les Imprimeries A. Herbin.

Fox, Leslie M. 1996. *Sustaining Civil Society*. Washington, DC: Civicus (The International Task Force on Enhancing the Resource Base of Civil Society).

Frederick, Howard H. 1993. Computer Networks and the Emergence of Global Civil Society. In *Global Networks*, edited by L. M. Harasim. Cambridge: MIT Press.

Freitag, Michel. 1995. *Le Naufrage de l'universite et autres essais d'epistemologic politique*. Québec/Paris: Nuit Blanche/Editions La Decouverte.

Freitag, Michel, and Éric Pineault (eds) 1999. *Le monde enchaîné*, edited by J. Pelletier, *Essais Critiques*. Québec: Nota bene.

Friberg, Mats, and Björn Hettne. 1988. Local Mobilization and World System Politics. *International Social Science Journal* 117 (August): 341–360.

Friedmann, John. 1986. The World City Hypothesis. *Development and Change* (January): 69–83.

Friedmann, John, and G. Wolff. 1982. World City Formulation: An Agenda for Research and Action. *International Journal of Urban and Regional Research* (September): 309–344.

Fumiaki, Mariya. 1995. United Power of Japan–U.S. Workers' Solidarity Attack Bridgestone Corp. *APWSL-JAPAN (Newsletter from Japan Committee of Asian Pacific Workers Solidarity Links)* 6 (20 November): 1–3.

Gaer, Felice D. 1996. Reality Check: Human Rights NGOs Confront Governments at the UN. In *NGOs, The UN, and Global Governance*, edited by T. G. Weiss, and L. Gordenker. Boulder, Co: Lynne Rienner.

Galtung, Johan. 1988. The Peace Movement: An Exercise in Micro–Macro Linkages. *International Social Science Journal* 117 (August): 377–381.

Gans, Herbert J. 1982. *The Urban Villagers: Group and Class in the Life of Italian-Americans* (2nd edn). New York: The Free Press.

Garau, Pietro. 1997. Experts' Meeting Launches European Observatory. *UNCHS: Habitat Debate* (March): 35.

Garilao, Ernesto D. 1987. Indigenous NGOs as Strategic Institutions: Managing the Relationship with Government and Resource Agencies. *World Development* (autumn): 113–120.

Garside, Patricia L. 1984. West End, East End: London, 1890–1940. In *Metropolis 1890–1940*, edited by A. Sutcliffe. Chicago, IL: The University of Chicago Press.

Geddes, Patrick. 1908. The Survey of Cities. *Sociological Review* (January).

George, Susan. 1999. À l'OMC, trois ans pour achever la mondialisation. *Le Monde Diplomatique* (July): 8, 9.

Germain, R.D., and Michael Kenny. 1998. Engaging Gramsci: International Relations Theory and the New Gramscians. *Review of International Studies* (January): 3–22.

Giddens, Anthony. 1984. *The Constitution of Society*. Berkeley: University of California Press.

Giddens, Anthony. 1985a. *The Nation-State and Violence*. Cambridge: Polity Press.

Giddens, Anthony. 1985b. Time, Space and Regionalization. In *Social Relations and Spatial Structures*, edited by D. Gregory and J. Urry. London: Macmillan.

Giddens, Anthony. 1990. *The Consequences of Modernity*. Cambridge: Polity Press.

Giddens, Anthony. 1991. *Modernity and Self-Identity: Self and Society in the Late Modern Age*. Stanford, CA: Stanford University Press.

Gill, Stephen. 1986. Hegemony, Consensus and Trilateralism. *Review of International Studies* 12: 205–21.

Gill, Stephen. 1990. *American Hegemony and the Trilateral Commission.* Cambridge: Cambridge University Press.

Gill, Stephen. 1991. Reflections of Global Order and Socio-Historical Time. *Alternatives*: 16.

Gill, Stephen. 1992. The Emerging World Order and European Change. In *New World Order?*, edited by L. Panitch, and R. Miliband. London: Merlin Press.

Gill, Stephen. 1994. Structural Change and Global Political Economy: Globalizing Élites and the Emerging World Order. In *Global Transformation: Challenges to the State System*, edited by Y. Sakamoto. Tokyo: United Nations University Press.

Gill, Stephen. 1997. Globalization, Democratization, and the Politics of Indifference. In *Globalization: Critical Reflections*, edited by J. H. Mittleman. Boulder, Co: Lynne Rienner.

Gill, Stephen. 1998. New Constitutionalism, Democratisation and Global Political Economy. *Pacifica Review* 10 (1): 23–38.

Gill, Stephen, and David Law. 1988. *The Global Political Economy: Perspectives, Problems and Policies.* Baltimore, MD: Johns Hopkins University Press.

Gill, Stephen, and David Law. 1993. Global Hegemony and the Structural Power of Capital. In *Gramsci, Historical Materialism and International Relation.*, edited by S. Gill. Cambridge: Cambridge University Press.

Gill, Stephen, Robert Cox and Kees van der Pijl. 1992. Structural Change and Globalizing Elites; Political Economy Perspectives in the Emerging World Order. Paper read at International Conference on 'Changing World Order and the United Nations System', at Yokohama, Japan, 24–27 March.

Gilloch, Graeme. 1996. *Myth and Metropolis: Walter Benjamin and the City.* Cambridge: Polity Press.

Glaab, Charles N., and A. Theodore Brown. 1967. *A History of Urban America.* New York: Macmillan.

Goheen, Peter. 1990. Symbols in the Streets: Parades in Victorian Urban Canada. *Urban History Review* 18 (3) (February): 237–243.

Goldblatt, David. 1997. At the Limits of Political Possibility: The Cosmopolitan Democratic Project. *New Left Review* 225 (September/October): 140–150.

Gordenker, Leon, and Thomas G. Weiss. 1996. Pluralizing Global Governance: Analytical Approaches and Dimensions. In *NGOs, The UN, and Global Governance*, edited by T. G. Weiss, and L. Gordenker. Boulder, Co: Lynne Rienner.

Gould, Elen. 1999. It's a WTO World. *Canadian Dimension* (December): 14–15.

Graeber, David. 2002. For a New Anarchism. *New Left Review*, Second Series (January to February): 61–74.

Graham, Laurie. 1995. Subaru-Isuzu: Worker Response in a Nonunion Japanese Transplant. In *Lean Work*, edited by S. Babson. Detroit: Wayne State University Press.

Griffin Cohen, Marjorie. 1992. The Lunacy of Free Trade. In *Crossing the Line: Canada and Free Trade with Mexico.* Vancouver: New Star Books.

Grinspun, Ricardo, and Maxwell A. Cameron. 1993. *The Political Economy of North American Free Trade.* Montréal/Kingston/London: McGill-Queen's University Press.

Groupe de Lisbonne. 1995. *Limites à la compétitivité: vers un nouveau contrat mondial.* Montréal: Boréal.

Güntzel, Ralph P. 1993. Québec Trade Union Internationalism: The Case of the

Confédération des Syndicats nationaux (CSN). *Zeitschrift für Kanada-Studien* 24 (2) (January): 127–145.

Gupta, Akhil, and James Ferguson. 1992. Beyond Culture: Space, Identity and the Politics of Difference. *Cultural Anthropologu* 7: 6–23.

Haas, Peter M. 1992. Introduction: Epistemic Communities and International Policy Coordination. *International Organization* 46: 1–35.

Habermas, Jürgen. 1996. Further Reflections on the Public Sphere. In *Habermas and the Public Sphere*, edited by C. Calhoun. Cambridge: MIT Press.

Hahnel, Robin. 2000. Speaking Truth to Power: Speaking Truth to Ourselves. *Z* (June): 44–51.

Hall, Peter. 1996. *Cities of Tomorrow: An Intellectual History of Urban Planning and Design in the Twentieth Century* (2nd edn). Oxford: Blackwell.

Hall, Peter. 1998. *Cities in Civilization*. New York: Pantheon Books.

Hamilton, Roger. 1994. Turning Residents into Citizens: Latin America's Reform Bandwagon Needs More Drivers – Lots More. *The IDB (Inter-American Development Bank)* (November): 6–7.

Hammack, David C. 1982. *Power and Society: Great New York at the Turn of the Century*. New York: Russel Sage Foundation.

Hardt, Michael, and Antonio Negri. 2000. *Empire*. Harvard, MA: Harvard University Press.

Harvey, David. 1985. *Consciousness and the Urban Experience: Studies in the History and Theory of Capitalist Urbanization*. Baltimore, MD: The Johns Hopkins University Press.

Harvey, David. 2000. *Spaces of Hope*. Berkeley: University of California Press.

Haussmann, Georges Eugène. 1979. *Mémoires du Baron Haussmann (Grands travaux de Paris: 1853–1870)*, 2 vols. Vol. 1. Paris: Guy Durier, éditeur.

Havard, William C. 1964. From Bossism to Cosmopolitanism: Changes in the Relationship of Urban Leadership to State Politics. *The Annals of the American Academy of Political and Social Sciences* 353 (May): 84–94.

Hays, Rachel. 1996. AFL-CIO Restructuring Favours Cross-Border Solidarity. *Borderlines. Information for Border and Cross-Border Organizers* 4 (9): 1, 7.

Hazan, Pierre. 2001. Riche Idée. *Libération*, 26 January: 56.

Headly, Joel Tyler. 1970 [1873]. *The Great Riots of New York 1712–1873*. New York: The Bobbs-Merrill Company.

Hecker, Steven, and Margaret Hallock. 1991. *Labor in a Global Economy*. Eugene, OR: University of Oregon Books and the Labor Education and Research Center.

Held, David. 1991. Democracy, the Nation-State and the Global System. *Economy and Society* 20 (2 May): 138–172.

Held, David. 1995. *Democracy and the Global Order: From the Modern State to Cosmopolitan Governance*. Cambridge: Polity Press.

Heredia, Carlos. 1994. NAFTA and Democratization in Mexico. *Journal of International Affairs* 48 (1): 13–38.

Herod, Andrew. 1995a. Labor as an Agent of Globalization and as a Global Agent. In *Globalization and its Politics: Critical Reappraisals*, edited by K. Cox. New York: Guilford Press.

Herod, Andrew. 1995b. The Practice of International Labor Solidarity and the Geography of the Global Economy. *Economic Geography* 71: 341–363.

Hideo, Watanabe. 1994. 'National Network in Solidarity with Migrant Workers'

Launched. *APWSL/Japan (Newsletter From Japan Committee of Asian Pacific Worker's Solidarity Links)* (July): 8–9.

Hiroko, Nitta. 1993. The Asian Women Workers' Center is Ten Years Old. *Resources Materials on Women's Labor in Japan* 12 (October): 1–4.

Hiroko, Shimaoka. 1992. Japan: Consummate Hell for Thai Women – Seeking Freedom From Slavery. *Resources Materials on Women's Labor in Japan* 11 (March): 4–6.

Hoare, Quintin, and Geoffrey Nowell Smith (eds). 1998. *Selections From the Prison Notebooks of Antonio Gramsci*. London: Lawrence and Wishart.

Hobsbawm, Eric J. 1984. The Transformation of Labour Rituals. In *Worlds of Labour: Further Studies in the History of Labour*, edited by E. J. Hobsbawm. London: Weidenfeld & Nicolson.

Hofstadter, Richard. 1959. *The Age of Reform*. New York: Alfred A. Knopf.

Hogness, Peter. 1989. One More Hole in the Wall; The Lunafil Strikers on Guatemala. In *Solidarity Across Borders*, edited by Peter Hogness. Chicago, IL: Midwest Center for Labor Research.

Holli, Melvin. 1976. Social and Structural Reform. In *The City Boss in America*, edited by A. B. Callow. New York: Oxford University Press.

Holton, R. 1998. *Globalization and the Nation State*. London: Macmillan.

Home, Stewart. 1996. Basic Banalities. In *What is Situationism? A Reader*, edited by S. Home. Edinburgh: AK Press.

Howell, Jude. 1997. Post-Beijing Reflections: Creating Ripples, But Not Waves in China. *Women's Studies International Forum* 20 (2): 235–252.

Hugo, Victor. 1985. *Oeuvres Complètes, Bouquins*. Paris: Robert Laffont.

Human Rights Watch. 1993. Human Rights in the APEC Region. *Human Rights Watch*.

Human Rights Watch. 1995. The Human Rights Watch Report on Women's Human Rights. New York: Human Rights Watch.

ICCSASW. 1991. *Annual Report*. Toronto: International Commission for the Coordination of Solidarity Among Sugar Workers.

ICCSASW. 1992. *Annual Report*. Toronto: International Commission for the Coordination of Solidarity Among Sugar Workers.

IDB. 1994. From Grassroots to Government. *IDB Extra* (Inter-American Development Bank): 8–9.

IDB (Inter-American Development Bank). 1996. IDB Women.

IDB. 1997a. *Echoes of Forging Links with NGOs*. Washington, DC: Inter-American Development Bank.

IDB. 1997b. How We Put it all Together. *IDB Extra 'Urban Renaissance'* (Inter-American Development Bank): 8.

IDB. 1997c. Rio's Urban Renaissance. *IDB Extra 'Urban Renaissance'* (Inter-American Development Bank): 1–8.

IDB. 1998. *Citizens Participation Increases Efficiency of Development*. Washington, DC/Cartagena: Inter-American Development Bank.

Interhemispheric Resource Center. 1996a. Missionaries with a Mixed Message. *Democracy Backgrounder* 1: 8.

Interhemispheric Resource Center. 1996b. Post-Nafta Labor Solidarity Advances Shakily. *Borderlines. Information for Border and Cross-Border Organizers* 4 (6): 1, 3–5.

Interhemispheric Resource Center. 1996c. Union Democracy Thwarted at Cuautitlán Ford Plant. *Borderlines. Information for Border and Cross-Border Organizers* 4 (9): 10.

Interim Committee to Consultative Non-Governmental Organizations 1978 [1948]. *Consultation Between the United Nations and Non-Governmental Organizations.* Vol. 3, *United Nations Studies.* Westport, CT: Greenwood Press.

IS. 1958a. Action en Belgique contre l'assemblée des critiques d'art internationaux. *Internationale Situationniste* (June): 29–30.

IS. 1958b. Définitions. *Internationale Situationniste* (June): 13–14.

IS. 1958c. Problèmes préliminaires à la construction d'une situation. *Internationale Situationniste* (June): 11–13.

IS. 1959a. L'urbanisme unitaire à la fin des années 50. *Internationale Situationniste* (December): 11–16.

IS. 1959b. Le détournement comme négation et comme prélude. *Internationale Situationniste* (December): 10–11.

IS. 1959c. Le sens du dépérissement de l'art. *Internationale Situationniste* (December): 1–8.

IS. 1960. Manifeste (17/5/60). *Internationale Situationniste* (June): 36–38.

IS. 1961. Critique de l'urbanisme. *Internationale Situationniste* (August): 5–11.

IS. 1962. Géopolitique de l'hibernation. *Internationale Situationniste* (April): 3–10.

IS. 1966. Le déclin et la chute de l'économie spectaculaire-marchande. *Internationale Situationniste* (March): 3–11.

IS. 1969. Réforme et contre-réforme dans le pouvoir bureaucratique. *Internationale Situationniste* (September): 35–43.

IS. 1997. Editorial Notes: The Avant-Garde of Presence. *October* 79 (winter): 14–22.

Ivain, Gilles. 1958. Formulaire pour un urbanisme nouveau. *Internationale Situationniste* 1 (June): 15–20.

Jacobs, Jane. 1993 [1961]. *The Death and Life of Great American Cities.* New York: The Modern Library.

Jameson, Fredric. 1991. *Postmodernism, or, The Cultural Logic of Late Capitalism.* Durham, NC: Duke University Press.

Jappe, Anselm. 2001. *Guy Debord,* Trans. Claude Galli. Paris: Denoel.

Jessop, Bob. 1995. The Regulation Approach, Governance and Post-Fordism: Alternative Perspectives on Economic and Political Change? *Economy and Society* 24 (3)(August): 307–333.

Johnson, S.P. 1993. *The Earth Summit: The United Nations Conference on Environment and Development.* London: Graham & Trotman.

Johnston, R.J. 1994. World Cities in a World System: Conference, Sterling, VA, April 1993. *International Journal of Urban and Regional Research* (March): 150–152.

Kaplan, Barry J. 1983. Metropolitics, Administrative Reform, and Political Theory: The Greater New York City Charter of 1897. *Journal of Urban History* 9 (2): 165–194.

Kappagoda, Nihal. 1995. *The Asian Development Bank.* Vol. 2, *The Multilateral Development Banks.* Boulder, Co: Lynne Rienner/The North South Institute.

Kaufmann, Vincent. 1997. Angels of Purity. *October* 79 (winter): 49–68.

Keck, Margaret, and Kathryn Sikkink. 1998. *Activists Beyond Borders: Advocacy Networks in International Politics.* Ithaca, NY: Cornell University Press.

Keiko, Yamamoto. 1992. Discrimination Against Women in Wages and Promotion – Nine Women File Suit Against Hitachi Manufacturing Co. *Resources Materials on Women's Labor in Japan* 10 (August): 1–6.

Kellner, Douglas. 2000. Globalization and New Social Movements: Lessons for Critical Theory and Pedagogy. In *Globalization and Education: Critical Perspectives*, edited by N.C. Burbules and C.A. Torres. London: Routledge.

Kenen, Peter B 1989. The Use of IMF Credit. In *The International Monetary Fund in a Multipolar World: Pulling Together*, edited by Catherine Gwin *et al.* Washington, DC: Overseas Development Council.

Khatib, Abdelhafid. 1958. Essai de description psychogéographique des Halles. In *Internationale Situationniste*, edited by G. Debord. Paris: IS.

Kidder, Thalia, and Mary McGinn. 1995. In the Wake of NAFTA: Transnational Workers Networks. *Social Policy* (summer): 14–21.

King, Anthony D. 1990. *Global Cities: Post-Imperialism and the Internationalisation of London, The International Library of Sociology*. London: Routledge.

Klein, Naomi. 2000a. *No Logo: Taking Aim at the Brand Bullies*. Toronto: Alfred A. Knopf.

Klein, Naomi. 2000b. The Vision Thing. *The Nation*, 10 July: 18–21.

Knox, Paul L. 1995. *World Cities in a World System*. Cambridge: Cambridge University Press.

Korten, David C. 1991. The Role of Nongovernmental Organizations in Development: Changing Patterns and Perspectives. In *Nongovernmental Organizations and the World Bank: Cooperation for Development*, edited by S. Paul and A. Israel. Washington, DC: The World Bank.

Kotanyi, Attila, and Raoul Vaneigem. 1961. Programme élémentaire du bureau d'urbanisme unitaire. *Internationale Situationniste* (August): 16–19.

Kreimer, Alcira, Thereza Lobo, Braz Menezes, Mohan Munasinghe, Ronald Parker, and Martha Preece. 1995. Rio de Janeiro – In Search of Sustainability. In *Towards A Sustainable Urban Environment: The Rio de Janiero Study*, edited by A. Kreimer, T. Lobo, B. Menezes, M. Munasinghe, R. Parker, and M. Preece. Washington, DC: The International Bank for Reconstruction and Development.

Kreml, William P., and Charles W. Kegley Jr. 1996. A Global Political Party: The Next Step. *Alternatives* (January to March): 123–134.

Labande, Christian. 1976. *La première internationale*. Paris: Union Générale d'Éditions.

Labelle-Rojoux, Arnaud. 2001. Une postérité politique ambigüe. *Magazine Littéraire* (June): 64–65.

Laclau, Ernesto, and Chantal Mouffe. 2001. *Hegemony and Socialist Strategy: Towards a Radical Democratic Politics* (2nd edn). London: Verso.

Lador-Lederer, J. Joseph. 1963. *International Non-Governmental Organizations and Economic Entities: A Study in Autonomous Organization and Lus Gentium*. Leyden: A.W. Sythoff.

Lanctôt, Jacques, and Michel Brulé (eds). 2001. *Le Québec de la honte*. Montréal: Lanctôt/Les intouchables.

Lap-Chew, Lin. 1996. Entre la protection et la prise de contrôle sur sa vie: stratégies pour contrer la traite des femmes. In *Voir le monde à travers les yeux des femmes. Allocutions des plénières du forum des ONG sur les femmes, Beijing 1995*, edited by E. Friedlander. New York: Women, Inc.

Lash, Scott, and John Urry. 1994. *Economies of Signs and Space*. London: Sage.

Lauritsen, John, and David Thorstad. 1974. *The Early Homosexual Rights Movement (1864–1935)*. New York: Times Change Press.

LaViolette, Nicole, and Sandra Withworth. 1994. No Safe Haven: Sexuality as a Universal Human Right and Gay and Lesbian Activism in International Politics. *Millennium* 23 (3): 563–588.

Le Corbusier. 1994 [1925]. *Urbanisme*. Paris: Flammarion.

Lefebvre, Henri. 1978 [1968]. *Le droit à la ville*. Paris: Anthropos.

Levin, Thomas Y. 1989. Dismantling the Spectacle: The Cinema of Guy Debord. In *On the Passage of a Few People Through a Rather Brief Moment in Time: The Situationist International, 1957–1972*, edited by E. Sussman. Cambridge/Boston: MIT Press/The Institute of Contemporary Art.

Lévy, Jean-Pierre. 1983. *La conférence des Nations Unies sur le droit de la mer*. Paris: A. Pédone.

Lewis, John P. 1985. Strengthening Effectiveness and Public Support. In *Twenty-Five Years of Development Co-Operation: A Review*, edited by R. M. Poats. Paris: Organization for Economic Cooperation and Development (Development Assistance Committee).

Linklater, Andrew. 2001. The Changing Contours of Critical International Relations Theory. In *Critical Theory and World Politics*, edited by R. W. Jones. Boulder, Co: Lynne Rienner.

Lipietz, Alain. 1993. *Vert espérance: l'avenir de l'écologie politique*. Paris: La Découverte.

Lipovetsky, Gilles. 1983. *L'ère du vide*. Paris: Gallimard.

Lipschutz, Ronnie D. 1992. The Emergence of Global Civil Society. *Millennium* 21(3) (winter): 389–420.

Lipschutz, Ronnie D., and Judith Mayer. 1996. *Global Civil Society and Global Environmental Governance: The Politics of Nature from Place to Planet*. Albany: State University of New York Press.

Lockwood, Charles. 1976. *Manhattan Moves Uptown*. Boston, MA: Houghton Mifflin Company.

López, Mercedes. 1991. An Interview with Cecilia Rodriquez of Mujer Obrera. *Correspondencia* (spring): 15–18.

Lovell, John. 1969. *Stevedores and Dockers: A Study of Trade Unionism in the Port of London 1870–1914*. London: Macmillan.

Lowi, Theodore J. 1964. *At the Pleasure of the Mayor: Patronage in New York City, 1898–1958*. London: The Free Press of Glencoe, Collier-Macmillan Limited.

Löwy, Michael. 1990. Fatherland or Mother Earth? Nationalism and Internationalism From A Socialist Perspective. In *Socialist Register 1989*, edited by L. P. and R. Miliband. London: Merlin Press.

Lui, Adonica Y. 1995. Political and Institutional Constraints of Reform: The Charity Reformers, Failed Campaigns Against Public Outdoors Relief, New York City, 1874–1898. *Journal of Policy History* 7 (3): 341–364.

Luijken, Anneke van, and Swasti Mitter. 1987. *Unseen Phenomenon: The Rise of Homeworking*. London: Change.

Luján, Bertha. 1996. El TLC a Dos años de Distancia. *Rostros y Voces de la Sociedad Civil* (April to May).

Lupsha, Peter A. 1976. Politics of Urban Change. In *The City Boss in America*, edited by A. B. Callow. New York: Oxford University Press.

Lyotard, Jean-François. 1993. The Other's Rights. In *On Human Rights: The Oxford Amnesty Lectures*, edited by S. Shute and S. Hurley. New York: Basic Books.

MacPherson, C.B. 1977. *The Life and Times of Liberal Democracy*. Oxford: Oxford University Press.

Magnusson, Warren. 1996. *The Search for Political Space: Globalization, Social Movements, and the Urban Experience*. Toronto: University of Toronto Press.

Maija, Abel. 1996. Brazil: Municipalities and Low-Income Sanitation. In *World Bank Participation Sourcebook*. Washington, DC.

Malamud, Carl. 1997. *A World's Fair for the Global Village*. Cambridge: MIT Press.

Malonew, James L. 1984. Who Needs the Sea Treaty? *Foreign Policy* 54 (spring): 44–63.

Maquila Solidarity Network. n.d. Defending their Right to Organize. *Solidarity with Maquila Workers*: 2–3.

Marc, Aleaandre, and Mary Schmidt. 1995. *Participation and Social Funds*, edited by E. Department. Vol. 4, *Participation Series*. Washington, DC: The World Bank.

Marston, Sallie A. 1989. Public Rituals and Community Power: St. Patrick's Day Parades in Lowell, Massachusetts, 1841–1874. *Political Geography Quarterly* 8 (3) (July): 255–269.

Marx, Karl. 1975. On the Jewish Question. In *Marx and Engels: Collected Works 1843–1844*. Moscow: International Publishers.

Masumi, Azu. 1995. The Fourth World Conference on Women: NGOs Will Continue Lobbying Actively. *APWSL/Japan (Newsletter From Japan Committee of Asian Pacific Worker's Solidarity Links)* (July): 4–5.

Mattelart, Armand. 1999. *Histoire de l'utopie planétaire*. Paris: La Découverte.

Maynard, John. 1999. A Sampo through Japan: Impressions of the NZ–Japan Postal Workers Exchange Visit. *APWSL/Japan (Newsletter From Japan Committee of Asian Pacific Worker's Solidarity Links)* (June): 1–2.

McClain, George D. 1992. Conflict as a Gift of God. *Social Questions Bulletin* (September to October): 1.

McLaughlin, John. 1996a. APWSL/Japan Supports New Otani Hotel Boycott in Los Angeles by HERE Local 11. *APWSL/Japan (Newsletter From Japan Committee of Asian Pacific Worker's Solidarity Links)* (July): 5.

McLaughlin, John. 1996b. APWSL/Japan Workers 'Alternative Tour' of Aotearoa/ NZ: Studies of the Effect of Privatization and Deregulation. *APWSL/Japan (Newsletter From Japan Committee of Asian Pacific Worker's Solidarity Links)* (November): 6–7.

McLaughlin, John. 1996c. HERE Local 11 Delegation Visits Tokyo, Osaka in Early April – Ties in with AFL-CIO President Sweeney's Japan Trip. *APWSL/Japan (Newsletter From Japan Committee of Asian Pacific Worker's Solidarity Links)* (April): 2–3.

McLaughlin, John. 1999. Some Impressions of the Third National Migrant Worker Forum Held in Tokyo. *APWSL/Japan (Newsletter From Japan Committee of Asian Pacific Worker's Solidarity Links)* (June): 5,7.

Melucci, Alberto. 1989 [1943]. *Nomads of the Present: Social Movements and Individual Needs in Contemporary Society*, edited by John Keane and Paul Mier Philadelphia, PA: Temple University Press.

Melucci, Alberto. 1995. Individualisation et globalisation; Perspectives théoriques. *Cahiers de recherche sociologique* 24: 184–205.

Merton, Robert K. 1976. The Latent Functions of the Machine: A Sociologist's View. In *The City Boss in America*, edited by A. B. Callow. New York: Oxford University Press.

Methodist Federation for Social Action. 1993. General Electric Campaign is Successful. *Social Questions Bulletin* (May to June): 3.

Michalet, Charles-Albert. 1976. *Le capitalisme mondial*. Paris: PUF.

Michel, James H. 1995. *Development Co-operation: DAC Annual Report*. Paris: Organization for Economic Cooperation and Development (Development Assistance Committee).

Michel, James H. 1996. *Development Co-Operation: DAC Annual Report*. Paris: Organization for Economic Cooperation and Development (Development Assistance Committee).

Midgley, Mary. 1999. Human Rights in Global Politics, edited by T. Dunne and N. J. Wheeler. Cambridge: Cambridge University Press.

Miles, Angela. 1996. *Integrative Feminisms: Building Global Visions 1960's–1990's*. New York and London: Routledge.

Miliband, Ralph. 1982. *Capitalist Democracy in Britain*. Oxford: Oxford University Press.

Miller, Zane, and Patricia M. Melvin. 1987. *The Urbanization of Modern America*. San Diego: Harcourt Brace Jonanovich.

Mitchell, William J. 1995. *City of Bits: Space, Place, and the Infobahn*. Cambridge, MA: MIT Press.

Mittleman, James H. 1998. Globalisation and Environmental Resistance Politics. *Third World Quarterly* 19 (5): 847–872.

Molotch, Harvey. 1976. The City as Growth Machine. *American Journal of Sociology* 82 (2): 309–330.

Monoson, S. Sara. 1990. The Lady and the Tiger: Women's Electoral Activism in New York City Before Suffrage. *Journal of Women's history* 2 (2) (autumn): 100–135.

Monroy, Mario B., (ed.). 1994. *Pensar Chiapas, Repensar México: Reflexiones de las ONGs Mexicanas Sobre el Conflicto*. México: Convergencia.

Moody, Kim. 1995. NAFTA and the Corporate Redesign of North America. *Latin American Perspectives* 22 (1) (winter): 95–116.

Morgan, Robin (ed.). 1984. *Sisterhood is Global: The International Women's Movement Anthology*. New York: Doubleday.

Morin, Edgard, and Anne Brigitte Kern. 1993. *Terre-Patrie*. (1st edn), *Points*. Paris: Seuil.

Morin, Edgard, and Sami Naïr. 1997. *Une politique de civilisation*: Paris: Arléa.

Morningstar, Chip, and F. Randall Farmer. 1991. The Lessons of Lucasfilm's Habitat. In *Cyberspace; First Steps*, edited by M. Benedikt. Cambridge: MIT Press.

Morris-Suzuki, Tessa. 2000. For and Against NGOs. *New Left Review* (Second Series) (2): 63–84.

Moscow, Warren. 1971. *The Last of the Big-Time Bosses: The Life and Time of Carmine De Sapio and the Rise and Fall of Tammany Hall*. New York: Stein & Day.

Moynihan, Daniel P. 1976. When the Irish Ran New York. In *The City Boss in America*, edited by A. B. Callow. New York: Oxford University Press.

Mumford, Lewis. 1961. *The City in History*. London: Penguin Books.

Munck, Ronaldo. 1992. Structures of Power, Movement of Resistance: An Introduction to the Theories of Urban Movements in Latin America.

Munck, Ronaldo. 2000. Labour in the Global: Challenges and Prospects. In *Global*

Social Movements, edited by R. Cohen, and S. M. Rai. London and New Brunswick: Athlone Press.

Myers, Gustavus. 1968 [1917]. *History of Tammany Hall*. (2nd edn), 298/56 vols. *Research and Source Works Series/American Classics in History and Social Science*. New York: Burt Franklin.

N'Dow, Wally. 1997. Editorial. *UNCHS: Habitat Debate* (March): 2. n.d. 2001.

Nash, Jörgen. 1964. The Mutant Manifesto. *The Times Literary Supplement*, 3 September: 782–783.

NEFAC. 2001. Anti-capitalist Resistance in the Streets of Prague. *The Northeastern Anarchist* (February): 11–15.

Newell, Peter. 2000. Environmental NGOs and Globalization: The Governance of TNCs. In *Global Social Movements*, edited by R. Cohen, and S. M. Rai. London and New Brunswick: Athlone Press.

NGO Forum on the World Economic Order. 1975. Scanning our Future: NGO Forum (ECOSOC).

Nitta, Hiroko. 1995. The Childcare Movement Exchange Programs beween Korea and Japan. *Resources Materials on Women's Labor in Japan* 15 (March): 1–5.

Nussbaum, M. 1996. Feminism and Internationalism. *Metaphilosophy* 27 (1–2): 202–208.

OECD. 1988. *Partenaires dans l'action pour le développement: les organisations non-gouvernementales*. Paris: Organization for Economic Cooperation and Development.

OECD. 1990. *Promoting Private Enterprise In Developing Countries*. Paris: OECD.

OECD. 1997. *Better Understanding our Cities; The Role of Urban Indicators*. Paris: Organization for Economic Cooperation and Development.

OECD (Development Assistance Committee). 1992. *DAC Principles for Effective Aid*. Paris: Organization for Economic Cooperation and Development.

Oliveira, Miguel Darcy de, and Rajesh Tandon. 1994. An Emerging Global Civil Society. In *Citizens Strengthening Global Civil Society*, edited by M. D. de Oliviera, and R. Tandon. Washington, DC: CIVICUS (World Alliance for Citizen Participation).

Ong, Aihwa. 1987. The Modern Corporation: Manufacturing Gender Hierarchy. In *Spirits of Resistance and Capitalist Discipline*, edited by A. Ong. Albany: State University of New York Press.

Ong, Aihwa. 1996. Strategic Sisterhood or Sisters in Solidarity? Questions of Communitarianism and Citizenship in Asia. *Industrial Journal of Global Legal Studies* 4: 106.

Oram, R.B. 1964. The Great Strike of 1889: The Fight for the Dockers, Tanner. *History Today* (August): 532–542.

Osorio, Victor. 1996. RMLAC: Five Years of Citizen Action. *Nuestra America* (summer).

Overbeek, Henk. 1990. *Global Capitalism and National Decline*. London: Unwin Hyman.

Pacific-Asia Resource Center. 1988. Will the Future be Ours?: We Propose a People's Plan for the 21st Century. *AMPO: Japan-Asia Quarterly Review*: 3–14.

Pagnucco, Ron, and David Atwood. 1994. Global Strategies for Peace and Justice. *Peace Review* 6 (4): 411–418.

PAN. 1997. Draft of NGO Charter on Transnational Corporations. Proposed by the People's Action Network to Monitor Japanese Transnational Corporations.

APWSL/Japan (Newsletter From Japan Committee of Asian Pacific Worker's Solidarity Links) (November): 5.

PAN. 1998. Draft of NGO Charter on Transnational Corporations. Proposed by the People's Action Network to Monitor Japanese Transnational Corporations, Part II. *APWSL/Japan (Newsletter From Japan Committee of Asian Pacific Worker's Solidarity Links)* (November): 5.

Parkhurst, Charles H. 1970 [1895]. *Our Fight With Tammany*. New York: Books for Libraries Press.

Participation and NGO Group. 1996. *The World Bank's Partnership with Nongovernmental Organizations*. Washington: Poverty and Social Policy Department (PSP), World Bank.

Pattison, George. 1966. Nineteenth-Century Dock Labour in the Port of London. *Mariner's Mirror* 52 (3) (August): 263–277.

Paul, Samuel, and Arturo Israel (eds). 1991. *Nongovernmental Organizations and the World Bank, Regional and Sectoral Studies*. Washington, DC: The World Bank.

Peel, Roy V. 1968 (1935). *The Political Clubs of New York City*. Long Island: Ira J. Friedman.

Pénicaut, Nicole. 2001. Combler le fossé. *Libération*, 26 January: 2.

Pénicaut, Nicole, and Christian Dutilleux. 2001. Davos et Potrto Alegre, deux sommets du monde. *Libération*, 26 January: 1–3.

Peterson, V. Spike, and Anne Sisson Runyan. 1993. *Global Gender Issues*, edited by G. A. Lopez, *Dilemmas in World Politics*. Boulder, Co: Westview Press.

Petrat, Supawadee. 1994. The Situation of Migrant Workers in Asia. *APWSL/Japan (Newsletter From Japan Committee of Asian Pacific Worker's Solidarity Links)* (December): 3–4.

Petrella, Ricardo. 1994. Pour un contrat social mondial. *Le Monde Diplomatique* (July): 20–21.

Petrella, Ricardo. 1995. Répondre à la révolte: un contrat mondial. *Transversales: Science/Culture* 32: 5–6.

Petrella, Ricardo. 1996. *Le bien commun. Éloge de la solidarité*, edited by P. Delrock (2nd edn), *Quartier Libre*. Paris: Labor.

Petrella, Ricardo. 1997. *Écueils de la mondialisation: Urgence d'un nouveau contrat social*. Montréal: Fides.

Phebus, Nicolas. 2002. Resistances sur le front du logement d'hier a aujourd'hui. Ruptures/NEFAC.

Philippis, Vittorio de, and Christian Losson. 2000. Assemblées annuelles du FMI et de la Banque mondiale. *Libération*, 27 September: 26–27.

Pietilä, Hikka, and Jeanne Vickers. 1994. *Making Women Matter: The Role of the United Nations* (2nd edn). London: Zed Books.

Pile, Stephen, and Michael Keith (eds). 1997. *Geographies of Resistance*. London: Routledge.

Poats, Rutherford M. 1985a. Crisis-Driven Reform. In *Twenty-Five Years of Development Co-Operation: A Review*, edited by R. M. Poats. Paris: Organization for Economic Cooperation and Development (Development Assistance Committee).

Poats, Rutherford M. 1985b. Twenty-Five Years of Development Co-Operation: A Review. Paris: Organization for Economic Cooperation and Development (Development Assistance Committee).

Poirier, Louis. 1992. Des liens de solidarite sociale. *ACN Dossier* 1(2) (May–June): 2.

Polak, J. 1991. *The Changing Nature of IMF Conditionality, Princeton University Essays in International Finance*. Princeton, NJ: Princeton University Press.

Polanyi, Karl. 1957. *The Great Transformation*. Boston, MA: Beacon Press.

Porter, Gareth, and Janet Welsh Brown. 1996. *Global Environmental Politics (1991)*. Boulder, Co: Westview Press.

Porter, Isabelle, and Jacinthe Gouin. 2002. Locataires en mode squat. *Recto Verso* (July–August): 7.

Price, Richard. 1998. Reversing the Gun Sights: Transnational Civil Society Targets Land Mines. *International Organizations* 52 (summer): 613–644.

Princen, Thomas, and Matthias Finger. 1994. *Environmental NGOs in World Politics: Linking the Local and the Global*. New York: Routledge.

Ramphal, Sir Shridath. 1997. A Vision More Compelling Now: The Commission on Global Governance (http://www.cgg.ch/atlee.htm, 31 July).

Red Chile de Acción por una Iniciativa de los Pueblos. 1996. Encuentro Sindical: Los trabajadores frente al NAFTA. *Nuestra America*, (February): 11.

Red Mexicana de Acción Frente al Libre Comercio. 1995. Referéndum de la Libertad. *Alternativas (Integración, Democracia y Desarrollo)* (September to October)

Red Mexicana de Acción Frente al Libre Comercio. 1996. Un Balance del Referéndum de la Libertad. *Alternativas (Integración, Democracia y Desarrollo)* (January to February)

Rheingold, Howard. 1993a. Habitat: Computer-Mediated Play. In *The Virtual Community*, edited by Howard Rheingold. Reading, MA: Addison-Wesley.

Rheingold, Howard. 1993b. *A Slice of Life in my Virtual Community*. Cambridge, MA: MIT Press.

Riordon, William L. (ed.). 1963. *Plunkitt of Tammany Hall: A Series of Very Plain Talks on Very Practical Politics, Delivered by Ex-Senator George Washington Plunkitt, from his Rostrum – The New York County Court House Bootblack Stand*. New York: E.P. Dutton & Co.

Risse-Kappen, Thomas, Stephen C. Ropp and Kathryn Sikkink. 1999. The Power of Principles: The Socialisation of Human Rights Norms into Domestic Practice. In *The Power of Principles: International Human Rights Norms and Domestic Change*, edited by Risse-Kappen *et al.* Cambridge: Cambridge University Press.

Ritchie, Cyril. 1996. Coordinate? Cooperate? Harmonise? NGO Policy and Operational Coalitions. In *NGOs, The UN, and Global Governance*, edited by T. G. Weiss, and L. Gordenker. Boulder, Co: Lynne Rienner.

Robbins, Bruce. 1998. Introduction Part I: Actually Existing Cosmopolitanism. In *Cosmopolitics: Thinking and Feeling Beyond the Nation*, edited by P. Cheah, and B. Robbins. Minneapolis: University of Minnesota Press.

Robert, Vincent. 1996. *Les chemins de la manifestation: 1848–1914, Collection du Centre Pierre Léon*. Lyon: Presses universitaires de Lyon.

Robertson, Rolan. 1992. *Globalization: Social Theory and Global Culture*. London: Sage.

Robinson, William I. 1992. The São Paulo Forum: Is There a New Latin American Left? *Monthly Review* 44 (December): 1–12.

Robson, William A. 1948. *The Government and Misgovernment of London*. London: George Allen & Unwin.

Ross, Ellen. 1983. Survival Networks: Women's Neighbourhood Sharing Before World War I. *History Workshop Journal* 15 (spring): 4–27.

Ross, George. 1995. *Jacques Delors and European Integration*. New York: Oxford University Press.

Ross, Kristin. 1997. Lefebvre on the Situationists: An Interview. *October* 79 (winter): 69–83.

Rowbotham, Sheila. 1996. Introduction. In *Mapping the Women's Movement: Feminist Politics and Social Transformation in the North*, edited by M. Threlfall. London: Verso.

Roy, Marianne. n.d. Solidarity in Québec: SPQ's Roots. *ACN/Dossier 37* (Special issue): 4.

Rucht, Dieter. 1993. Think Globally, Act Locally? Needs, Forms and Problems of Cross-national Cooperation among Environmental Groups. In *European Integration and Environmental Policy*, edited by J. D. Liefferink, P. D. Lowe, and A. P. J. Mol. London: Belhaven Press.

Rupp, Leila J. 1997. *Worlds of Women: The Making of an International Women's Movement*. Princeton, NJ: Princeton University Press.

Sadler, Simon. 1998. *The Situationist City*. Cambridge: MIT Press.

SalAMI. 2000. Mobilisations et résistances civiles contre le Sommet des Amériques et le projet de Zone de libre-échange des Amériques: Plan d'action et propositions de SalAMI. Http://www.alternatives.ca/salami/html/zlea.html: SalAMi.

Salmen, Lawrence F., and A. Paige Eaves. 1991. Interactions between Nongovernmental Organizations, Governments and the World Bank: Evidence from Bank Projects. In *Nongovernmental Organizations and the World Bank: Cooperation for Development*, edited by S. Paul, and A. Israel. Washington, DC: The World Bank.

Salter, J.T. 1935. *Boss Rule: Portraits in City Politics*. New York: Whittlesey House/ McGraw Hill.

Samson, Claudette. 2000a. Il faudra 3.8 kms de clôture. *Le Soleil*, 2 November:A-3.

Samson, Claudette. 2000b. Un sommet de sécurité. *Le Soleil*, 2 November:A-1, A-2.

Sante, Luc. 1992. *Low Life*. New York: Vintage/Random House.

Sartre, Jean-Paul. 1970. Masses, Spontaneity, Party. In *Socialist Register 1970*, edited by R. Miliband and J. Salville. London: Merlin Press.

Sassen, Saskia. 1998. *Globalization and Its Discontents*. New York: The New Press.

Sassen, Saskia. 2000. *Cities in a World Economy* (2nd edn). Thousand Oaks, CA: Pine Forge Press.

Sassen, Saskia. 2002. The Repositioning of Citizenship: Emergent Subjects and Space for Politics. *Berkeley Journal of Sociology: A Critical Review* 46: 4–26.

Savage, Mike, and Andrew Miles. 1994. *The Remaking of the British Working Class 1840–1940*, edited by G. C. Tom Scott, John Davis, and Joanna Innes, *Historical Connections*. London: Routledge.

Schilen, Sandy, Jan Peterson and Sangeetha Prushuthoman. 1997. The Huairou Commission and Women, Homes and Community Super Coalition: A New Way of Partnering to Expand Women's Leadership in Policy Initiatives. *UNCHS (Habitat)* (March): 25–26.

Schlesinger, Arthur Meier. 1983. *The Rise of the City*, edited by A. M. Schlesinger, and D. R. Fox. Vol. X, *History of American Life*. New York: Macmillan.

Schneer, Jonathan. 1994. London's Docks in 1900: Nexus of Empire. *Labour History* 59 (3) (winter): 20–33.

Scholte, Jan Aart. 1993. *International Relations of Social Change*. Buckingham: Open University Press.

Scholte, Jan Aart. 1996. The Geography of Collective Identity in a Globalizing World. *Review of International Political Economy*, (winter): 565–607.

Scholte, Jan Aart. 1998. The IMF Meets Civil Society. *Finance and Development* (September): 42–46.

Schwartz, M.A. 1997. Cross-Border Ties Among Protest Movements – The Great Plains Connection. *Great Plains Quarterly* 17 (2): 119–130.

Schwartz, Norman, and Anne Deruyttere. 1996. Community Consultation, Sustainable Development and the Inter-American Development Bank: A Concept Paper. IDB, Social Programs and Sustainable Development Unit, Indigenous Peoples and Community Development Unit.

SDA Unit (World Bank). 1990. *The Social Dimensions of Adjustment in Africa: A Policy Agenda*. Abidjan/New York/Washington: African Development Bank/UNDP/World Bank.

Seiichi, Yamasaki. 1995. Kathmandu APWSL Council Meeting: Strong Representation of Women Workers at the Grass Roots. *APWSL/Japan (Newsletter From Japan Committee of Asian Pacific Worker's Solidarity Links)*, (July): 2–4.

Seiichi, Yamasaki. 1996. New Otani Dispute: Union and Community Relations Strengthened by HERE Visit. *APWSL/Japan (Newsletter From Japan Committee of Asian Pacific Worker's Solidarity Links)* (February): 5.

Seiichi, Yamasaki. 1997. APWSL Japan Alternative Tour to U.S.A.: Touching Base with the U.S. Labor Movement. *APWSL/Japan (Newsletter From Japan Committee of Asian Pacific Worker's Solidarity Links)*, (February): 3–5.

Seiichi, Yamasaki. 1999. NZ Postal Workers Visit Japan: A Successful Example of Workers Meeting. *APWSL/Japan (Newsletter From Japan Committee of Asian Pacific Worker's Solidarity Links)* (June): 3.

Sennett, Richard. 1992. *The Conscience of the Eye: The Design and Social Life of Cities*. New York: W.W. Norton.

Shaw, Martin. 2000. *The Global State, Cambridge Studies in International Relations*. Cambridge: Cambridge University Press.

Shields, Rob. 1991. *Places on the Margin: Alternative Geographies of Modernity*. London: Routledge.

Shrage, Laurie. 1994. *Moral Dilemmas of Feminism: Prostitution, Adultery and Abortion*. London: Routledge.

Sikkink, Kathryn. 1993. Human Rights, Principled Issue-Networks, and Sovereignty in Latin America. *International Organization* 47(3): 411–441.

Sklair, Leslie. 1999. Globalization. In *Sociology: Issues and Debates*, edited by S. Taylor. London: Macmillan.

Sklair, Leslie. 2001. *The Transnational Capitalist Class*. Oxford: Blackwell.

Smith, H. Llewellyn, and Vaughan Nash. 1984 [1890]. *The Story of the Dockers' Strike Told by Two East Londoners*. edited by F. M. Leventhal, *The World of Labour*. New York and London: Garland Publishing.

Smith, Jackie. 1999. Global Politics and Transnational Social Movement Strategies: The Transnational Campaign Against International Trade in Toxic Wastes. In *Social Movements in a Globalizing World*, edited by D. Della Porta, H. Kriesi, and D. Rucht. London: Macmillan.

Smith, Jackie *et al.* 1997. Social Movements and World Politics: a Theoretical Framework. In *Transnational Social Movements and Global Politics*, edited by J. Smith, C. Chatfield, and R. Pagnucco. Syracuse: Syracuse University Press.

Smith, Michael P. 1994. Transnational Migration and the Globalization of Grassroots Politics. *Social Text* 39 (summer): 15–33.

Smith, Michael P., and Luiz E. Guarnizo (eds.) 1998a. *Transnationalism From Below*, edited by M. P. Smith. Vol. 6, *Comparative Urban and Community Research*. New Brunswick: Transaction Publishers.

Smith, Michael P., and Luis E. Guarnizo. 1998b. The Locations of Transnationalism. *Comparative Urban and Community Research* 6: 3–34.

Smith, Russel E., and Mark A. Healy. 1994. Labor and Mercosur: A Briefing Book. Paper read at Labor, Free Trade and Economic Integration in the Americas: National Labor Union Responses to a Transnational World, 25–27 August at Duke University.

Southerners for Economic Justice. 1993. *1992 Program Review*. Durham, NC:SEJ.

Spooner, Dave. 1989. *Partners or Predators: International Trade Unionism and Asia*. Hong Kong: Asia Monitor Resource Center.

Spybey, T. 1996. *Globalization and World Society*. Cambridge: Polity Press.

Stedman Jones, Gareth. 1971. *Outcast London: A Study in the Relationship Between Classes in Victorian Society*. Oxford: Clarendon Press.

Stedman Jones, Gareth. 1974. Working Class Culture and Working Class Politics in London 1870–1900: Notes on the Remaking of a Working Class. *Journal of Social History* 7 (4): 460–509.

Stern, Robert A.M., Gregory Gilmartin, and Massengale John Montague. 1983. *New-York 1900: Metropolitan Architecture and Urbanism, 1890–1915*. New York: Rizzoli International Publishing.

Stone, Allucquère Rosanne. 1995. *The War of Desire and Technology at the Close of the Mechanical Age*. Cambridge, MA: MIT Press.

Sutcliffe, Anthony. 1984. Introduction: Urbanization, Planning, and the Giant City. In *Metropolis 1890–1940*, edited by A. Sutcliffe. Chicago, IL: The University of Chicago Press.

Tarrow, Sidney. 2001. Beyond Globalization: Why Creating Transnational Social Movements is so Hard and When it is Most Likely to Happen: Global Solidarity Dialogue. http://www.antenna.nl-waterman/tarrow.html.

Taylor, Anthony. 1995. 'Common-Stealers', 'Land-Grabbers' and Jerry-Builders': Space, Popular Radicalism and the Politics of Public Access in London, 1848–1880. *International Review of Social History* 40 (August): 383–407.

The Economist. 1999. The Non-governmental Order. *The Economist*, 11 December: 20–21.

The Women's Environmental Network. 1994. *Save the World with WENDi*. London: WEN.

The World Bank. 1979. *World Bank Standards and Procedures*. Washington, DC: The World Bank.

The World Bank. 1988. *The World Bank Annual Report*. Washington, DC: The World Bank.

The World Bank. 1991. *Urban Policy and Economic Development: An Agenda for the 1990s, World Bank Policy Papers*. Washington, DC: The World Bank.

The World Bank. 1994a. Partners in Reform: The Special Program of Assistance for Africa (SPA). *Findings* (October).

The World Bank. 1994b. *World Bank Development Report 1994: Infrastructure for Development*. Washington, DC: The World Bank.

The World Bank. 1996a. West Central Africa: Building Ownership for Environ-
mentally Sustainable Development. *Findings (Africa Region, World Bank)* (June),
http://www.worldbank.org/aftdr/findings/english/find76.htm.

The World Bank. 1996b. *The World Bank Participation Sourcebook*. Vol. 19, *Environ-
mentally Sustainable Development*. Washington, DC: The World Bank.

The World Bank. 2000a. *The World Bank, NGOs and Civil Society*. Washington, DC:
The World Bank Group.

The World Bank. 2000b. *NGO Meeting with Mr. Wolfensohn, Prague*. Washington,
DC: The World Bank Group.

Thill, Georges. 1995. D'une dépendance globale à une solidarité planétaire responsable. *La Revue Nouvelle* 10 (October 1995): 52–64.

Thompson, E.P. 1982. Notes on Exterminism, the Last Stage of Civilization. In
Exterminism and Cold War, edited by New Left Review. London: Verso.

Thompson, F.M.L. 1988. *The Rise of Respectable Society: A Social History of Victorian Britain, 1830–1900*, edited by F. M. L. Thompson, *The Fontana Social History
of Britain Since 1700*. London: Fontana

Thompson, Paul. 1967. *Socialists. Liberals and Labour: The Struggle for London
1885–1914*. London: Routledge & Kegan Paul.

Thorp, William L. 1985. The DAC's Expanding Influence. In *Twenty-Five Years of
Development Co-Operation: A Review*, edited by R. M. Poats. Paris: Organization
for Economic Cooperation and Development (Development Assistance
Committee).

Tobin, James. 1978. A Proposal for International Monetary Reform. *The Eastern
Economic Journal* 4 (3–4 July/October): 153–159.

Todd, Jesse T. 1993. Battling Satan in the City: Charles Henry Parkhurst and Municipal Redemption in Gilded Age New York. *American Presbyterian* 71 (4)(winter):
243–252.

Tofler, Alvin. 1970. *Future Shock*. New York: Random House.

Toshiko, Kadokawa. 1996. The Heart-to-Heart Solidarity of Workers Begins
from People-to-People Encounters in Daily Life. *APWSL/Japan (Newsletter
From Japan Committee of Asian Pacific Worker's Solidarity Links)* (November):
10–11.

Truong, Thanh-dam. 1990. *Sex, Money and Morality: Prostitution and Tourism in
Southeast Asia*. London: Zed Books.

Tschumi, Bernard. 1998. *Architecture and Disjunction*. Cambridge, MA: MIT Press.

Tuan, Yi-Fu. 1977. *Space and Place: The Perspective of Experience*. Minneapolis:
University of Minnesota Press.

UNCHS. 1988. *Global Strategy for Shelter to the Year 2000 (Summary)*. Nairobi:
United Nations Center for Human Settlements (Habitat).

UNCHS. 1990a. Global Strategy for Shelter: National Actions Indicators. *UNCHS
(Habitat) Shelter Bulletin*, July: 2.

UNCHS. 1990b. *Human Settlements Basic Statistics*. Nairobi: United Nations Center
for Human Settlements.

UNCHS. 1991a. *Global Strategy for Shelter to the Year 2000: Implementation of the
first phase*. Nairobi: United Nations Center for Human Settlements (Habitat).

UNCHS. 1991b. Global Strategy for Shelter: Enabling Leaders and Community participation. *UNCHS (Habitat) Shelter Bulletin* (July): 2–4.

UNCHS. 1993. Fourteenth Session, Commission on Human Settlements: A Clear
Vision. *Habitat News* (August): 5–8.

UNCHS. 1996. *An Urbanizing World: Global Report on Human Settlements 1996.* Oxford/Nairobi: Oxford University Press/United Nations Center for Human Settlements.

UNCHS. 1997a. Cooperation with Partners in the Context of Habitat II. *UNCHS: Habitat Debate* (March): 9–10.

UNCHS. 1997b. Youth for Habitat. *UNCHS: Habitat Debate* (March): 32.

UNDP. 1996. Habitat II: City Summits to Forge the Future of Human Settlements in an Urbanizing World. *UN Chronicle* (spring): 40–48.

Valin, Fern, and Jim Sinclair. 1992. Solidarity, Not Competition In *Crossing the Line: Canada and Free Trade with Mexico*, edited by J. Sinclair. Vancouver: New Star Books.

van der Pijl, Kees. 1984. *The Making of a Transnational Ruling Class.* London: Verso.

van der Pijl, Kees. 1989. The International Level. In *The Capitalist Class: An International Study*, edited by T. Bottomore and R. J. Brym. New York: New York University Press.

van der Pijl, Kees. 1997. Transnational Class Formation and State Forms. In *Innovation and Transformation in International Studies*, edited by S. Gill and J. Mittleman. Cambridge: Cambridge University Press.

van der Pijl, Kees. 1998. *Transnational Class Formation.* London: Routledge.

van Hoolthon, F, and Marcel van der Linden. 1988. *Internationalism in the Labour Movement 1830–1940.* Vol. II. Leiden: E.J. Brill.

Vaneigem, Raoul. 1961. Commentaires contre l'urbanisme. *Internationale Situationniste* (August): 33–37.

Vaneigem, Raoul. 1967. *Traité de savoir-vivre à l'usage des jeunes générations.* Paris: Gallimard.

Vaneigem, Raoul. 1996. *Nous qui desirons sans fin*, edited by J-Y. Clement. Vol. 59, Folio/Actuel. Paris: Gallimard.

Vaneigem, Raoul. 1999. *Pour une internationale du genre humain*, edited by J-Y. Clément, *Amor Fati.* Paris: Le Cherche Midi.

Vaneigem, Raoul. 2001. *Déclaration universelle des droits de l'être humain, Amor Fati.* Paris: Le Cherche Midi.

Vertovec, Steve. 1999. Conceiving and Researching Transnationalism. *Ethnic and Racial Studies* 22 (2)(March): 447–462.

Vertovec, Steve, and Robin Cohen. 1999. Migration, Diasporas and Transnationalism. In *Migration, Diasporas and Transnationalism*, edited by S. Vertovec and R. Cohen. Cheltenham: Edward Elgar.

Vienet, René. 1998 [1968]. *Enragés et situationnistes dans le mouvement des occupations, nrf.* Paris: Gallimard.

Walkowitz, Judith R. 1992. *City of Dreadful Delight: Narratives of Sexual Danger in Late-Victorian London.* Chicago, IL: The University of Chicago Press.

Wallerstein, Immanuel. 1987. World-System Analysis. In *Social Theory Today*, edited by A. Giddens and J. Turner. Stanford, CA: Stanford University Press.

Wallerstein, Immanuel. 1989 [1968]. Révolution dans le système mondial. *Les temps modernes* 514–515 (May to June): 154–176.

Walton, John. 1987. Urban Protests and the Global Political Economy: The IMF Riots. In *The Capitalist City: Global Restructuring and Community Politics*, edited by M. P. Smith and J. R. Feagin. Oxford: Blackwell.

Warah, Rasna. 1997. The Partnership Principle: Key to implementing the Habitat Agenda. *UNCHS: Habitat Debate* (March): 1, 4–5.

Waterman, Peter. 1988. The New Internationalism: A More Real Thing Than a Big, Big Coke? *Review: Fernand Braudel Center* 10 (3): 289–328.

Waterman, Peter (ed.) 1992a. *The Old Internationalism and the New: A Reader on Labour, New Social Movements and Internationalism.* The Hague: Institute of Social History.

Waterman, Peter. 1992b. Women of the World, Unite! But Which? And for What? In *The Old Internationalism and the New: A Reader on Labour, New Social Movements and Internationalism,* edited by P. Waterman. The Hague: Institute of Social History.

Waterman, Peter. 1995. New 'Social Unionism: A Model for the Future?'. *SA Labour Bulletin* (November): 68–76.

Waterman, Peter. 1996. Labour and Feminist Contributions to a Global Solidarity Culture in South Africa (Part 1). *Transnational Associations/ Associations Transnationales,* (November): 22–39.

Waters, M. 1995. *Globalization.* London: Routledge.

Webb, Sydney, and Beatrice Webb. 1989. *The History of Trade Unionism.* London: Chiswick Press.

Werbner, P. 1999. Global Pathways. Working Class Cosmopolitans and the Creation of Transnational Ethnic Worlds. *Social Anthropology* 7 (1): 17–35.

White, Lyman C. 1951. *International Non-Governmental Organizations: Their Purposes, Methods, and Accomplishments.* New Brunswick, NJ: Rutgers University Press.

White, Norval, and Elliot Willensky. 1978. *AIA Guide to New York City.* Edited by A. I. Architects. New York: Macmillan.

Willetts, Peter (ed.). 1982. *Pressure Groups in the Global System, The Transnational Relations of Issue-Orientated Non-Governmental Organizations.* New York: St Martin's Press.

Wilson, Bob, and Dissanayak Wimal. 1996. *Global Local: Cultural Production and the Transnational Imaginary.* Durham, NC: Duke University Press.

Wolfensohn, James D. 1997. *The Challenge of Inclusion: Address to the Board of Governors, Hong Kong, China September 23.* Washington DC: The World Bank.

Wollen, Peter. 1989a. Bitter Victory: The Art and Politics of the Situationist International. In *On the Passage of a Few People Through a Rather Brief Moment in Time: The Situationist International, 1957–1972,* edited by E. Sussman. Cambridge/ Boston: MIT Press/The Institute of Contemporary Art.

Wollen, Peter. 1989b. The Situationist International. *New Left Review* 174 (March to April): 67–95.

Yoko, Akimoto. 1998. Exchange Visit with Two Activists from Thailand. *APWSL Japan* (November): 3.

Young, Ken, and Patricia L. Garside. 1982. *Metropolitan London: Politics and Urban Change 1837–1981.* London: Edward Arnold.

Yukie, Araya. 1998. Introducing the Asian Women Workers' Center. *APSWL Japan: Newsletter from Japan Committee of APWSL* (February): 4.

Zamora, Rubén. 1995. Towards a Strategy of Resistance. *NACLA: Report on the Americas* 29 (1): 6–9.

Zink, Harold. 1968. *City Bosses in the United States.* New York: AMS Press.

Index